WEST METRO BIKE ROUTES

See inside back cover for EAST METRO BIKE ROUTES

41

RIDES

1-20 BIKE TOURS
See pages 26 to 63

RIDES

A-G MOUNTAIN BIKE RIDES
See pages 118 to 126

RATINGS FOR BIKE TOURS

⊜ Easier – Mostly paved, off-road trails

〰 Moderate – Mostly on bike-friendly streets

⩕ Experienced – On roads, longer, less protected

LENGTH

Mileage listed below is for a full tour, loop, or distinct area. OW (one way) and RT (round trip) mileage is given for linear trails. Note: Longer rides are easily made by connecting two or more routes.

10

Sample Description (tour user guide pages 26 & 27)

> **O** BIKE TOUR with RATING and LENGTH
>
>> Oa. Regional Park/Trail or shorter loop described and mapped within tour

1 COON RAPIDS RIDER	〰	20.5 MILES
⊜ 1a. Coon Rapids Dam Regional Park		3.3 miles
⊜ 1b. Bunker Hills Regional Park		5.7 miles
2 NORTH HENNEPIN REGIONAL TRAIL	⊜	14.4 MILES RT
⊜ 2a. Elm Creek Park Reserve		20.0 miles
3 FRIDLEY FLYER	〰	17.7 MILES
⊜ 3a. Long Lake Regional Park		5.0 miles
⊜ 3b. Rice Creek West Regional Trail		5.5 miles RT
⊜ 3c. Mississippi River Regional Trail		8.0 miles OW
4 MINNEAPOLIS GRAND ROUNDS	〰	32.7 MILES
⊜ 4a. Minnehaha Parkway		9.8 miles RT
5 GREATER MINNEAPOLIS GREENWAYS	⊜	38.0 MILES
6 MINNEAPOLIS LAKE DISTRICT	⊜	15.8 MILES
⊜ 6a. Cedar Lake Trail		8.8 miles RT
⊜ 6b. Lake of the Isles		2.9 miles
⊜ 6c. Lake Calhoun		3.1 miles
⊜ 6d. Lake Harriet		2.8 miles
7 HENNEPIN EXPLORER	⩕	39.6 MILES
8 EVERY WHICH WAY TO THE LUCE	〰	31.2 MILES
⊜ 8a. Medicine Lake Loop		8.1 miles
〰 8b. Big Loop without Medicine Lake		24.4 miles
9 ON THE ROAD TO FREEDOM	⩕	31.9 MILES
⊜ 9a. Baker Park Reserve		6.2 miles
〰 9b. Road Route without Baker Park		23.8 miles
⊜ 9c. Lake Rebecca Park Reserve		6.5 miles
10 LUCE LINE STATE TRAIL	〰	69.8 MILES OW
⊜ 10a. Vicksburg Trailhead to Winsted		29.0 miles
〰 10b. Winsted to Thompson Lake (Cosmos)		34.0 miles
11 BLOOMINGTON OR BUST	〰	19.2 MILES
⊜ 11a. Hyland Lake Park Reserve		5.0 miles
〰 11b. All mapped routes to Hyland Park		31.1 miles OW
12 SWIM ROUND LAKE MINNETONKA	⩕	29.2 MILES

13 LRT NORTH TRAIL	⊜	18.0 MILES OW
⩕ 13a. LRT North and LRT South Loop		41.4 miles
⊜ 13b. Carver Park Reserve		8.5 miles
14 LRT SOUTH TRAIL	⊜	11.5 MILES OW
15 CHASKA CHASER	⊜	13.2 MILES
⊜ 15a. Total miles of paved path		25.0 miles
16 MINNESOTA VALLEY STATE TRAIL	⩕	27.0 MILES OW
⊜ Minnesota River to Murphy's Landing		10.0 miles RT
17 EDEN PRAIRIE – BIKES NOT BOMBS	〰	20.8 MILES
18 BURNSVILLE BIKE BY WAYS	〰	18.4 MILES
19 BIKING FOR THE BIRDS	〰	29.5 MILES
⊜ 19a. Fort Snelling Dirt Ride		11.4 miles
20 PLANES, TRAINS & AUTOMOBILES	〰	17.0 MILES

MOUNTAIN BIKE RIDES Rating for terrain/distance

2 N. HENNEPIN REG. TRAIL (turf trail)	⊜	14.4 MILES RT
9 Winter biking at BAKER PARK	〰	4.0 MILES
16 MINNESOTA VALLEY STATE TRAIL	⩕	50.0 MILES RT
19 BIKING FOR THE BIRDS		
19a. Fort Snelling Dirt Ride	⊜	11.4 miles RT
A ELM CREEK PARK RESERVE	⊜-〰	5.0 MILES
B LAKE REBECCA PARK RESERVE	⊜-〰	4.0 MILES
C BLOOMINGTON BLUFF TRAIL	〰	20.0 MILES RT
D TERRACE OAKS PARK	〰-⩕	3.4 MILES
E BUCK HILL MTN. BIKE & BMX	〰-⩕	3.0 MILES
F MURPHY HANREHAN PARK	⩕	6.0 MILES
G LOUISVILLE SWAMP	⊜	11.5 MILES

DAY TRIPS

41 LAKE WOBEGONE TRAIL	⊜	55.0 MILES RT

When I see an adult on a bicycle, I do not despair for the future of the human race.

H. G. Wells

Fred's Best Guide to

TWIN CITIES BICYCLING

By
Richard 'Fred' Arey

MINNESOTA
OUTDOORS
PRESS

Fred's Best Guide to
TWIN CITIES BICYCLING

Minnesota Outdoors Press
Richard Fred Arey • 534 Laurel Avenue #6

651-290-0309
Saint Paul, Minnesota 55102

Additional copies of this book and Twin Cities Winter Recreation may be obtained by sending $18.50 per copy – or two copies for just $32! – (price includes tax, shipping and handling) to the publisher at the above address. Make checks payable to Minnesota Outdoors Press. Allow up to three weeks for delivery.

I GET BY WITH A LITTLE HELP FROM MY FRIENDS.
Cover art and design – David Mataya
Production and design – Rob Schanilec – my main man
Word processing – Rob Schanilec
Text, maps, some photos and illustrations – Fred
Proofing – Paula Schanilec and Chaunce Stanton
Photos – Credits adjacent to each photograph

Revised and expanded, 1999
10   9   8   7   6   5   4   3   2   1

Library of Congress Cataloging-in-Publication Data

Arey, Richard Fred
   Twin Cities Bicycling – Revised Edition
   Fred's Best Guide to Twin Cities Bicycling
   Richard Fred Arey
   p.   cm.
ISBN 0-9620918-4-7 $15.95

1. Bicycle touring – Twin Cities Metropolitan Area – Guide
   books
2. Minnesota – Twin Cities – Bicycling Guide
3. History – Bicycling – Minnesota

Watch for these upcoming Minnesota Outdoors Press books.
1. *A Pictorial History of Twin Cities Parks and Recreation*
2. *Twin Cities Summer Recreation*
3. *Duluth Recreation*

And if you have too much money lying around, please call me about my limited edition book WATERFALLS OF THE MISSISSIPPI with colored wood engravings by Gaylord Schanilec.

Dakota and Ojibwa place names are from Paul Durand's excellent book, *Where the Waters Gather and the Rivers Meet*. Send $17.00 to Paul at 15341 Red Oaks Road SE, Prior Lake, MN 55372, to obtain your copy. Many of the geographical place name histories are from Warren Upham's landmark book, *Minnesota Geographic Names*, available from the Minnesota Historical Society. The Thomas McGrath poem (How could I have come so far?…) is from *Selected Poems: 1938-1988* © 1988 by Thomas McGrath. Reprinted by permission of Copper Canyon Press. PO Box 271, Port Townsend, WA 98368. I would also like to thank everyone that reviewed and commented on my text and maps.

LIABILITY DISCLAIMER
Routes described and mapped in this book were compiled from a variety of sources. Minnesota Outdoors Press and Richard Fred Arey assume no liability for bicyclists travelling on these routes. The maps and descriptions are intended to aid in the selection of routes, but do not guarantee safety while riding these routes.

HAVE FUN, WEAR A HELMET, RIDE AT YOUR OWN RISK

DEDICATIONS

To Mom and Dad — who have always kept the faith
and been there when I needed them. This is for you.

> *How could I have come so far?*
> *(And always on such dark trails!)*
> *I must have travelled by the light*
> *Shining from the faces of all those I have loved.*
>
> Thomas McGrath

And for everyone else who has heard me talk about a
Twin Cities Parks and Recreation book for the last
decade or so — Voila! This doesn't seem that tough
does it? Three down, three to go.

This is for those who were there at the beginning —
Jerry Hass, Roxanne Hart and Marty Bucher.

And for all those who have biked, skied, paddled,
walked and sailed along with me through the years.

Hey, Ho. Let's Go!

Do you remember your first bike?

Minnesota Historical Society (MHS), St. Paul, 1956

PICTORIAL HISTORY OF BICYCLING

Bicycling, until lately, has been looked upon by many as a sport for the youth, or as a "craze," soon to pass out of fashion. But slowly and surely it has been dawning upon the public mind that this great invention is really a vehicle that is destined to supplant, in many instances, the horse and buggy — is doing so and pointing to greater possibilities.

MINNESOTA WHEELMAN, September, 1885

Do you remember your first bicycle?

The history of bicycling goes back some 150 years, but for me, nothing is more memorable than the first view of my bright red Schwinn under the Christmas tree. Except, perhaps, the first ride on my second bike, when I became so enamored with how the gears were shifting that I rode smack into a parked car.

The bicycle, the most efficient form of transportation ever devised, has a long and colorful history. In the 1890s, cyclists led the national "Good Roads" movement. Summit Avenue became the first paved street in St. Paul at the urging of local bike racers.

The first road maps were developed by bicyclists looking for the best roads out of town. The bicycle also helped energize the movement for women's emancipation. In 1896, Susan B. Anthony declared, "I stand and rejoice every time I see a woman ride by on a wheel."

Technical innovations were legion and included the development of gears, cyclometers, sprockets and pneumatic tires. Cecil Behringer, a Minnesotan and former bicycle racer, patented a titanium treatment process he used in building an ultralight racing bike.

What goes around comes around. Separated bike paths seemed like a good innovation in the 1970s — about 80 years after the first ones were built on Como Avenue and around Lake Harriet. Bicycle cops, bike couriers, mandatory bike registration, and bike tours that span the globe have all made the news over the last few years. They also made the news a century ago.

And what about those nutty winter bicyclists who seem to have popped up out of every other snowdrift? If they're really serious they'll revive another old Twin Cities tradition. At the stroke of midnight each New Year's Eve, cyclists from Minneapolis and St. Paul would race over the High Bridge, to Northfield and back, to see who would complete the year's first century ride.

Will history repeat itself yet again?

1997 — Leonardo da Vinci designed weapons and machines that were far ahead of their time but he did not invent the bicycle. *New Scientist* magazine reveals the hoax of the 20th century doodle that made its way into several bike history books and magazine articles.

1818 — German inventor Karl von Drais patents the two-wheel hobbyhorse with a pivoting front wheel for steering. It is propelled by the feet while straddling the vehicle — like a 19th century Fred Flintstone.

1843 — An early bicycle story — unlikely to be true — revolves around an 1843 newspaper article describing a 140-mile round-trip ride, on what was possibly a tricycle, from Dumfries to Glasgow, Scotland. The rider's name is not given but crowds gathered on his return and he is fined five schillings when he knocks over a child in the ensuing ruckus.

1864 — Hotshot young engineering students, René and Aimé Olivier, in collaboration with Pierre Michaux, produce a small number of two-wheeled velocipedes driven by cranks and pedals atttached to the front wheels. Michaux is a blacksmith experienced in making carriages from malleable cast iron – a new technology the Olivier brothers hoped to exploit. Michaux-brand velocipedes, the world's first commercially available bicycles, begin production in 1867.

Pierre Lallement on his 1866 velocipede — arguably the world's first true bicycle.

Smithsonian Institute.

Nov. 20 1866 — Pierre Lallement, a New Haven, Connecticut resident and recent U.S. immigrant from France, takes out the first patent anywhere for a rotary-action, crank-driven, two-wheeled velocipede. The bicycle has arrived in America.

Advertisement from 1896 Northwest Cycle Show program.

One of the famous Bell Brothers bicyclists, c. 1885.

1869 — The first bicycle craze hits the wilds of Minnesota, a mere decade after statehood's arrival on May 11, 1858. Velocipedes, also known as boneshakers, are reported to have raced in St. Paul at Armory Hall.

March 4 1869 — The *St. Cloud Visitor* reports that certain parties have purchased a velocipede and will keep it at City Hall for those who desire to ride it.

Aug. 11 1870 — James Starley patents the "Ariel," an all metal, mass produced, reasonably priced high-wheeler from England. The high-wheeler, also known as an "ordinary," is similar to a velocipede but employs a far larger front wheel for greater speed.

1877-1878 — The first known "safety" bike (high-wheelers being notoriously difficult to ride and subject to "headers" that catapulted the bicyclist headfirst into the ground) was built by H. Bate of England. Both wheels are the same size, there is a center saddle, and pedals attached to a sprocket and chain drive the rear wheel like today's bikes.

May 1881 — The Minneapolis Cycling Club organizes with 12 members. It claims affiliation with the League of American Wheelmen (LAW) that held its first meet in Rhode Island (attended exclusively by high wheelers) the previous year.

Sept. 24 1884 — The second annual meet of the Minnesota Wheelmen includes a one mile, bicycle against roller skate race, with cup to winner. Any doubt about who won?

1885 — J. K. Starley (James' nephew) produces the Rover, the first commercially successful safety bike using a diamond frame, direct steering and a brake. Soon, frame modifications allow women to once again be bicyclists as the original velocipedes had provided.

Sept. 22 1885 — The third annual meeting of the Minnesota division of the LAW is marked by the publication of volume one of the *Minnesota Wheelman*. The 16-page pamphlet notes that there are 408 bicycles in the state including "about 150 in Minneapolis." And a section on the Rights of Wheelmen points out that "bicycles and tricycles are carriages subject to the same rules and regulations and enjoying the same rights and privileges on the public highways as those drawn by horses."

The pamphlet also mentions that the Minneapolis Parks Commission has passed a law prohibiting bicyclists. But they note that "Minneapolis wheelmen are serene as yet, for the parks are good places to keep out of with a bicycle. About the time they are ripe for the wheelmen, the wheelmen will enjoy them. Mark the prediction."

Michelin Tire Corporation

1886 High-wheeler catalog has chapter on "Learning to Fall." Mark Twain says, "Get a bicycle. You will not regret it, if you live."

1888 John Dunlop takes a piece of rubber tubing, like a garden hose, joins the ends together and glues it onto the rim of his son's tricycle. He attaches a baby's milk bottle tube as a valve and the pneumatic tire is born. On June 18, 1891, Edouard Michelin goes the next step and produces a removable tire that is attachable without glue. Today's bike is now complete except for the derailleur.

1890 By the early 1890s, safety bicycles become common, and prices fall (high wheelers could be as expensive as a house!) to the point where the middle class can enjoy them. Bicycle clubs like Flour City Cyclists sprout up around the Twin Cities. Bicycle theft becomes a matter of no small concern and one thief who claimed he was, "just giving it a try," is sent to the workhouse at Como Park for three months.

1892 John S. Johnson of Minneapolis becomes one of America's first national cycling champions setting world's records in races of 100 yards to five miles. In September, 1892, he becomes the first person to break the two minute mile with a time of 1:56.6. He later set world records in speed skating as well.

Jan. 24 1894 Farmers and bicyclists join together at the first Minnesota Good Roads Convention held in St. Paul. Professor Pendergast addresses the congress saying, "Wheelmen are no longer confined to the cities. Bicycles, now within the reach of all, are no strangers among farmers. The golden days of which the poets have sung are upon us."

1895 The Minneapolis YWCA sponsors an all-women bicycle club with 60 members.

1890 Flour City Cyclists Clubhouse at 1611 Park Avenue, Minneapolis

MHS Collections

Three women bicyclists and friend on 1896 bicycle path around Lake Harriet.

Minneapolis Park Commission Report

Dottie Farnsworth

1896 The first bicycle path is installed around Lake Harriet by the Minneapolis Park Board. Not to be outdone, the St. Paul Park Board installs seven-foot-wide bike paths on both sides of Como Avenue Parkway and installs racks for 1,500 bicycles at Como Park. Local bicycle clubs get excited about these prospects and propose a bikeway linking Minneapolis and St. Paul funded by user fees from the estimated 25,000 local cyclists.

April 2 1896 Henry Ford takes his first handmade "car" out for a spin in Detroit. The gasoline "quadricycle" consists of a buggy frame mounted on four bicycle wheels and powered with a two-cylinder engine.

1896 Deere and Webber Co. is just one of the many local bike manufacturers that pop up during this first heyday of bicycling.

1896 Bicycle speed records are being set constantly and Minneapolis racer Dottie Farnsworth edges out Mate Christopher, "breaking the world record all to pieces by making 21 miles and seven laps" in an hour. The understated report continues by exclaiming, "a gait of 21 miles an hour is an encroachment on an express train that would excite enthusiasm anywhere."

1896 In England, John S. Johnson breaks the European record for the paced, flying start mile with a time of 1:44. Minnesota nice is no advantage overseas, however. Johnson loses a one-on-one race in front of 15,000 spectators when he stops to allow his adversary to change a punctured tire.

John S. Johnson, "The White Flyer"

Northwestern Horseman and Sportsman

Mrs. Archie Matheis, winner of the Minnesota "Special Meritorious Medal" 1897 competition.

Century Road Club Manual

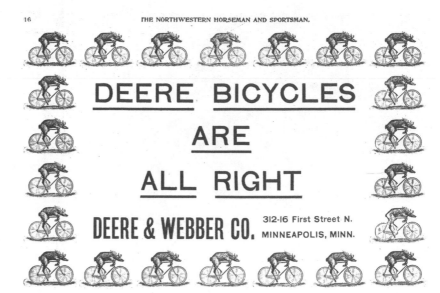
Advertisement from 1896 magazine. Deere and Webber later became the John Deere Co.

1896   Susan B. Anthony proclaims, "the wheel has done more to emancipate women than anything else in the world. I stand and rejoice every time I see a woman ride by on a wheel. It gives a woman a feeling of freedom and self-reliance."

April 1897   The Minneapolis Park Board decides to equip two of its officers with bicycles for the Lake Harriet–Minnehaha Boulevard beat. Reports say, "there is a lively scramble among the officers to see who will do the Board's riding this season."

Aug. 8 1897   Mrs. Archie Matheis becomes the first woman in Minnesota to ride a double century — 200 miles! — in a single day.

Aug. 3 1899   At 2:54 a.m., Gus "Rainmaker" Hansen sets the American record for 1,000 miles on a bicycle with a time of 92 hours and 36 minutes. Known for his knack of bringing rain at the start of a long ride, Gus is also remarkable for eating rhubarb pie as part of his training regiment. He sets the 1,000 mile record riding loops on the cycle path network connecting Fort Snelling with Chowan's Corners near Lake Minnetonka.

1897 bicycle path, Minnehaha Parkway

Minneapolis Park Commission Report

Josephine Parquette and Charles Affleck on a bicycle built for two. St. Paul, 120 W. Congress, 1900. (They married in 1901.)

1899-1900
The St. Paul City Council passes a bicycle ordinance requiring a lighted lantern at night while the Minneapolis City Council passes a law requiring bike licenses. Over 33,000 are sold the first year at 50 cents apiece.

Jan. 1 1900
The annual 100-mile, midnight race between Minneapolis and St. Paul riders is hotly contested. This year, the first century of the new century is at stake and St. Paul cyclists Thomas Bird and James McIlrath take the prize.

June 1902
The *Guide to Minneapolis Bicycle Paths* is published by Rev. Isaac Houlgate. The 57 miles of mapped paths mark the zenith of the Minneapolis path system. "Minneapolis is recognized as a wheelman's paradise," says the *Minneapolis Journal.*

M ~ *Jos McStrath Jr.*

The Pleasure of Your Company is Requested

at the

SECOND ANNUAL DINNER

of the

CENTURY ROAD CLUB OF AMERICA,

At

One O'clock P. M., Nov. 13th, 1898,

At the Long Meadow Gun Club, Minnesota Bottoms.

1904
Just two years later, the *Minneapolis Journal* reports the beginning of the end for the first bicycle craze. It reports that "several local paths will be destroyed this summer," and trees planted in their place. Trolleys and the arrival of the automobile mark the transition.

Taylors Falls was a popular destination for Twin Cities cyclists in 1900.

6
Day
Bike
Race

Sixth
International
Race

Feb. 20
thru 26
1936

MINNEAPOLIS · AUDITORIUM
SPONSORED BY MINNEAPOLIS MILK FUND

15c

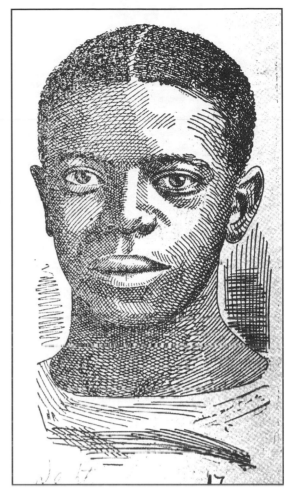

Major Taylor

1905   A *Minneapolis Journal* editorial argues that, "while comparatively few people now go wheeling for pleasure, the bicycle is more than ever the working-man's horse."

1929   The years 1910 to 1930 are the dark ages for bicycling in America. Perhaps the most noteworthy event is the publication of Major Taylor's autobiography, *The Fastest Bicycle Rider in the World: The Story of a Colored Boy's Indomitable Courage and Success Against Great Odds*. Jackie Robinson is generally credited with breaking the color line in professional sports in baseball in 1947, but a half century earlier Major Taylor defied all the odds when he won the world professional sprint championship in 1899 and the U.S. National title in 1900. Taylor first raced in the Midwest.

1931   The Six Day Races begin their run at the Minneapolis Auditorium. Two person teams from throughout Europe and North America compete. The rules provide that one of the racers has to be on the track at all times. The races become extremely popular and in 1936 nearly 40,000 attend the annual event.

1933   Schwinn introduces balloon-tired Excelsior bicycles for kids and helps revive interest in bicycling. With fat tires and ruggedness to spare, Excelsiors reappear in the late 1970s as the first mountain bikes on Mount Tamalpais near San Francisco.

1934   The Gopher Wheelmen bicycle racing club is formed and meets nightly at Lake Calhoun. Today this club is the oldest in Minnesota, and founding member Kenny Woods is still active and bicycling.

1941   With the coming of World War II and fuel rationing, bicycling's fortunes continue to rise. In 1941 a bicycle rental concession is opened near the Lake Harriet Grandstand.

1948   The State of Minnesota produces its first *Bicycle Safety Manual*. There is a section on bike hikes and bike parades. Bicycle accident statistics for 1947 indicate 333 car-bike crashes with eight fatalities (six in the five to fourteen age group). Accidents at intersections account for 69 percent of the total while "disregarding stop signs" and "stunting" are listed among the common causes.

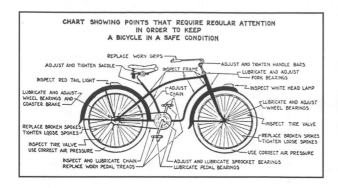

Sept. 25 1955 The Gopher Wheelmen score a major upset by winning the 50-mile Elgin to Chicago Bicycle Race — the oldest in America at the time.

1967 Bicycling's popularity continues to grow for adults as well as for kids. In 1967 the Minneapolis Park Board reopens a bike path around Lake Harriet. The Board also initiates a car-free parkway program on Sundays that is quite popular for the next several years.

Feb. 2 1970 Nearly 800 cyclists complete the First Annual Mid-American Grand Prix Marathon Bicycle Race (otherwise known as the Ground Hog Invitational) around Lake Harriet. Two cyclists decide they have a better route and cut across the lake.

April 18 1972 A bicyclist collides with a pedestrian on a combined bike-walk path around Lake Harriet. The fatal accident spurs the Minneapolis Park Board to separate all walking and biking paths.

Ken Woods, one of the founders of the Gopher Wheelmen, on his "giraffe" unicycle. Ken earned a living from the 1930s into the 1950s bike racing and trick riding around the country.

Oct. 9 1972 The Countryview Bicycle Trail, lauded as Minnesota's first state bike trail, is dedicated. The 22-mile "trail" runs on low traffic roads between Lake Phalen and Stillwater.

Boys bicycling down flooded levee. Stillwater, MN ca. 1945.

Governor Wendell Anderson, wife Mary and son Brett dedicate the Countryview Bicycle Trail.

1973 The Mideast Oil Embargo hits the United States. Gas lines form, stations are closed on Sundays and Americans first face up to their total dependence on imported oil.

Aug. 22 1973 Carl Ohrn, a transportation planner with Barton-Aschman Associates, presents a proposal for an 1,856-mile bikeway system in the Twin Cities. Stating that the average door-to-door speed for auto trips is only 20 miles per hour, he estimates that 8 percent of the 3 million daily metro area trips would be made by bikes if a good system was built.

Sept. 1974 The Minneapolis Public Works Department installs Minnesota's first dedicated bike lanes along University Avenue and Fourth Street at the University of Minnesota campus.

1976 Packed gravel is laid down on the first 6½ miles of the Luce Line State Trail and this becomes Minnesota's second developed rail-to-trail conversion. (The Douglas Trail near Rochester opened in 1975.) Rail trails have eclipsed state parks in popularity, and to keep up with the demand, there are now over 50 built or planned in Minnesota.

1977 Cecil Behringer builds a 200-meter wood velodrome near Shakopee. A metallurgical engineer with several patents, Behringer got his start as a Western Union bike messenger in 1933 and went on to become the Minnesota bike racing champion in 1936.

1978 Minnesotan Chris Kvale and his brother Kevin bike from California to New York City in a record 14½ days.

Feb. 14 1980 The first annual statewide bicycle conference is held at the ArrowWood Resort in Alexandria. Educating motorists, statewide bicycle licensing, and teens on bike patrols are among the topics discussed.

1982 Designed in America and built in Japan, Specialized comes out with the first production mountain bike — the Stumpjumper. Within two years mountain bikes account for a third of all adult bike sales in the United States.

1984 The Minnesota state legislature gives MN DOT the authority to hire a State Bicycle Coordinator and form the Minnesota State Bicycle Advisory Board. Jim Dustrude bikes to his first day of work on Wednesday, September 5, 1984.

Dipping their front tires into the Pacific Ocean, Dan Buettner and crew conclude their record journey. Along for the ride are, left to right, Dan Buettner, Martin Engel, Ann Knabe and Bret Andersen.

Aug. 8 1986 Roseville resident Dan Buettner leaves Prudhoe Bay, Alaska, on the start of his first continent-spanning excursion. He doesn't stop biking until he reaches Ushuaia, Argentina, on June 14, 1987, where the four-person crew celebrates with a king crab dinner. The 15,536 mile trip establishes the first of his world records.

Summer 1987 Hennepin County opens Minnesota's first pilot mountain bike program at Bryant Lake Park on a 3½ kilometer trail.

Nov. 1 1987 Greg LeMond, the first American to win the Tour de France (1986), purchases his new home in Wayzata. He is still recovering from a hunting accident that nearly kills him and takes up cross-country skiing in the off-season.

May 19 1989 The Hennepin Parks Board continues to lead the way in local parks programming and officially approves the first experimental mountain bike trail season at Murphy Hanrehan Park Reserve.

A young Greg LeMond leads the pack at the Nature Valley Criterium around Kenwood Park, Minneapolis. August, 1980. Greg told me that he met his future wife this weekend.

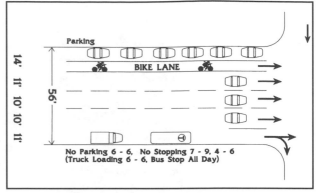

New downtown Minneapolis bike lane diagram.

July 24 1989 — Racing from Versailles into Paris in a stunning 26 minutes, 57 seconds, Greg LeMond wins the Tour de France for the second time. In what is one of the most amazing sporting comebacks of all time, LeMond beats out Laurent Fignon of France by eight seconds — the smallest margin of victory ever in the world's greatest bicycle race.

1990 — Governor Rudy Perpich puts Minnesota on the world cycling map by building the velodrome at the National Sports Center in Blaine. The facility is hailed as the finest racing track in the country.

1990 — Under Minnesota Congressman Martin Sabo's leadership, the 1990 Congress directs the U.S. Department of Transportation to identify the potential of the bike as a mode of transportation. The U.S. DOT releases the multi-volume *National Bicycling and Walking Study* as a result.

Sept. 15 1990 — Just weeks after winning his third Tour de France, Greg LeMond enters his first mountain bike race. On "Fire Tower Hill," he pulls away from his competitors and wins the 35-mile Chequamegon Fat Tire Festival.

1991 — Looking to expand the alternatives for "Bike to Work Day," Jeff Obst coins the phrase B-BOP (Bike, Bus Or carPool) Day. In direct response to the Gulf War (millions of dollars and lives spent to protect U.S. access to cheap oil and almost nothing spent on methods to limit our addiction), RFA launches the first employer-based B-BOP Challenge where participants pledge to B-BOP twice a month, once a week, or more for a four-month period. Since 1991, B-BOP programs have sprung up around the U.S.

1991 — Minnesota Congressman James Oberstar is instrumental in passage of the Intermodal Surface Transportation Efficiency Act (ISTEA or "ice tea") — the most profound national support of bicycling since the Good Roads Movement of a century ago.

Feb. 1992 — *PLAN B*, the nation's first Comprehensive State Bicycle Plan, is produced in Minnesota.

Aug. 1992 — Bike lanes are striped on Summit Avenue in St. Paul from Lexington Avenue west to the Mississippi River. This is the first Minnesota application of sophisticated "straight-through" bicycle striping that is common in many European cities.

Aug. 17 1993 — Fifteen countries, 272 days, 11,877 miles and 4.7 million pedal turns later, Africa Trek, led by Dan Buettner, pulls up to the southern tip of South Africa. Five continents down — two to go.

July 1994 — Tom Becker leads the city of Minneapolis into the 21st century with an unprecedented system of downtown bicycle lanes. Check out Hennepin Avenue, where two-way bicycle lanes share traffic with over 20,000 other vehicles every day.

Feb. 17 1995   A groundbreaking ceremony inaugurates the Cedar Lake Trail. America's first bicycle freeway sports divided, nonstop, one-way lanes heading into and out of downtown Minneapolis. The Cedar Lake Trail (see RIDE 6) connects the city's most popular recreational bike trails with the most concentrated employment node in the state. This is BIG! And once again it shows how history has a way of repeating itself. In 1896 — almost one hundred years earlier — one-way, separated cycle paths first connected downtown St. Paul with Como Park.

Sept. 13 1998   The Saint Paul Classic Bike Tour is enjoyed by 4,900 cyclists, making it the second largest ride ever in Minnesota. The smiling masses are cheered by the Mississippi River and charmed by Saint Paul's friendly neighborhoods. Organizers plan to close the entire route to cars for the 10,000 (cyclists!) in 2000 ride. Call 612-372-3424 to make history!

B-BOP into the next century. Phone 651-602-1602 to learn how.

Jerry Hass, 1995

America's "first bicycle freeway" — the Cedar Lake Trail — offers nonstop service into downtown Minneapolis. See RIDE 5.

Jerry Hass, 1995

BIKE SAFETY – POP QUIZ

Test your knowledge of bicycle safety. The following questions were developed with the help of the **Minnesota Community Bicycle Safety Project** (612-625-9719) and Cynthia McArthur. Answers below.

1. Bicycles are legal vehicles subject to the same traffic laws as cars.

    True   False

2. What percent of bicycle crashes involve collisions with motor vehicles?

    a. 10%   b. 40%   c. 70%   d. 90%

3. Almost half of the children under age nine killed on bicycles die when they bike out of a driveway without looking or yielding.

    True   False

4. Riding on off-road paths is safer than riding on the street.

    True   False

5. Bicycle registration is required by law in the following cities:

    a. Bloomington   b. Minneapolis   c. St. Paul

6. About three percent of all bicycle riding is at night. What percent of fatalities occur at night?

    a. 4%   b. 25%   c. 60%   d. 75%

7. A white light (visible from 500') and a red reflector (visible to 600') are required by Minnesota law. Why are flashing rear lights so popular?

    a. They meet state law.

    b. They are highly visible.

    c. They last "forever" on one battery.

Match the percent of car-bike collisions that occur in each of the following situations:

8. _____ Cyclists fail to yield (pulling out of driveway, at controlled intersection, etc.).

9. _____ Motorists fail to yield (either at a stop sign or when turning left).

10. _____ Being hit from behind.

11. _____ Riding the wrong way against traffic.

12. _____ No lights on bike at night.

13. _____ Opening car doors.

    a. 5%
    b. 7%
    c. 10%
    d. 18%
    e. 30%
    f. 60%

14. What is wrong with this picture?

15. Could you replace your bike for $10.00?

    Yes   No

QUIZ ANSWERS

1. True
2. a. 10%
3. True
4. Statistics vary, but experts generally agree that bike path collisions are more frequent, whereas on-street accidents result in more injuries.
5. b. Minneapolis
6. c. 60%
7. d. All of the above
8. e. 30%
9. e. 30%
10. b. 7% Rear-ending often occurs at night. Experienced riders will use a mirror which is also good on country roads where there is no shoulder.
11. c. 10% It is against the law to ride against traffic and motorists will not expect you.
12. d. 18%
13. a. 5%
14. The bicyclist is riding the wrong way, not wearing a helmet, listening to Barry Manilow and singing, "look Ma, no hands."
15. Probably not but registering your bike will significantly increase the chances of recovering your bicycle. It costs a mere $10.00 and can help to quickly identify injured bicyclists, especially kids. Phone 612-625-9719 or stop by a Motor Vehicle Deputy Registrar, local police department or bike shop to register your bike.

BIKING SAFELY

Minnesota SAFE KIDS in St. Paul (651-291-9150) has helmets at group discount prices for children and adults

If experience is the best teacher then I should be an expert on bike safety. I have been hit by a car at an intersection, run into an opening car door while biking along a line of parked cars, and done a complete flip over the handlebars of a mountain bike after hitting a large rock hidden in some tall grass. Most of my bike accidents happened many years ago, and for the most part, they were my fault. **Truth is, poor cycling skills — not cars — are to blame for most injuries to bicyclists.** In fact, 90 percent of all bike crashes do not involve a motor vehicle.

Bicycling is a fun, life-long activity. Most accidents are easily avoided by following some simple rules. You must be predictable, be seen, and anticipate the worst. However, as Elvis Costello once sang, "accidents will happen," and that is perhaps the best reason to wear a helmet.

BE PREDICTABLE

Obey traffic signs and signals.
Nothing makes motorists more angry than bicyclists blowing past them at a red light. You will run into these same folks later at public bike facility meetings.

Ride on the right with traffic.
Ride in a straight line.

Choose the best way to turn left.
Most experienced cyclists prefer to do it like a car. LOOK, signal, move into the left lane and turn left. At busy, multiple lane intersections you may opt for using cross-walks like a pedestrian.

BE SEEN

Use headlights, taillights, reflectors and reflective vests at night.
Bright neon colors and whites help day or night.

Use hand signals.
Right turns can be signalled in one of two ways. Hold left arm up and bent 90° at elbow or extend right arm straight out. Keep one hand on handlebar.

Go slowly on walks and paths.
Pedestrians have the right of way. Yell, "On your left," when passing.

ANTICIPATE THE WORST

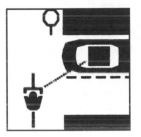

Make eye contact.
Believe that motorists do not see you. Never assume that motorists will:
- Stop at red lights.
- Go straight (even if they have not signaled a turn).
- Look when backing out of a driveway.
- Stay in their lane.

Avoid road hazards.
Slow down. Cross railroad tracks at right angles.

Wear a helmet.

Intersections are dangerous.
Watch for left-turning vehicles and driveway pull-outs.

BICYCLE COMMUTING

We're not blocking traffic, we are traffic!

Cyclist at 1997 Critical
Mass ride in Minneapolis

Small steps can make a big difference. By using just one less gallon of gas each week you will eliminate over 1,000 pounds of pollution each year.

MN Department of Transportation

As many as 2,000 bicyclists now commute into downtown Minneapolis. Bicycling provides no-wait, no-transfer, door-to-door service — just like a car — and this is just one of its attractions.

Most trips (over 75 percent) in the Twin Cities are not work-related. Travelling by bicycle has the same benefits whether you are commuting to the bank, the store or your buddy's place.

It's cheap.

This partly explains the influx into downtown Minneapolis. Some people simply cannot afford to own, operate and park a car downtown.

It's fun.

I would bet this is the number one reason people commute by bike — whether it is to work, the store or a friend's house. Cedar Lake Trail, West River Road and miles of striped bike lanes have been added in Minneapolis. By the year 2000 forty more miles of bikeways will be built out to the western suburbs. See RIDE 5 and get in gear.

It's good exercise.

You don't have to worry about squeezing in time for the club. And the scenery is a lot better.

CHOOSING A ROUTE

Use the maps on the following pages and any additional street maps (see sidebar on MAP SOURCES page 22) to help choose a good route. Once you have determined a good route, practice it once on a weekend. Consider the following:

- Length (2 to 8 miles is typical)
- Your comfort level in traffic
- Personal safety in unfamiliar neighborhoods
- Scenery (try a prettier route on your way home)
- Combining trips on the way home to include shopping, socializing, etc.

DRESS FOR SUCCESS

Dress for the weather and dress comfortably. Take your time. Europeans wear the most stylish clothes while bicycling and never seem to work up a sweat. Some thoughts:

- Pick a "casual day" as your bike day
- Keep an extra set of clothes/shoes at work
- Wear a bright colored shell or reflective vest at twilight
- Bring a polypropylene head band and gloves
- Wear a helmet

BIKE NECESSITIES

- Bright, white clothing
- Helmet that fits
- U-lock
- Fenders
- Reflectors and lights
- Rear rack, saddlebags
- Bell or horn
- Mirror
- Bike registration tag

The well-dressed, fully-equipped bicycle commuter in action.

SAINT PAUL BIKE COMMUTER ROUTES

BN TRAIL to Beam Av.

EDGERTON

ARCADE

ROSE LAWN

GATE-WAY STATE TRAIL

35E

EDGERTON

PROSPERITY

VICTORIA ST.

ARLINGTON

Phalen Park

MARYLAND

Como Park

JACKSON ST.

BRAINERD

CUYUGA

JOHNSON PKWY

PROSPERITY

COMO AV.

HORTON AV.

BURR

Swede Hollow Trail

7TH ST

STILLWATER

GATEWAY DR.

COMO AV.

RICE ST. busy!

TEDESCO

7TH ST busy!

JOHNSON PKWY

HAZEL

SYCMOR

STATE CAPITOL

LAFAYETTE RD.

3RD

3RD STREET

McKNIGHT RD.

UNIVERSITY AV. busy!

PARK

CEDAR

JACKSON

KELLOGG

INDIAN MOUNDS BLVD.

94

CONSTITUTION

7TH

WARNER RD.

BURNS AV.

94

3M

CATHEDRAL

KELLOGG BLVD

CIVIC CTR

WARNER busy!

UPPER CREEK TRAIL

AFTON RD.

SUMMIT AV.

SUMMIT

GRAND

7TH

BATTLE CREEK

GRAND HILL

SMITH

WABASHA ST. busy!

LOWER AFTON RD.

I-35E BIKEWAY

HIGH BRIDGE

CONCORD ST.

61

PT. DOUGLAS BIKEWAY

RANDOLPH

VIEW

GEORGE

OAKDALE ST.

STRYKER

STATE

HUMBOLDT

DOWNTOWN

EDGCUMBE

Mississippi River

SMITH AV.

DODD

DODD ROAD

OAKDALE AV.

JACKSON

WINTER ST.

MT. AIRY

RICE ST. busy!

COMO

CHARLES

UNIV. AV. bad!

SHEPARD

35E

PARK

CEDAR

35E

94

12TH ST.

JACKSON

EAST 7TH

J. IRELAND BLVD

94

ST. PETER

CEDAR

7TH

ST. ROBERT

KELLOGG

SELBY

KELLOGG

WABASHA

WARNER

SUMMIT

WEST 7TH

CIVIC CENTER

SHEPARD

WABASHA

N

All streets shown on map are suitable for experienced bicyclists. Busier streets are noted on the map. All downtown streets are busy on weekdays.

• • Paved Paths.

© 1995 by Richard Arey. Have fun. Take care. Ride at your own risk.

WEB SITE & MAP SOURCES

Good street maps are essential companions for bicycle riding and route finding. Check your city and county for street maps and bicycle route maps.

Web Sites

Web sites can be good sources for bike maps and tons of other information. Check out the chapter on BICYCLE ORGANIZATIONS (page 137) and ANNUAL BIKE EVENTS (page 133) for several more local sites.

- Pioneer Press at www.pioneer-planet.com/archive/bikeguide
- Star Tribune at webservl.star-tribune.com/freetime/duff/bike
- The WWW Bicycle Lane at www. bike-lane.com is "ground zero for bike links"
- Harris Cyclery at www.sheldonbrown.com/harris/index.html is the Net bicycle encyclopedia
- Upper Midwest Cycling at www.umcy-cling.com is good for local racing events
- Pete's BikIndex at www.bikindex.com is great for gear

MN DOT

Metro East, Metro West and Southeast Minnesota Bikeways Phone 651-296-2216 These maps are being updated and should be available by the summer of 1999.

Metropolitan Maps

University of Minnesota
Bicycle Guide and Commuter Map
This 1997 map rates all streets within about 8 miles of campus. Phone 612-625-9719.

Metropolitan Council
Regional Parks Map
Phone 651-602-1140
Web Site: www.metrocouncil.org
My favorite seven county car map.

Little Transport Maps

Twin Cities' Bike Map
This 1999 map highlights the better bike routes throughout the metro area and many of the mountain bike areas.

Minnesota Bike Atlas

Twin Cities Bike Club (612-924-2443)
The fifth edition, published in 1997, is good for road rides over 40 miles.

County Maps

Dakota County (612-891-7030)
Web site: www.co.dakus/parks
Washington County (651-430-4300)
Washington and Dakota County have miles of broad-shouldered country roads.

City Maps

Cities that have bikeway maps include:
- Brooklyn Center (612-569-3340)
- Brooklyn Park (612-493-8335)
- Burnsville (612-895-4500)
- Eagan (651-681-4660)
- Eden Prairie (612-949-8300)
- Hastings (651-437-4127)
- Lakeville (612-985-4600)
- Roseville (651-628-0088)
- Woodbury (651-739-5972)

DO PARK

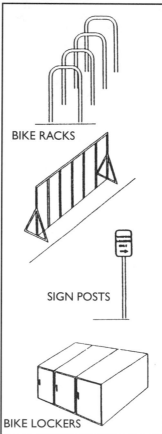

BIKE RACKS

SIGN POSTS

BIKE LOCKERS

DON'T PARK ⊗

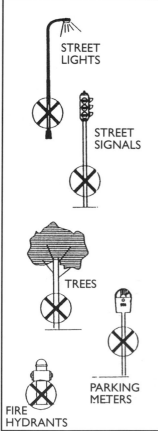

STREET LIGHTS

STREET SIGNALS

TREES

PARKING METERS

FIRE HYDRANTS

BICYCLE PARKING

If you have a four or five hundred dollar (or more!) bicycle, your biggest concern is not how you get to work but whether your bike will be there to get you home. Here are your options.

- Bicycle Registration — This is your best chance to recover a stolen bike should all else fail (612-625-9719).

- Inside Storage — Some companies allow employees to bring their bicycles into the office. Check with building management as well.

- Bicycle Lockers — Over 200 lockers are now available in downtown Minneapolis. Contact Municipal Parking at 612-339-2560. Hennepin County (612-348-7560), various MTC Park-and-Ride lots (651-602-1602), the University of Minnesota (612-625-9000) and downtown St. Paul (651-266-6579) all have, or will soon have, bike lockers to rent.

- U-Locks — Case hardened steel and anti-theft designs make these the best. Lock to approved stationary objects.

- Old Bikes — Using a "winter beater" bicycle can save the worry of losing an expensive bike.

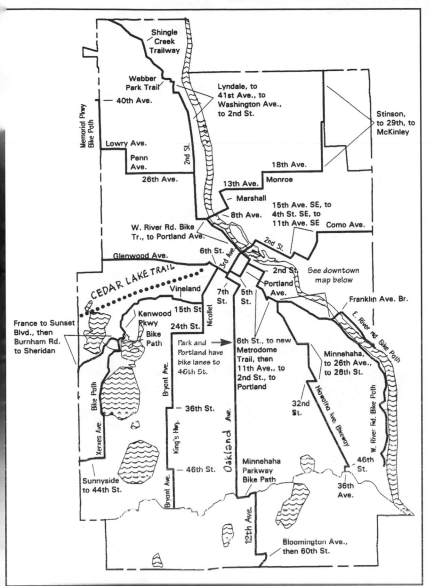

MINNEAPOLIS BIKE COMMUTER ROUTES

The routes shown at left are suggestions only and individual streets vary considerably in their ability to accommodate bicyclists. Use this map in combination with a more detailed street map to plan your commute.

BICYCLE REGISTRATION

Bike registration is mandatory in Minneapolis and your bicycle *may be impounded* if you fail to do so. The $10 fee helps pay for facility improvements. Register your bike at one of these locations or call 612-625-9719.

- Any motor vehicle licensing office
- Hennepin County Government Center
- Minneapolis Parks office at 3800 Bryant Avenue S.

MINNEAPOLIS BICYCLE ADVISORY BOARD

This bike advocacy group consists largely of city staff and has been very successful. Phone 612-673-2411 for details. See BICYCLE ORGANIZATIONS chapter for bike advocacy groups in St. Paul, Hennepin County and elsewhere.

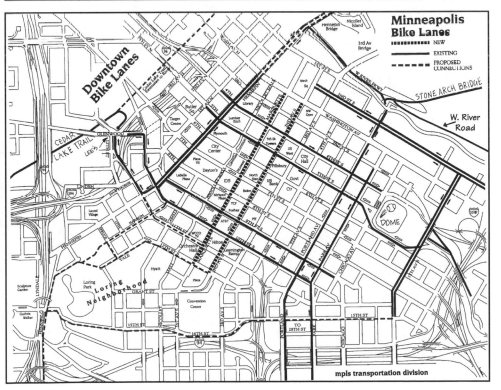

DOWNTOWN BIKE LANES

The striped bike lanes in downtown Minneapolis are almost without precedent for a major American city. They are primarily located on the <u>left</u> side of one-way streets. This feels a little awkward at first but was intentionally designed to avoid conflicts with buses, truck deliveries and opening car doors. The two-way bike lanes amidst Hennepin Avenue may be unique on the planet and are definitely worth a try.

NICOLLET MALL

This unique roadway is currently closed to all bicyclists but couriers.

MINNEAPOLIS BIKEWAYS

See RIDE 5 for an overview of the amazing network of rail-trails leading into Minneapolis that are being converted to bikeways.

Paul Stafford, Minnesota Office of Tourism

There are hundreds of miles of paved off-road trails in the seven county metro area. Most of them are along lakes, parkways, and rivers like the Cannon Valley Trail shown here. See RIDE 38.

RECREATIONAL BIKE TOURS

Do it!	*Just do it!*	*You can do it!*
Jerry Rubin, 1970	Nike Commercial, 1994	Mom, always

The Twin Cities are blessed with as great a network of on-road and off-road routes as any metropolitan area in the country. Bicycle riding is a joy. Pick a route you've never done and follow mom's advice.

These routes have been designed to capture the scenic, historic and cultural highlights of each locale while providing a safe biking experience. Since most cycling accidents are the result of poor biking skills, and only 10 percent involve an automobile, you may want to quickly review the chapters on BIKING SAFELY and BIKE COMMUTING.

Use the WEST METRO BIKE ROUTES map (inside front cover) and EAST METRO BIKE ROUTES map (inside back cover) to locate the following rides.

Many regional parks have their own short off-road path systems for families with very young children. Hennepin Parks (612-559-9000) rents bikes at a number of parks. If you are looking for a longer ride, it is easy to combine two or more routes for as long an excursion as you desire.

The Twin Cities has a number of excellent bicycle shops that can help you select the proper bicycle and help maintain it. Don't get hung up on having the priciest gear or the most stylish clothing — get something that fits and is comfortable. Then get on with it.

If you would like some company on these tours, hook up with one of the local bicycle riding clubs. (See BICYCLE ORGANIZATIONS, page 137.) Portions of these routes are included on regularly scheduled club rides or as part of a yearly event. (See ANNUAL BIKE EVENTS, page 133.)

A well-maintained bike is essential for safe, comfortable bicycling. You will bike with added confidence if you have taken an introductory bike maintenance class At a minimum, carry the equipment and know how to fix a flat.

YOUR GUIDE TO THIS GUIDEBOOK

See RIDE 1, pages 26 and 27, for sample user's guide to bike tour maps, symbols and route connections.

EVERY TIME YOU RIDE

- Check tire pressure and inflate properly
- Spin each wheel to be sure it doesn't rub
- Be certain any quick release mechanisms are tight
- Test brakes
- Make sure bicycle lights are working if night riding

DON'T LEAVE HOME WITHOUT

- Helmet and sunglasses
- Water bottle(s) filled!
- Handlebar bag with plastic map holder
- Maps (one of route and one detailed street map)
- U–Lock and key
- Spare quarters, identification
- Snacks and/or cash
- Windbreaker — white, bright or with reflective stripes
- Gloves, hat
- Handkerchief, paper towels
- Suntan lotion and bug spray

Tool Kit and Skills to Use
- Tire pump
- Tire irons
- Spare tube
- Patch kit
- 6" crescent wrench
- Swiss army knife
- Allen keys, spoke wrench
- Chain link remover

Remember — headlights, taillights and reflectors are required by law at night.

BIKING FOR COMFORT

1. Ride a bike that has the right size frame and seat height. This is the reason to buy bikes at bike shops, not department stores.

2. Stoke up with a good meal that is rich in carbohydrates and low in fat.

3. Stretch before riding, using smooth gentle movements and holding each stretch for 20 or 30 seconds. Repeat at the end of your ride.

4. Pedal easy the first (and last) ten minutes of each ride.

5. Most cyclists pedal far too slowly and in too high a gear. Gear down to make it easier to pedal and get your cadence up to 70 or 80 pedal revolutions per minute.

6. Drink water before you are thirsty and at least one bottle every hour.

7. Shift your hand positions often and/or use padded bars or gloves to keep hands relaxed.

8. Avoid saddle sores by using a gel–filled or sheepskin seat. Position the seat parallel to the ground. Lift your butt off the seat when the ride is bumpy. Buy a good pair of cycling shorts — the sleek fit is for comfort more than looks.

9. Keep feet level on pedals. Avoid pointing toes downward while pedaling.

10. Ride downhill with the wind at your back and a DQ on the horizon.

COON RAPIDS RIDER

Anoka County. Connects with RIDES 2, 3 and 7.

LENGTH RATING

NEW

This notes a new path or ride that was not in last edition of this book.

CAUTION

🌊 20.5 mile loop described includes both paved path systems

⬤ 3.3 mile round trip path at Coon Rapids Dam Regional Park

⬤ 5.7 miles of off-road path at Bunker Hills Regional Park

⬤ 8.0 miles **Mississippi River Regional Trail** goes from Coon Rapids Dam south to Rice Creek Regional Trail. See RIDE 3.

Take the sidewalk path on Hanson Boulevard and take care crossing the Highway 10 interchange. Car parking fee at Coon Rapids Dam.

An easy route that connects the two main recreation destinations in the city. The paved path along the river in Coon Rapids Dam Regional Park is a delight and it is well worth walking your bike across the dam to feel the power of the Mighty Mississippi. And cowa bunga! On the north end of the town the surfs up at the Bunker Hills Wave Pool. Call the city at 612-767-6462 for a city map with the complete trail system.

GO!

Start your ride at the **COON RAPIDS DAM REGIONAL PARK** (612-757-4700). To reach the park take Coon Rapids Boulevard northwest 2 miles from the intersection of Highways 10 and 47. Turn left (south) on Egret Boulevard to park entrance.

NSP donated the dam to Hennepin Parks in 1969 and this continues to be the park's biggest highlight. If you happen to have a really long fishing pole in your tool bag, try trolling for carp on the river or stocked trout in **CENAIKO LAKE**.

After a warm-up lap at the Coon Rapids Dam Park head north on Egret Boulevard and left on Robinson Drive. Pretty **SUBURBAN** through here.

6.7 mi

Take the bridge over the creek in **LION'S COON CREEK PARK** and turn right onto the paved **SAND CREEK TRAIL**. This path has a wooded intimate feeling that is not necessarily enhanced by the neighborhood kids zipping through here. The path has recently been resurfaced but if you are in a hurry you will save 1.7 miles if you continue up Hanson and take **121st AVENUE** over to Foley.

Mileage given is cumulative and generally to the first bold faced **PLACE** mentioned in text. In this instance the rider will have cycled 3.3 miles in Coon Rapids Dam Regional Park and 3.4 miles further to Lion's Coon Creek Park for a total of 6.7 miles.

11.2 mi

Enter **BUNKER HILLS REGIONAL PARK** (612-757-3920) and go up the road a couple hundred feet until you see the paved path on the right. In the distance you may hear the soft strains of a Beach Boys medley. Kendall Bunker had a homestead here in the 1850s. Bunker Hills, like much of Anoka County, lies on the low, sandy topography of the Anoka sandplain. The "hills" are sand dunes that have been stabilized by planting pine and spruce trees.

For the biggest loop, ride through the park and take County Road 116 over to where the trail starts in the northwest corner. If you time your ride just right, you should be able to **CATCH THE WAVE** on your return.

17.6 mi

The sand, waves and stables may have you itching for a "surf and turf" meal but, hey, this is a **DAIRY QUEEN!** Go for the peanut buster parfait.

19.3 mi

Take note of **ERLANDSON PARK** and call your Coon Rapids council member to speed the completion of the trail that will someday connect Sand Creek with a trail to Coon Rapids Dam Park along Coon Creek.

20.5 mi

BACK TO **GO!** Heck, take another spin along the Mississippi or head south on RIDE 3.

Total miles bicycled.

RATINGS FOR RIDES

⬤ Easier – Mostly paved, off-road trails

🌊 Moderate – Mostly on bike-friendly streets

⚡ Experienced – On roads, longer, less protected

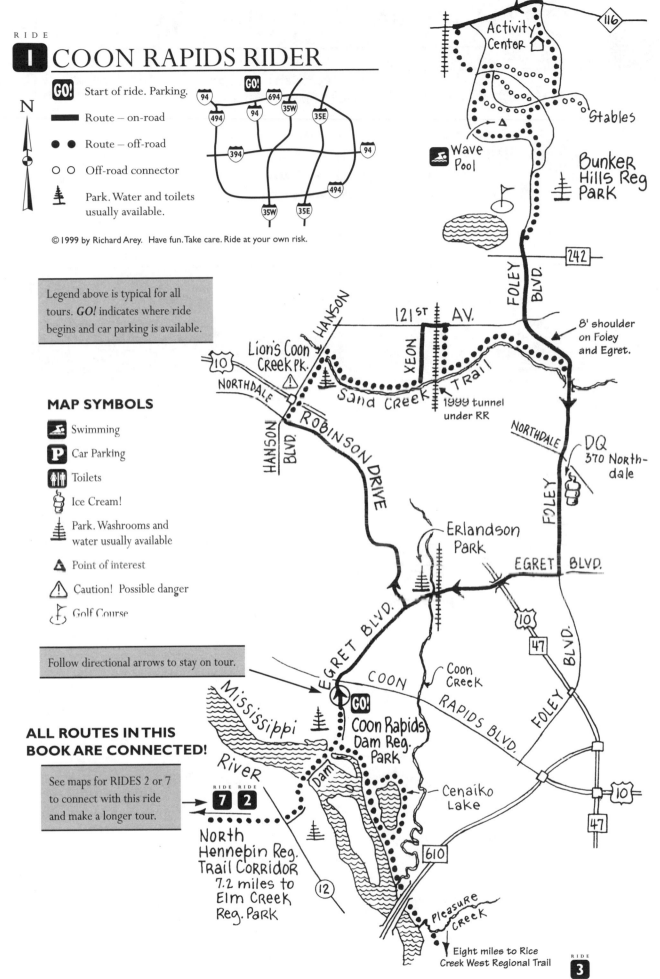

RIDE 1 COON RAPIDS RIDER

GO! Start of ride. Parking.

━━━ Route – on-road

•• •• Route – off-road

○ ○ Off-road connector

Park. Water and toilets usually available.

© 1999 by Richard Arey. Have fun. Take care. Ride at your own risk.

Legend above is typical for all tours. *GO!* indicates where ride begins and car parking is available.

MAP SYMBOLS

Swimming

P Car Parking

Toilets

Ice Cream!

Park. Washrooms and water usually available

△ Point of interest

⚠ Caution! Possible danger

Golf Course

Follow directional arrows to stay on tour.

ALL ROUTES IN THIS BOOK ARE CONNECTED!

See maps for RIDES 2 or 7 to connect with this ride and make a longer tour.

RIDE 7 **RIDE 2**

Activity Center

Stables

Bunker Hills Reg Park

Wave Pool

242

Foley Blvd.

8' shoulder on Foley and Egret.

121ST AV.

HANSON

Lion's Coon Creek Pk.

10

NORTHDALE

HANSON BLVD.

ROBINSON DRIVE

XEON

Sand Creek Trail

1999 tunnel under RR

NORTHDALE

DQ 370 North-dale

FOLEY

Erlandson Park

EGRET BLVD.

10

47

FOLEY BLVD.

EGRET BLVD.

GO!

Coon Rapids Dam Reg. Park

Mississippi River

Dam

COON RAPIDS BLVD.

Coon Creek

Cenaiko Lake

610

North Hennepin Reg. Trail Corridor 7.2 miles to Elm Creek Reg. Park

12

10

47

Pleasure Creek

Eight miles to Rice Creek West Regional Trail

RIDE 3

116

- 27 -

RIDE 2 NORTH HENNEPIN REGIONAL TRAIL

Hennepin and Anoka County. Connects with RIDES 1, 3, 7 and A.

LENGTH RATING

- 14.4 miles – **North Hennepin Regional Trail** round trip
- 20 miles – Elm Creek Park Reserve (See RIDE A)
- 37.2 miles – North Hennepin Trail and both county parks
- 7.2 miles – Hennepin Parks has now opened the parallel turf trail at **North Hennepin Regional Trail** to mountain bikes. It is an east (flat) introduction to off-road cycling.

All four rides are excellent for families.

CAUTION Hennepin Parks annual or daily parking fee required.

> *The North Hennepin Regional Trail joins Elm Creek Park Reserve and the Coon Rapids Dam Regional Park to provide a seamless recreational experience for all levels of cyclists. Elm Creek won Mpls. St. Paul magazine's 1998 award for Best In-Line Skating trail. The North Hennepin Trail is one of the area's oldest separated paths and will be widened and resurfaced in 2000. When first proposed in 1972, demographic studies showed it to be an iffy deal at best. Now these types of trails are the hottest thing going.*

GO! Start at **COON RAPIDS DAM REGIONAL PARK** (612-424-8172) on the <u>west</u> side of the river in Brooklyn Park. Take Highway 252 north from I-694 about four miles. Turn left (west) on 93rd Avenue, proceed three blocks and take a right (north) on Russell Av. (County Road 12) to park entrance.

Check out the West Visitor Center that offers a number of programs and displays relating to the natural history of the Mississippi. Live animal displays include bullheads, a fox snake and the "state threatened" Blanding's turtle.

Be sure to check out the Coon Rapids Dam walkway and Anoka County park facility which includes some great shore fishing and scenic bike paths.

1.5 mi Head west on the **NORTH HENNEPIN TRAIL** (612-424-5511). You can make a short detour to visit Brooklyn Park's **HISTORICAL FARM**. It is open for tours on summer Sunday afternoons from 1 to 4 p.m. (612-493-8368).

3 mi **OAK GROVE CITY PARK** has picnic facilities, some nice woods and two ponds.

Large stands of trees break up the flat landscape that was once used for potato farming. The sandy soil is favored by pocket gophers that like to tunnel underneath the path and cause the occasional sag. The suburbs are largely kept at bay until you approach **ZACHARY LANE**.

7 mi Crossing over Zachary Lane you enter **ELM CREEK PARK RESERVE** (612-424-5511). There are 20 miles of paved trails and a 5-mile mountain bike course that provides an easy introduction to the sport. Wildlife is abundant in Hennepin Parks' largest reserve. Herons, duck, beaver and deer can all be seen from the rolling trail.

The **EASTMAN NATURE CENTER** in the northwest corner of Elm Creek Park offers numerous displays, programs and an observation deck over a large marsh. The center was named for Whitney Eastman, a conservation advocate and charter member of the 600 (bird species sighted) Club in North America. Butterfly tagging is just one of the many programs offered. A monarch butterfly tagged here was later discovered by a researcher in Mexico some 2,000 miles away.

Elm Creek offers many other diversions including a creative play area, swimming, picnicking and bike rentals.

23 mi BACK TO *GO!*

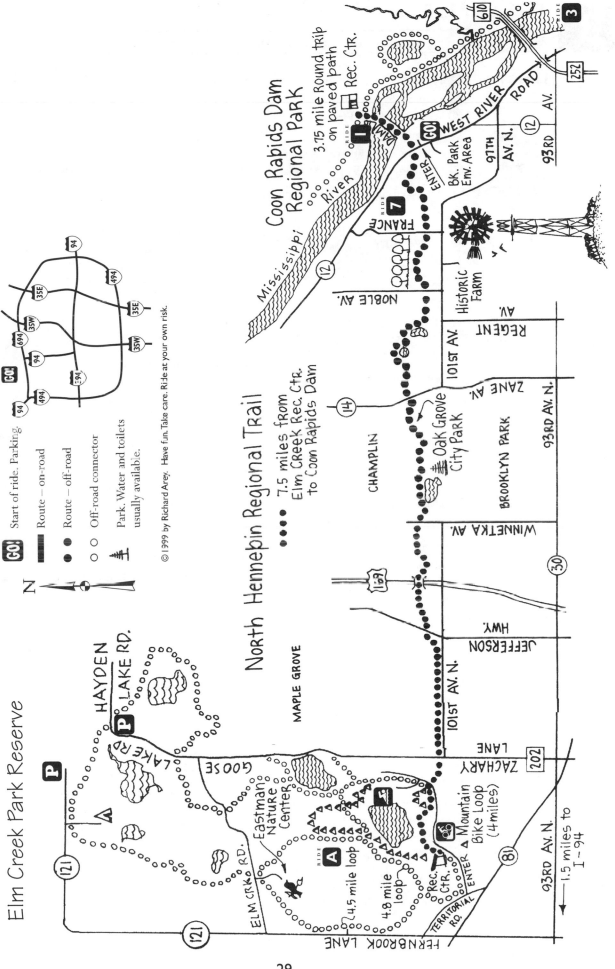

2 NORTH HENNEPIN REGIONAL TRAIL

Elm Creek Park Reserve

North Hennepin Regional Trail

Coon Rapids Dam Regional Park

3.75 mile Round trip on paved path

7.5 miles from Elm Creek Rec. Ctr. to Coon Rapids Dam

GO Start of ride. Parking.

▬▬▬ Route — on-road

●●● Route — off-road

○○○ Off-road connector

⚲ Park. Water and toilets usually available.

© 1999 by Richard Arey. Have fun. Take care. Ride at your own risk.

FRIDLEY FLYER

3

Anoka and Ramsey Counties. Connects with RIDES 1, 2, 4 and 25.

LENGTH
RATING

〰 17.7 miles – Full loop as described, add 6.1 miles for river loop.

◗ 5 miles – Paved paths in Long Lake Regional Park

◗ 5.5 miles – Round trip on Rice Creek Regional Trail

◗ 6.1 miles – Round trip on new Mississippi River paths,
   I-694 south to 37th Av. Camden Bridge

◗ 8.0 miles – One way on **Mississippi River Regional Trail**

NEW

CAUTION   Some gravel paths and short steep pitches along Rice Creek east of Central. Careful crossing Highway 65. Use sidewalk for two blocks along Silver Lake Road.

Beautiful stretches of paved paths along Long Lake, Rice Creek and the Mississippi River are now safely linked. Instead of doing a loop you may prefer to retrace your steps upon reaching 42nd Avenue, or continue south along the Mississippi River until you reach St. Anthony Parkway and the Minneapolis Grand Rounds bike loop.

GO!   Start at **LONG LAKE REGIONAL PARK** (651-777-1707). Take I-694 to 35W north to Highway 96. Exit 96 and go west to Old Highway 8. Turn left (south) on 8 and proceed to entrance on right.

This is a full-service park with plenty to do even if you don't go bicycling. There is a swimming beach with modern bathhouse, a picnic pavilion, creative play area, and nature trails for hiking. Stop by the old New Brighton train station for a dose of history. Cross the new footbridge over Rice Creek on the north end of the park and follow Mississippi Street a short distance to the path that starts on your right.

1.2 mi   Beginning at Long Lake Road the paved path parallels the railroad tracks. Follow this until you reach the intersection of 69th Avenue and Stinson. Head left (south) and you will intersect **RICE CREEK REGIONAL TRAIL**. The first stretch of trail is gravel so you may prefer to take the paved path on 69th Avenue to Central where Rice Creek Trail paving begins.

4.0 mi   Bike up out of the ravine and cross Central Avenue at 69th. Rice Creek was named for **HENRY M. RICE**, a United States Senator. Rice was a resident of St. Paul but in 1849 (the same year Minnesota became a territory) he bought land and built a country residence near here.

Follow the swiftly flowing stream as it oxbows through the pretty wooded ravine. Canoeing the creek is more difficult than it may appear. I have seen two canoes broken in half on visits here.

5.6 mi   **COLUMBIA ARENA** appears as you approach University Avenue. There is public parking here.

6.4 mi   You leave Rice Creek as it tumbles over a rocky rapids below a train trestle.

8.5 mi   The path forks near Mississippi Street. You can head north eight miles to Coon Rapids Dam or bike east over to East River Road and then south past **ISLANDS OF PEACE** county park. (The riverside paths were designed as a retreat for handicapped people and biking is not allowed.) You will pick up a path again just before reaching I-694 and take this under the freeway to **ANOKA COUNTY RIVERFRONT PARK**. Picnic facilities and an exercise course punctuate the flat landscape.

Architecture buffs will enjoy peeking in at the **WATER WORKS** buildings located along the path just south of the park. The romantic brick structures look more like chateaus than utility sheds. You may continue south to the Camden Bridge and loop back on the trails on the west side of the Mississippi.

10.5 mi   The 42nd Avenue bridge takes you up and over the vast railroad yards. Enjoy the view south to the **MINNEAPOLIS SKYLINE**.

13.9 mi   Wide paved shoulders make biking a breeze as you head back home. On a hot summer afternoon you might enjoy a dip at the **MOORE LAKE BEACH**.

17.7 mi   Caution is advised at Silver Lake Road. Take the sidewalk for two blocks. **BEACH ROAD** takes you back into Long Lake Park. Look closely and you may spot the stone foundation of an 1880s roundhouse on the right side of the path. **BACK TO** *GO!*

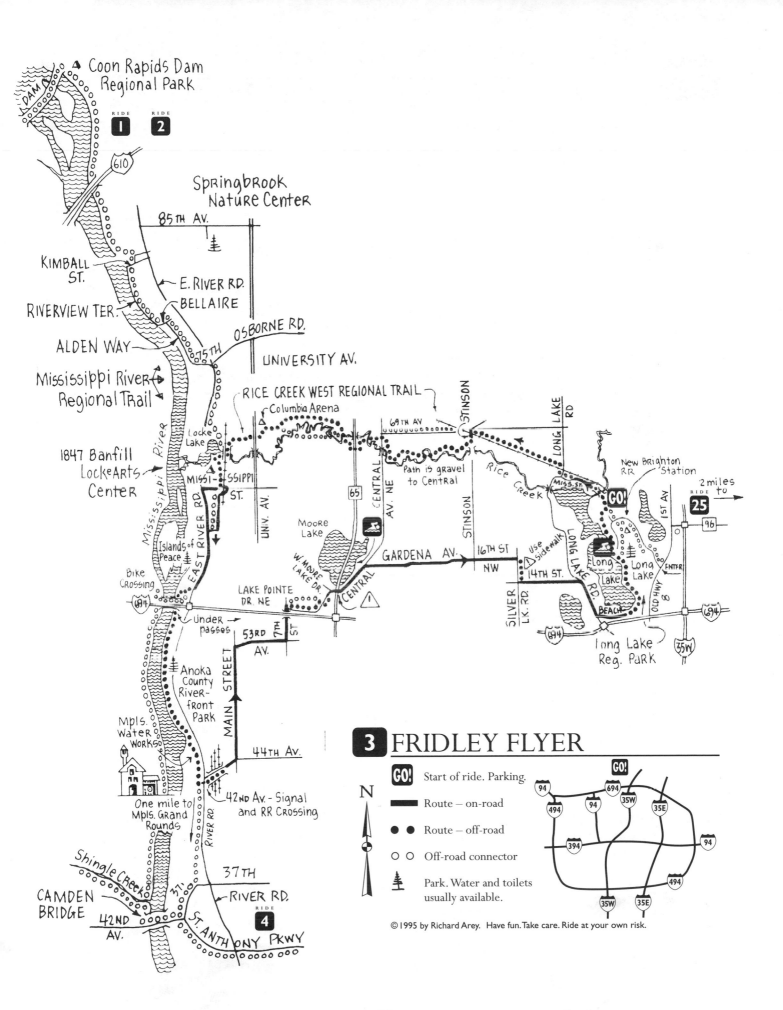

Coon Rapids Dam
Regional Park

RIDE **1** RIDE **2**

610

Springbrook
Nature Center

85TH AV.

KIMBALL
ST.

E. RIVER RD.
BELLAIRE

RIVERVIEW TER.

OSBORNE RD.

ALDEN WAY

75TH

UNIVERSITY AV.

Mississippi River
Regional Trail

RICE CREEK WEST REGIONAL TRAIL

STINSON

Columbia Arena

69TH AV

LONG LAKE RD.

Locke
Lake

New Brighton
RR Station

1847 Banfill
Locke Arts
Center

Mississippi River

Path is gravel
to Central

Rice Creek

MISS. ST.

GO!

2 miles
to

RIDE **25**

96

MISSI- SSIPPI
ST.

UNIV. AV.

65

CENTRAL AV. NE

STINSON

1ST AV

ENTER

Moore
Lake

Islands of
Peace

EAST RIVER RD.

W. MOORE LAKE DR.

GARDENA AV.

16TH ST
NW

Use sidewalk

Long
Lake

Long
Lake

Bike
Crossing

694

Lake Pointe
DR. NE

CENTRAL

14TH ST.

SILVER LK. RD.

OLD HWY 8

BEACH

694

Under
passes

53RD
AV.

7TH ST.

Long Lake
Reg. Park

494

35W

Anoka
County
River-
front
Park

MAIN STREET

RIVER RD.

44TH AV.

Mpls.
Water
Works

42ND AV. - Signal
and RR Crossing

One mile to
Mpls. Grand
Rounds

Shingle Creek

37TH
RIVER RD.

CAMDEN
BRIDGE

42ND
AV.

37TH

ST. ANTHONY PKWY

RIDE **4**

3 FRIDLEY FLYER

GO! Start of ride. Parking.

N

——— Route – on-road

●● Route – off-road

○○ Off-road connector

🌲 Park. Water and toilets
usually available.

© 1995 by Richard Arey. Have fun. Take care. Ride at your own risk.

MINNEAPOLIS GRAND ROUNDS

Hennepin County. Connects with RIDES 3, 5, 6, 7, 8, 11, 19, 20, 27, 30 and 39.

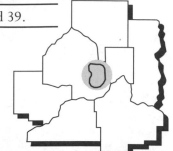

LENGTH 〰 32.7 miles – Full Grand Rounds as described
RATING ◗ 9.8 miles – Minnehaha Parkway, round trip
◗ 9.2 miles – West River Parkway, round trip
◗ 12.7 miles – Wirth and Memorial Parkways, round trip

CAUTION The 15th Av. SE to Como Av. to Stinson Blvd. section is busy.

> *"I would have the City itself a work of art"* H.W.S. Cleveland — *Minneapolis, April 20, 1888.*
>
> *And so it is. Here is the bike ride that delivers it all — gleaming lakes, long majestic boulevards, dancing Minnehaha Falls (when running), and the country's third coast — the Mississippi River. On March 14, 1891, a Special Committee of the Minneapolis Parks Commission, under the leadership of Dr. William Watts Folwell, made the first call for enlarging the park system by creating a "Grand Rounds — a main encircling boulevard or parkway, connecting and passing through several of the larger park areas." By 1918, Wirth, Victory Memorial and St. Anthony parkways had all been developed to join The Lakes, Minnehaha Creek and the Mississippi River. This is one of the most impressive systems in the country, and yet, it has never been truly finished. For decades after 1918 there were plans to connect the "Missing Link of the Grand Rounds Parkway System" through the U of M campus. It still hasn't happened. So sing a few stanzas of "Will the Circle be Unbroken" as you wind your way up from the river to Stinson Boulevard.*

GO! Start your tour at 36th Street and **EAST LAKE CALHOUN PARKWAY**. This is quite near the spiritual, historical and recreational heart of Minneapolis. Within a block or so are the sites of an early Dakota Indian village, the first white residence, and the resting place of H.W.S. Cleveland — the godfather of Minneapolis parks.

1.0 mi Head south and at the first intersection take William Berry Parkway to **LAKE HARRIET PAVILION**.

2.5 mi Follow the separated bikeway clockwise around Lake Harriet to **MINNEHAHA PARKWAY**. The bike path along the Creek is in rough shape but is one of the prettiest in the metro area.

6.1 mi **LAKE NOKOMIS** is reached. If you missed the **DAIRY QUEEN** on Cedar Avenue you have another **DQ** opportunity shortly. The 2.9 mile bike path around Nokomis is not included in the overall Grand Rounds mileage. Beach is on west shore.

8.2 mi **MINNEHAHA FALLS** is located about a block south of Godfrey Parkway. The falls were the inspiration for Henry Longfellow's epic poem, *The Song of Hiawatha,* though he never visited here.

8.6 mi Head up West River Parkway and you will start catching some views of the **MISSISSIPPI RIVER GORGE**. Just north of Franklin Avenue, a long downhill run brings you right next to the river.

13.2 mi Take **FOURTH STREET** up out of the gorge and across the Washington Avenue bridge. Marvel at

Frank Gehry's stainless steel-clad **WEISMAN ART MUSEUM** gleaming above the Mississippi.

15.5 mi **STINSON BOULEVARD** is reached after winding through campus. You have just negotiated the "Missing Link of the Grand Rounds."

21.5 mi St. Anthony Parkway leads to a fine vista at Deming Heights Park. The **CAMDEN BRIDGE** over the Mississippi River allows another distant view of the downtown skyline.

22.4 mi **VICTORY MEMORIAL PARKWAY** was dedicated on June 11, 1921, in honor of the Hennepin County casualties during World War I.

26.4 mi Straight and stately Memorial Parkway begins to curve as it approaches Golden Valley Road and the **45th PARALLEL OF LATITUDE**. Locate the marker at the southeast corner of Wirth Parkway and Golden Valley Road. You are now standing halfway between the North Pole and the equator!

28.4 mi Continue down Wirth Parkway through beautiful **THEODORE WIRTH PARK** — named after the man who took down the "Keep Off the Grass" signs in 1906 and led the Minneapolis park system into the age of recreation. Mileage is to the entrance of **ELOISE BUTLER WILDFLOWER GARDEN**.

29.3 mi Cross I-394 and in a couple blocks you will cross Cedar Lake Trail and take a left onto the bike path at the head of **CEDAR LAKE**.

32.7 mi Follow the famous lakes **BACK TO** *GO!*

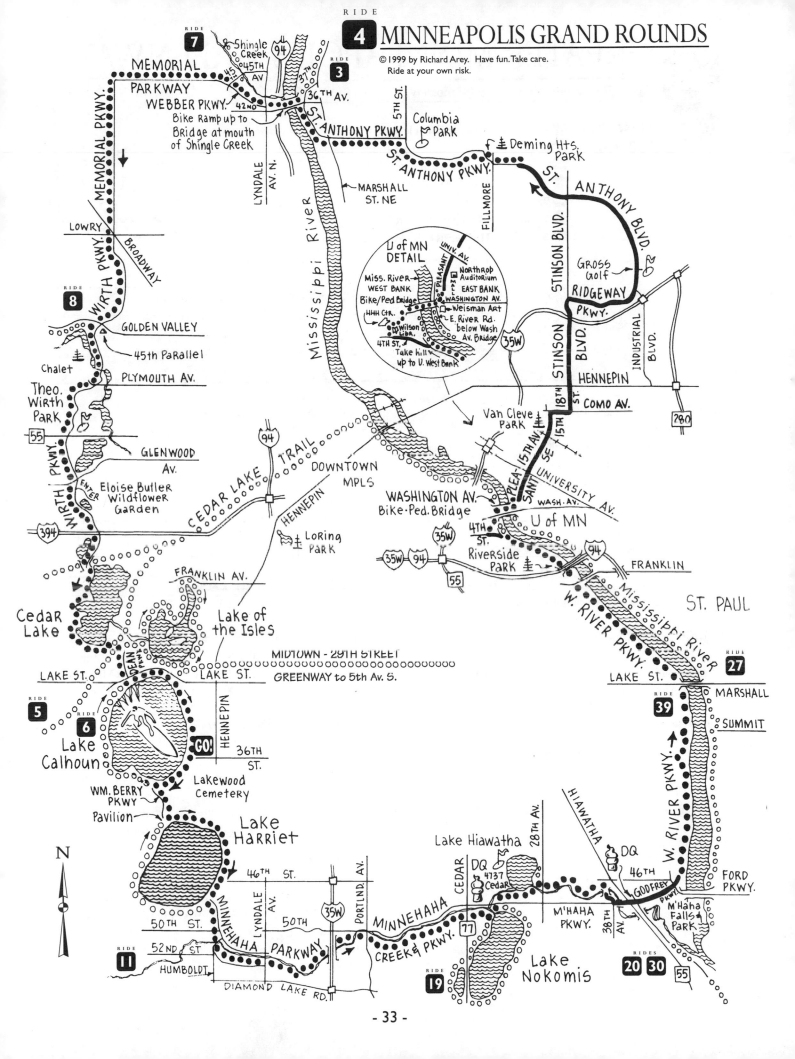

MINNEAPOLIS GRAND ROUNDS

RIDE **4**

© 1999 by Richard Arey. Have fun. Take care.
Ride at your own risk.

GREATER MINNEAPOLIS GREENWAYS

Hennepin County. Connects with most WEST METRO RIDES.

LENGTH
RATING

◖ 1.8 miles – **Bassetts Creek Trail** 8 foot to 14 foot paved
◖ 4.4 miles – **Cedar Lake Trail** 10 foot paved each way
◖ 4.0 miles – **Hutchinson Spur** 10 foot paved
◖ 5.5 miles – **LRT East Corridor** 12 foot paved
◖ 9.0 miles – **Luce Line Trail East** 10 foot paved
◖ 5.6 miles – **Midtown Greenway** 16 foot paved
◖ 3.8 miles – **University Bikeway** 12 foot paved

CAUTION   Most of these bikeways are scheduled to be completed in 1999 but delays may arise.

*F*orget about partying like it's 1999. It's time to bicycle like it's 1999. The network of greenways and bikeways that comes together this year is exciting and inspirational. When complete you will be able to bike from Chaska to the State Fairgrounds on off-road paths; from Hopkins, Plymouth, Maple Grove and Brooklyn Park to downtown Minneapolis on paved trails. You'll be able to hop on a bicycle on Como Avenue in St. Paul and travel off-road to the Cosmos — Minnesota, that is.

BASSETTS CREEK TRAIL

Minneapolis Public Works, 612-673-2411

This trail follows Bassetts Creek south from Plymouth Avenue and Xerxes in Theodore Wirth Park to Bryn Mawr Park and an overpass connection to the **CEDAR LAKE TRAIL**. Scheduled completion date is Fall of 1999.

CEDAR LAKE TRAIL

Cedar Lake Park Association, 612-377-9522 or
Minneapolis Public Works, 612-673-2411

America's first bicycle freeway opened in 1995. It will be extended east through the downtown Minneapolis warehouse district to the Mississippi River (and the trails to the **STONE ARCH BRIDGE**) by summer of 1999.

It is also being extended north (Bassett's Creek Trail), west (Hutchinson Spur) and south (Kenilworth Trail). This is the key commuter link from the 'burbs into the big city. The association's board and volunteers are constantly upgrading the park with prairie restorations, historical interpretation and much more.

HUTCHINSON SPUR – CEDAR TRAIL

Hennepin Parks, 612-559-9000

This trail links the Cedar Lake Trail to the LRT South and East trails. It goes from Highway 100 and Vernon Avenue along the Burlington Northern Railroad corridor west to 28th Street. It then heads southwest to hook up with the LRT Trails at the Hopkins Depot Coffeehouse on the southeast corner of Highway 169 and Excelsior. Fall of 1999 completion.

LRT EAST CORRIDOR

Hennepin Parks, 612-559-9000

This trail is under construction as I write. Trivia fans should note that the base for this trail is the pulverized remains of St. Paul's Civic Center. Makes you wonder where the Dome will end up. The first stretch will open spring of 1999 while the connection to the Kenilworth/Midtown Confluence may have to wait until Fall. This is a worthy but not altogether scenic trail. It does go near **WOLFE PARK**, one of the Cities' best water parks.

LUCE LINE TRAIL EAST

Hennepin Parks, 612-559-9000

After finally resolving some pesky wetland and railroad issues the Luce Line Trail is nearly ready to make the final move from I-494 to Theodore Wirth Park. Along the way (and a great side trip) it picks up the beautiful, paved **MEDICINE LAKE TRAIL** which hugs the shoreline. Year 2000 is the better bet for completion.

MIDTOWN GREENWAY

Midtown Greenway Coalition, 612-724-3288

George Puzak came up with the original concept and a strong grassroots effort has helped put the Midtown Greenway on the map. By 1999 the first phase from Chowen Avenue to 5th Avenue South will be built. The trail follows the 29th street below-grade railway corridor and is being enlivened with some great public art.

UNIVERSITY BIKEWAY

University of Minnesota, 612-625-1333

This project will link the paved trails on the Stone Arch Bridge with St. Paul's **COMO AVENUE BIKEWAY PROJECT** (scheduled for completion in 1999-2000). The center portion of this "Transitway Bike Path" is already built. A paved path will follow the rail corridor east from the Stone Arch Bridge to Mariucci Hockey Arena. The bikeway continues to Raymond Avenue in St. Paul.

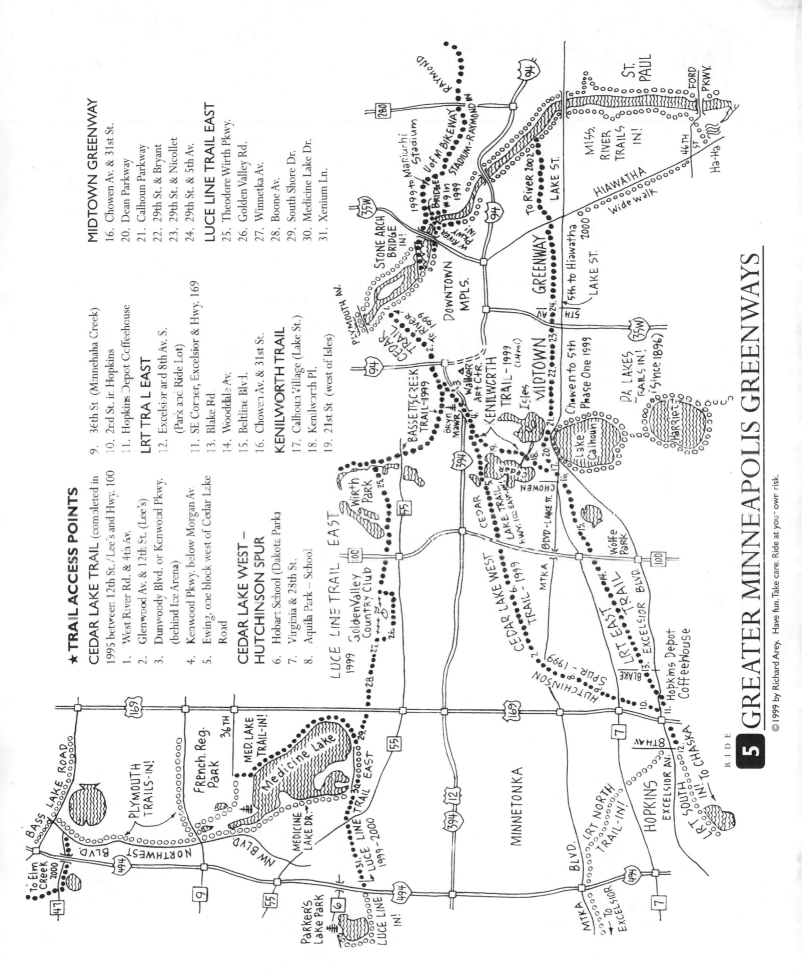

★ TRAIL ACCESS POINTS

CEDAR LAKE TRAIL (completed in
1995 between 12th St./Lee's and Hwy. 100

1. West River Rd. & 4th Av.
2. Glenwood Av. & 12th St. (Lee's)
3. Dunwoody Blvd. or Kenwood Pkwy. (behind Ice Arena)
4. Kenwood Pkwy. below Morgan Av.
5. Ewing, one block west of Cedar Lake Road

CEDAR LAKE WEST –
HUTCHINSON SPUR

6. Hobart School (Dakota Park)
7. Virginia & 28th St.
8. Aquila Park – School

9. 36th St. (Minnehaha Creek)
10. 2rd St. in Hopkins
11. Hopkins Depot Coffeehouse

LRT TRAIL EAST

12. Excelsior and 8th Av. S. (Park and Ride Lot)
11. SE Corner, Excelsior & Hwy. 169
13. Blake Rd
14. Wooddale Av.
15. Beltline Blvd.
16. Chowen Av. & 31st St.

KENILWORTH TRAIL

17. Calhoun Village (Lake St.)
18. Kenilworth Pl.
19. 21st St. (west of Isles)

MIDTOWN GREENWAY

16. Chowen Av. & 31st St.
20. Dean Parkway
21. Calhoun Parkway
22. 29th St. & Bryant
23. 29th St. & Nicollet
24. 29th St. & 5th Av.

LUCE LINE TRAIL EAST

25. Theodore Wirth Pkwy.
26. Golden Valley Rd.
27. Winnetka Av.
28. Boone Av.
29. South Shore Dr.
30. Medicine Lake Dr.
31. Xenium Ln.

RIDE

5 GREATER MINNEAPOLIS GREENWAYS

© 1999 by Richard Arey. Have fun. Take care. Ride at your own risk.

MINNEAPOLIS LAKE DISTRICT

Hennepin County. Connects with RIDES 4, 5, 7, 8 and 11.

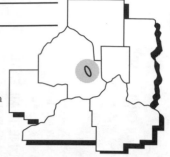

LENGTH   Mileage for each lake given below

RATING   ⬤ Everyone loves The Lakes. New on-road bike lanes

CAUTION On nice weekends and weekday afternoons everyone is out here. Watch your speed and yell, "on your left," when passing. New parking fees are easily avoided by bicycling here. (Minneapolis Parks, 612-661-4800)

*T*he Lakes! We have all been here before. And no wonder. These urban gems are the backyard playground of the Twin Cities. Thanks to the vision of H.W. S. Cleveland, these lakes and surrounding parkways were set aside for public use over a century ago. The unbroken prairie has long since been filled in with large homes, and the lakeside resorts of the 1880s are now the site for swarms of good-looking people circling the shining blue orbs on cycles and skates, strollers and sneakers. Dakota Chief Cloudman established the first village on the southeast shore of Lake Calhoun in 1828. Henry David Thoreau kicked around these same shores in 1861, writer Brenda Ueland grew up here and singer David Pirner wheeled past these lakes before his band Soul Asylum hit it big in the early 1990s.

GO!   Start at the lake of your choice.

1.7 mi one way   **CEDAR LAKE**   Named for the red cedars that once grew alongside the lake and have since been replanted. The **CEDAR LAKE TRAIL** (3.5 miles long) on the north end of the lake provides nonstop service into Minneapolis. This short but spectacular trail has native prairie plantings and an expansive feel with the dramatic Minneapolis skyline looming above.

2.9 mi loop   **LAKE OF THE ISLES**   Known by the Dakota as **WI-TA TOM NA**, or "Lake of Four Small Islands." Two of the islands were lost when Lake of the Isles was dredged and reshaped prior to 1900. Raspberry Island remains and was the site of a heron rookery until 1992. The curving shoreline and impressive residences make Lake of the Isles the most scenic and stately of the lakes. The nearby **PURCELL HOUSE** is a tour de force prairie-style home, open the second Saturday each month (phone 612-870-3131 for reservations).

3.1 mi loop   **LAKE CALHOUN**   "Lake of the White Earth," or **MDE MA-KA SKA**, is the name the Dakota used. It was named Lake Calhoun in 1886 after John Caldwell Calhoun, the Secretary of War, who ordered the establishment of Fort Snelling. Gideon and Samuel Pond were missionaries who built a small cabin overlooking the lake (a marker notes the spot on the southeast part of the lake). This was the first white residence in Minneapolis.

Thoreau tromped around here in 1861 and noted the "myriads of mosquitoes and wood ticks," and that the site of Pond's mission was "overgrown with sumac and covered with gopher heaps." The Lake Calhoun Pavilion was built on this spot in 1879, followed by the Lyndale Hotel, a mansion and now the golden dome of St. Mary's Greek Orthodox Church.

Lake Calhoun draws the youngest crowds. There is a refreshment stand on the northeast corner of the lake.

2.8 mi loop   **LAKE HARRIET**   Distinguished by the Dakota from Lake Calhoun as **MDE UN-MA** or "The Other Lake." It was later named after Harriet Lovejoy Leavenworth, the wife of Fort Snelling's first Commander. The whimsical **LAKE HARRIET PAVILION** rises from the north end of the lake and concessions can be found here along with a menu of summer concerts. The separated bike and pedestrian paths taken for granted in Minneapolis came as a result of a fatal collision between a bicyclist and a walker on a combined path here in 1972.

There are several other attractions around Lake Harriet including historic **STREET CAR RIDES** (612-228-0263), the magnificent tile interior of the **LAKEWOOD CEMETERY MEMORIAL CHAPEL**, bird watching at **T.S. ROBERT'S BIRD SANCTUARY,** a stroll through the **ROSE GARDENS**, and award-winning ice cream at **SEBASTIAN JOES**. Serious bicyclists now have their own on-road bike lane. Some come to refill their water bottles at the **SPRING** and move on.

RIDE 8 7 4

Wirth Lake

Bassetts Creek Trail

GLENWOOD AV.

WIRTH PKWY.

ENTER

Spring Water Well

Theo. Wirth Park

Eloise Butler Wildflower Garden

Cedar Lake Trail

PENN

94

RIDE 5

Target Ctr.

Lee's Bar

Access at Glenwood & 12th

AV.-Bike Lane

HENNEPIN

Nicollet Mall

1ST AV.

WASHINGTON

7TH ST.

MPLS. DOWNTOWN

Basilica

Loring Bar

Loring Park

12TH

Loring Greenway

394

WAYZATA

KENWOOD

Sculpture Garden

100

Brownie Lake

Cedar Lk. Trail

KENWOOD PKWY

Guthrie → Walker ART Center

15TH

CEDAR LK. RD.

CEDAR LK. RD.

CEDAR LK.

22ND ST.

Cedar Lake

FRANCE

CEDAR

PENN

PKWY

Sebastian Joes

FRANKLIN   AV.

IRVING

LK. PL.

Purcell Hse c 2328 Lk. PLACE

24TH ST.

Decent Bike Route

★ Cedar Lk. Trail Access
• Hwy. 100, south of tracks
• Cedar Lk. Rd. and Ewing
• Kenwood Pkwy. below Morgan Av.

LK OF IS. PKWY.

21st

3.

Lake of the Isles

25TH ST.

27TH

LK OF ISL. PKWY.

Midtown Greenway

HENNEPIN

LAKE   ST. 2.

4.

Calhoun Club

DEAN PKWY.

LAKE

5 LAGOON

1.

To Hopkins

EXCELSIOR

RIDE 5

Minikahda (private)

NEW

Kenilworth Trail Access
1. Chowen and 31st Streeet
2. Calhoun Village
3. 21st St.

FRANCE

W. LK. CALHOUN PKWY.

P

P

Lake Calhoun

LAKE

U P T O W N

HENNEPIN

Pond Bros. Cabin Site June 1834

RIDE 6 MINNEAPOLIS LAKE DISTRICT

━━━ Route – on-road
●● Route – off-road
○○ Off-road connector
🌲 Park. Water and toilets usually available.

N

© 1999 by Richard Arey. Have fun. Take care. Ride at your own risk.

Volley ball

36TH   ST.   H

Hubert Humphrey at Rest

Lakewood Cemetery & Chapel

Midtown Greenway Trail Access
1. Chowen and 31st Street
4. Dean Pkwy.
5. Calhoun Pkwy.

WM. BERRY PKWY.

RFLD. RD.

P

P

Spring water pump

Harriet-Como Streetcar line & Station

Sebastian Joes 44th & Upton

42ND

SHERIDAN

Robert's Bird Sanctuary

P

Lyndale Park Peace Garden

Rose Garden 42ND ST.

Decent Bike Route

Beard's Plaisance & Picnic Hill

UPTOWN

44TH

47TH

Harriet Pavilion

KINGS   HWY.

46TH ST.

Lake Harriet

BRYANT

W. LK. HARRIET PKWY.   RIDE 11

5 miles to Minnehaha Falls

MINNEHAHA PKWY.

50TH

The Malt Shop

- 37 -

HENNEPIN EXPLORER

Hennepin County. Connects with RIDES 1, 2, 4, 8 and A.

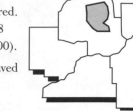

LENGTH Full loop is 39.6 miles. Some traffic and navigational skills required. By 2000 or so, Hennepin Parks will complete their off-road, 11.8 mile path system from Elm Creek to French Park. (612-559-9000).

NEW New 2.2 mile paved trail along Medicine Lake and a new 3.5 mile paved trail circles Rice Lake in Maple Grove and eliminates the need to use Rice Lake Road.

RATING Palmer Lake paved path loop (2.7 miles)

Shingle Creek path from 45th to 63rd avenues (3.5 miles one way)

Elm Creek Park Reserve paved path (20 miles). Ten miles are new.

CAUTION Worst stretch is Medicine Lake Road where you may want to use the sidewalk.

A long, scenic tour linking several communities and their best off-road paths. The Shingle Creek and Palmer Lake trails are undiscovered gems. You will be surprised at how rural the North Hennepin Trail is and may want to do an extra loop in Elm Creek Park Reserve. Enjoy the lake vistas as you return through Maple Grove and Plymouth.

GO! Start at the **45TH PARALLEL OF LATITUDE** stone marker on the southeast corner of Golden Valley Road and Wirth Parkway. You are exactly halfway between the Equator and the North Pole.

0.9 mi Wirth Parkway becomes **VICTORY MEMORIAL PARKWAY** as you march northward. One elm was planted in honor of each of the 555 (later 568) Hennepin County servicemen who died during World War I. The magnificent living archway of elms has been diminished by disease, at least until the hackberry replacements have time to fill in.

3.8 mi Watch for 45th Avenue on your left. Take this across **SHINGLE CREEK** and immediately turn left onto the paved path next to the creek. (If you like, you can make a detour by continuing <u>east</u> on the paved path to the mouth of Shingle Creek and the Mississippi River. The first shingle mill in the county, built in 1852, was located here.)

Continue north along pretty Shingle Creek and remember that the Dakota knew this as **O-MNI-NA** (a calm place, a shelter), **WA-KAN** (a spirit, sacred), **WA-KPA-DAN** (a small stream).

7.8 mi Just past 69th Avenue you enter the **PALMER LAKE NATURE AREA**. Watch for huge waves of migrating waterfowl should you visit early spring or late fall. The path picks up Shingle Creek again on the north side of the marsh.

15.1 mi Brooklyn Park's **HISTORICAL FARM** is a living record of Minnesota farm life from 1890 to 1910. It is open for tours on summer Sunday afternoons from 1 to 4 p.m. Phone 612-493-8368.

15.4 mi A **NEW TRAIL** is being built from Shingle Creek to the Historical Farm and **NORTH HENNEPIN TRAIL**.

19.8 mi **ELM CREEK PARK RESERVE** is Hennepin Parks' largest preserve with over 5,400 acres. There are 20 miles of paved bike/hike trails and a swimming beach. This ride only crosses a corner of the park.

21.3 mi Exit the park on **TERRITORIAL ROAD** (right) and then head south (left) on Fernbrook. You may want to stop at City Hall to pick up a map of Maple Grove as the next stretch is a little tricky. (**NEW PATH** – late in 1999 – will connect Elm Creek Park with Bass Lake Road.)

Across the street from City Hall a paved path begins. Follow the route shown. If you get lost you can skip the lakeside trails and take Rice Lake Road and then East Fish Lake Road to Wedgewood. If you don't get lost, take a short detour to **FISH LAKE PARK**. There are picnic facilities overlooking the lake and a short bike trail.

32 mi **CLIFTON FRENCH REGIONAL PARK** is named for Hennepin Parks' first parks superintendent. A great new 12' paved path has been built along the east side of Medicine Lake.

36.2 mi Forget the hassle of Medicine Lake Road with a Brownie Delight at **DAIRY QUEEN**.

39.6 mi After enjoying the occasional skyline views on Sandburg and Golden Valley Roads, its **BACK TO** *GO!*

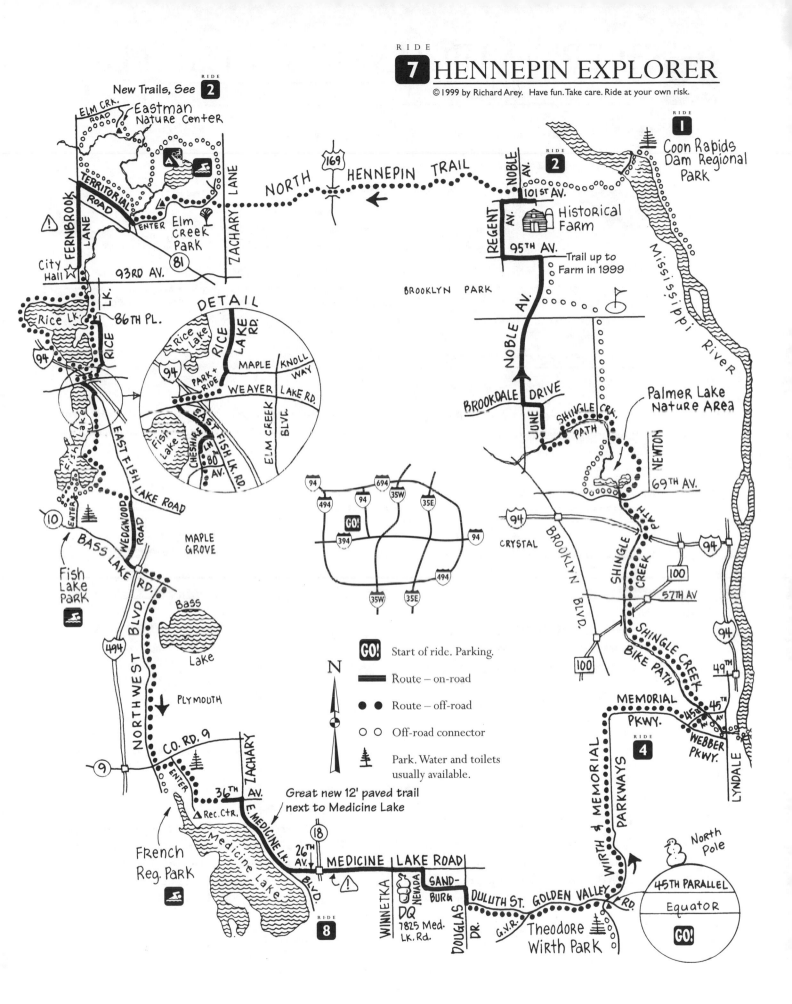

EVERY WHICH WAY TO THE LUCE

Hennepin County. Connects with RIDES 4, 5, 6, 7, 9 and 10.

LENGTH   〰 31.2 miles – Big loop plus Medicine Lake as described below
RATING   ◑ 8.1 mile loop around Medicine Lake
       〰 24.4 miles – Big loop without Medicine Lake

Intermediate – quite a few hills but no major traffic.

A new paved path goes from County Road 16 (McGinty Road) north
to Linner Road. It crosses above Stone Road just west of I-494. Take
the ramp up and you can eliminate the confusing road connection.

CAUTION   Roads have shoulders or low traffic counts. Sunset Trail has big hills.

This mid-length tour connects one of the newest trails, the Cedar Lake Trail, with the metro area's oldest conversion, the Luce Line State Trail. The route capitalizes on some long stretches of bike-friendly roads for an enjoyable afternoon ride. Highlights include the historic C.H. Burwell House, the Medicine Lake loop and the return ride through Theodore Wirth Park. Nice fall color ride.

GO! The parking lot on the west side of **CEDAR LAKE** is an arbitrary choice and perhaps most people will simply bicycle to the route. See RIDE 6 for detailed map showing location of Cedar Lake.

.8 mi Bike/pedestrian bridge over the Cedar Lake Trail. Nice **SKYLINE VIEW** of downtown Minneapolis.

5.3 mi Penn Cycle Shop is on the corner at Cedar Bend if you need any last minute fine tuning. Down the block is the **CHEEP SKATE ROLLER RINK** for a wheely good time.

7.2 mi The **C.H. BURWELL HOUSE**, built in 1883, is on the National Register of Historic Places. Even better, the grassy slope down to Minnehaha Creek makes for a lovely picnic site. Charles Burwell was manager of the flour and grist mill that was first used for milling lumber in 1852. The lovely East-Lake-style home is open for tours in summer on Thursday and Friday afternoons and the first and third Saturday of the month from noon to 3 p.m.

8.3 mi **MEADOW PARK** – has water, washrooms and play area!

8.5 mi **TRAIL TO LINNER** at Stone Road and I-494.

13.3 mi Follow the winding streets closely (or take the new trail) and you'll find the trailhead for the **LUCE LINE STATE TRAIL**. Head West young man and don't stop until you have entered the Cosmos. Cosmos, Minnesota, that is. See RIDE 10.

22.1 mi Stop by the **FRENCH REGIONAL PARK** Visitor Center for more refreshments, take a swim, or goof off a little at the rather amazing creative play area. (My friend thought we were approaching a zoo when she first saw it.) The park is named after Hennepin Parks' first Superintendent, Clifton E. French. Clif guided the acquisition of what has become one of the finest park systems in the country. And he is a great guy to boot.

29.3 mi Enjoy the modern skyline views of Minneapolis — especially nice when reflecting the late afternoon sun — as you cruise down Glenwood Avenue on your way to **THEODORE WIRTH PARK**. Theodore Wirth combined the vision of H.W.S. Cleveland with the park land purchases of Charles Loring to forge the great system of Minneapolis parks and parkways we enjoy today. He came to town in 1906 and ushered in the modern era of recreation. Wirth began by removing the "keep off the grass" signs and ended his career some four decades later with a proposal for a vast metropolitan parks system that is now being realized.

31.2 mi As you bike down the path toward Cedar Lake make one last stop at the small parking lot just north of I-394 (west side of parkway). Across the way is the largest red maple in the city. A short walk behind you is a fascinating tamarack bog. Perhaps another time. **BACK TO** *GO!*

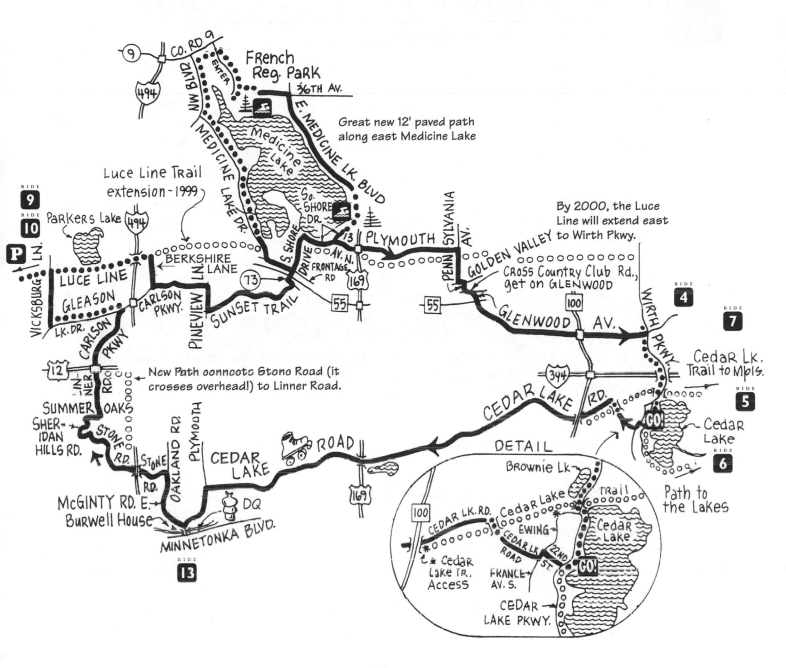

Great new 12' paved path along east Medicine Lake

Luce Line Trail extension - 1999

By 2000, the Luce Line will extend east to Wirth Pkwy.

Cross Country Club Rd., get on GLENWOOD

New Path connects Stone Road (it crosses overhead!) to Linner Road.

Cedar Lk. Trail to Mpls.

Path to the Lakes

DETAIL

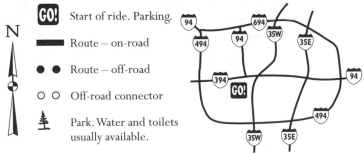

ON THE ROAD TO FREEDOM

Hennepin County. Connects with RIDES 8, 10 and 12.

LENGTH
RATING

31.9 miles – Luce Line Trail out plus Baker Park loop

6.2 miles paved path – Baker Park Reserve

23.8 miles – Road route without Baker Park loop

6.5 miles – Paved path at Lake Rebecca Park Reserve

CAUTION   Big hills abound and traffic is moderate but there are 5 foot to 8 foot shoulders on Country Roads 6, 19 and 24. County Road 19 has quite a bit of traffic on summer weekends.

If you got this book for Christmas, stop by Baker Park Reserve where they have opened a four-mile-long trail for **winter mountain biking**. Use parking lot on County Road 201. Phone Hennepin Parks at 612-559-9000 to obtain a special use permit.

A glorious ride when the trees are ablaze. This tour takes you to Lake Independence and stands of mature hardwood are seen on much of the surprisingly rural route. Bicyclists have the option of taking either the Luce Line off-road path or the road out to Baker Park Reserve. Families may just want to do a lap or two at Baker Park Reserve and finish their day with a dipped cone at Dairy Queen or a dip in Lake Independence.

More adventurous bicyclists can go north on County Road 19 and west on County Road 11 (no shoulder!) to beautiful Lake Rebecca Regional Park. Lake Rebecca sports the finest fall foliage in the Hennepin Parks system.

GO!

Start at the **LUCE LINE STATE TRAIL** (651-296-6157) parking lot on the west side of Vicksburg Lane, south of County Road 6. Take Vicksburg Lane north to County Road 6 and head west. Past Highway 101 the houses are replaced by rolling farms, wetlands and woodlots. NOTE: A second option is to follow the Luce Line out to Budd Avenue.

5.3 mi   First stop is **WOLSFELD WOODS SCIENTIFIC and NATURAL AREA.** Watch for Trinity Lutheran Church and pull into the parking lot. This is perhaps the finest remaining example of the "Big Woods" (named "Bois Grand" by early French explorers) left in Minnesota. Do not even think of bicycling in here! In spring — when wild flowers brighten the forest floor — or for fall colors, it is definitely worth locking up your bike and taking a stroll. Red oaks over 200 years old and near-record-size sugar maples are your reward.

6.6 mi   Enter **BAKER PARK RESERVE** on the paved trail off County Road 6. The park was donated by Morris T. Baker in 1957 and was first in the long line of great Hennepin County Parks. Most activity is focused on Lake Independence. Biking around Lake Katrina and the surrounding marsh showcases the natural beauty of Baker Park. Watch for trumpeter swans on the lake as you bike along the southern and western portion of the loop.

9.4 mi   If you're in the mood you can exit the park and catch a cone at the **DAIRY QUEEN** on the northeast corner of County Road 29 and Highway 12.

11 mi   Main entrance to **BAKER PARK** is on the left. Bicycle rental, swimming, camping, picnic facilities — and a mess of summer people — can be found here. If the lines are short, I highly recommend a glide on the cable ride at the creative play area.

19.4 mi   Follow the scenic contours of County Roads 19, 201 and 24 around the northern edge of Baker and over to scenic **HOLY NAME LAKE**. The quaint Italianate-style Holy Name Church is a landmark signalling your reentry to suburbia.

23.8 mi   BACK TO *GO!*

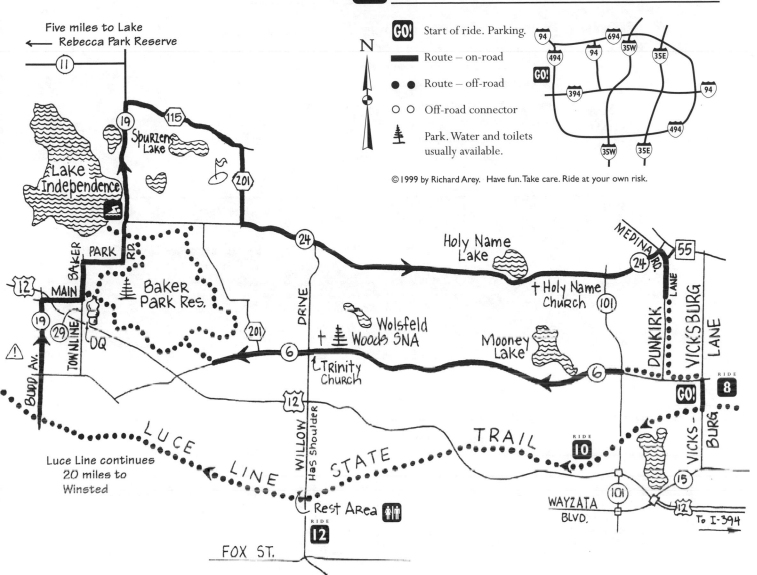

RIDE 9 ON THE ROAD TO FREEDOM

GO! Start of ride. Parking.

━━━ Route – on-road

•••• Route – off-road

○ ○ Off-road connector

🌲 Park. Water and toilets usually available.

© 1999 by Richard Arey. Have fun. Take care. Ride at your own risk.

Five miles to Lake Rebecca Park Reserve

Spurzem Lake

Lake Independence

Baker Park Res.

Holy Name Lake

Holy Name Church

Wolsfeld Woods SNA

Trinity Church

Mooney Lake

Luce Line continues 20 miles to Winsted

LUCE LINE STATE TRAIL

Rest Area

RIDE 12

FOX ST.

RIDE 10

RIDE 8

GO!

Vicksburg Lane

Dunkirk Lane

Medina Rd.

WAYZATA BLVD.

To I-394

LAKE REBECCA REGIONAL PARK

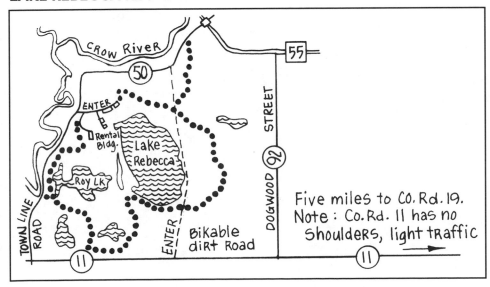

CROW RIVER

ENTER

Rental Bldg.

Lake Rebecca

Roy Lk.

TOWN LINE ROAD

ENTER

Bikable dirt Road

DOGWOOD STREET

Five miles to Co. Rd. 19.
Note: Co. Rd. 11 has no Shoulders, light traffic

LUCE LINE STATE TRAIL

Hennepin, Carver, McLeod, Meeker. Connects with the Cosmos (Minnesota, that is).

**LENGTH
RATING**

- 72 miles – Entire **Luce Line Trail**, one way when complete
- 29 miles – One way, Vicksburg Lane to Winsted (packed gravel)
- 34 miles – One way, Winsted to Thompson Lake (turf and dirt)
- 9 miles – One way, Vicksburg *east* to Wirth Park (paved by 2000)

Two new bridges and an improved trail surface have greatly improved biking opportunities west of Winsted and especially west of Hutchinson. Closer to home, Hennepin Parks is ready to pave the nine mile stretch from Wirth Park to the Vicksburg Trailhead in 1999-2000.

PHONE   DNR Trails and Waterways, 651-296-6157.

Although this trail leads to the Cosmos, it was built on the broken dreams of W.L. Luce. In 1902 Mr. Luce began construction on a 1,000-mile rail service from Minneapolis to Brookings, South Dakota. By 1915 or so, an electric train was carrying city folks out to dances at the Stubbs Bay Hotel and Pavilion. But financial difficulties ensued and the line was terminated at Glueck, Minnesota, in 1927. The railway was abandoned in 1971. Through the efforts of the first Luce Line Trail Association, the trail was authorized for construction in 1973 and built starting in 1976.

The Luce Line State Trail is said to follow a route used by the Dakota Indians nearly two centuries ago. It provides an excellent escape from the ever-expanding suburbs. The landscape is rolling and wooded at first, becoming level farmland west of Watertown. In August, watch for the many native prairie flowers blooming along the way.

GO!   **TRAILHEAD** with parking and toilets is located at Vicksburg Lane just south of County Road 6. Mile posts below are heading <u>west</u>.

5.4 mi   This first stretch to **WILLOW DRIVE** is one of the prettiest and easily the most heavily used. The trail traverses an area of lakes, marsh and hardwood forested moraines just north of Lake Minnetonka. The **REST AREA** just west of Willow Drive has picnic tables, water and outdoor toilets.

7.0 mi   A small parking lot is located on the west side of **STUBBS BAY ROAD**.

19.0 mi   **WATERTOWN** rests on the banks of the South Fork Crow River. The trail leading here is still quite pretty with occasional canopies of trees and nice views over **OAK LAKE**. A short detour on the quiet streets of Watertown can include a water stop at **VETERANS MEMORIAL PARK** downtown.

29.0 mi   Pastures and fields are broken by small knolls covered with oak trees on your way to **WINSTED.**

Thrushes, killdeer, finches and pheasant will be your most likely trail companions this far out. A beautiful curving path around Winsted Lake takes you into the quiet old town founded in 1887.

37.0 mi   **SILVER LAKE.** The packed limestone path ends at Winsted. The surface is turf and dirt out to Hutchinson.

44.0 mi   **HUTCHINSON** has a fine 2-mile, paved path through town and along Otter Lake and the Crow River. Hutchinson may some day be the small town bike capitol of the Midwest. A cooperative project between MN DOT and the country of Finland is using the town for a case study on bike-friendly development.

64.0 mi   A better path now leads to the **COSMOS**. This tiny town was organized in 1870 under the ancient Greek name for the universe as an orderly and harmonious system.

63.0 mi   A pleasant stretch of path leads to the **TRAIL'S END** at Cosmos County Park on Thompson Lake.

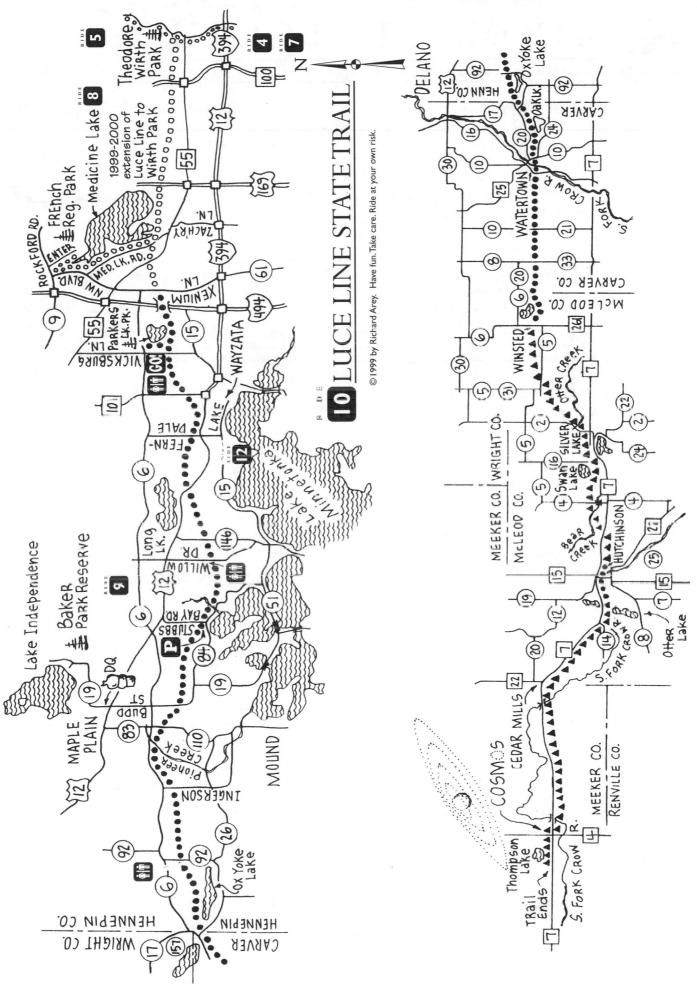

LUCE LINE STATE TRAIL

RIDE **10**

© 1999 by Richard Arey. Have fun. Take care. Ride at your own risk.

RIDE

BLOOMINGTON OR BUST

Hennepin County. Connects with RIDES 4, 6, 14, 17, 19, B and C.

LENGTH
RATING

19.2 miles – Loop around Hyland Lake Park Reserve described below
5.0 miles – Paved path in Hyland Lake Park Reserve
TO HYLAND LAKE PARK RESERVE VISITOR CENTER
11.7 miles – From 50th and Minnehaha Parkway in Minneapolis
12.2 miles – From Excelsior and 8th Avenue in Hopkins
7.2 miles – From Staring Lake Park in Eden Prairie

CAUTION Shady Oak Road has a shoulder and some traffic. Watch directions and street signs closely on routes into Bloomington.

Many people heading for Bloomington end up at the Mall of America and come out a little poorer, if not busted. I recommend a different target, the natural center of town being the 1,000 acres of lakes, woods and wildlife that comprise Hyland Lake Park Reserve. (See RIDE B) This oasis in the middle of Minnesota's third largest city is deservedly popular. A creative play area, fishing, picnicking and pleasure boats are yours to enjoy. You can even rent a bike on the premises if necessary. Pack up your tire patch kit and head on down.

GO! Start at the main parking lot in **HYLAND LAKE PARK RESERVE** (612-941-4362). Park entrance is reached by taking Highway 100 (Normandale Blvd.) south from I-494 to 84th Street. Turn right (west) and follow 84th to East Bush Lake Road. Go south to entrance on left. Of course, if you had biked down you would have saved yourself the car parking fee.

1.8 mi Head up and over to the paved path that follows the west side of **BUSH LAKE** along Bush Lake Road to Veness Road. There are some nice picnic grounds here.

A 3.5 mile side trip (not included in following mileage) up to the virgin stands of oak, maple and basswood in **TIERNEY WOODS** is well worth it. Lock up your bike, take a stroll and imagine the 300 square miles of Big Woods that once swept from Faribault up to St. Cloud.

10.8 mi Retrace your steps to Veness Road and then head south along Bloomington Ferry Road. You skirt the bluffs along Auto Club Road and are teased by a couple nice views across the Minnesota River Valley. Normandale and 98th take you to **MARSH LAKE PARK**. A 100-foot-long earth dam preserves a wildlife refuge and controls the flow of flood

waters. I spotted a loon diving for fish here one August afternoon.

11.8 mi Watch closely for a service access road off France Avenue (on the north edge of campus) that takes you to the **NORMANDALE JAPANESE GARDEN**. This small contemplative place was exquisitely designed by Takao Watanabe, a landscape artist from Tokyo.

18 mi **MT. NORMANDALE LAKE** shimmers in the reflection of the sleek office towers that rise above 84th Street. Look cool as you do a lap around these popular paths.

17.1 mi The only on-street biking on this route is the hard uphill on East Bush Lake Road. (This could explain the ski jump you bike past.) There is a shoulder, but sadly, no elevator. Eventually you reach the entrance to **RICHARDSON NATURE CENTER** (612-941-7993). Bluebirds and deer herds are just part of the attraction. Stop back some time when you can take a stroll as bikes are not allowed inside.

17.3 mi The City of Bloomington has just finished a million dollar renovation of **BUSH LAKE SWIMMING BEACH**. Check it out.

19.2 mi BACK TO *GO!*

- 46 -

11 BLOOMINGTON OR BUST

© 1999 by Richard Arey. Have fun. Take care. Ride at your own risk.

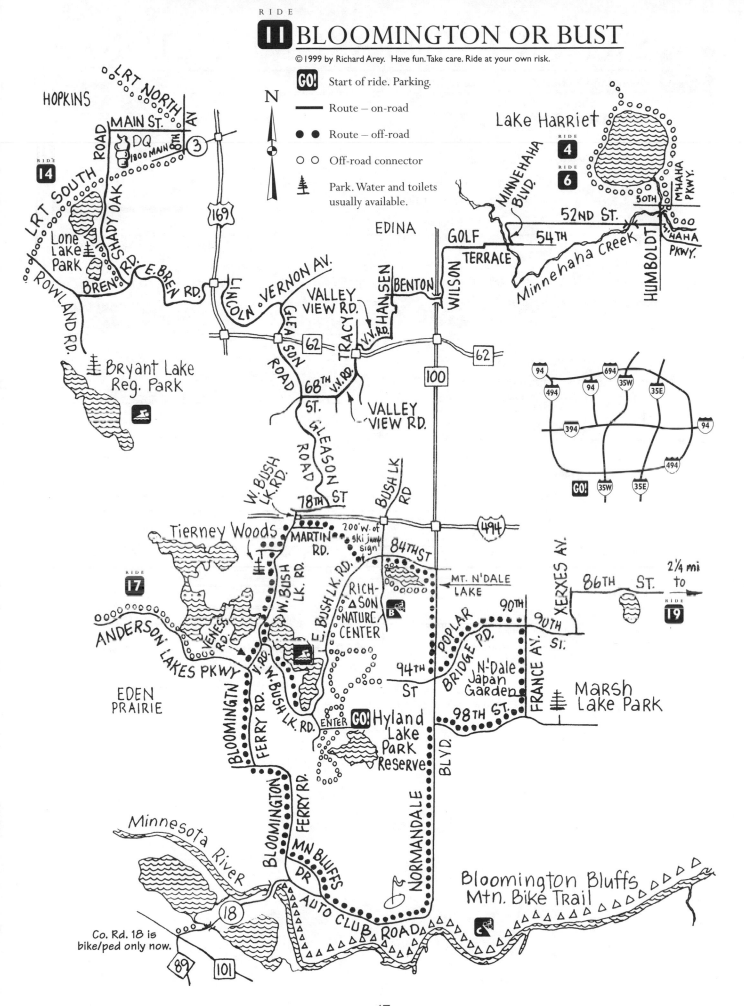

GO! Start of ride. Parking.

Route – on-road

• • Route – off-road

○ ○ Off-road connector

Park. Water and toilets usually available.

SWIM ROUND LAKE MINNETONKA

Hennepin County. Connects with RIDES 8, 9, 10 and 13.

LENGTH 29.2 miles to stop at each beach

RATING   Experienced riders only. LRT route is flat and easy.

CAUTION County Road 19 and North Shore Drive get busy.

NEW County Road 15 is busy but has a good shoulder (except for one very short stretch) and goes right along the lake.

*M*ore than just a guide to all the public swimming beaches on Lake Minnetonka — this is a great bike route for experienced riders in any season. Fall colors make the route especially memorable and the springtime flower displays at Noerenberg Park are well worth stopping for. History buffs should note that the Dakota names "minne" — water, and "tonka" — big, were combined by Territorial Governor Alexander Ramsey after a visit in 1852 and that the Native American name for the lake has been lost in time.

GO! Start at the **MINNETONKA CITY HALL** (612-939-8200) parking lot just west of I-494 on Minnetonka Boulevard. This lot is always open to the public.

1.7 mi Minnetonka Boulevard is a little rushed (an off-road trail is planned) so you'll be glad to see the Lake Shore Boulevard turn. Take this to Park Lane and **LIBB'S LAKE BEACH**. Start swimming.

5.0 mi Follow the quiet, winding streets over to the **DEEPHAVEN SWIMMING BEACH**. Dip your front tire into the lake while you ponder where **PRINCE** christened his lady friend in the movie *Purple Rain*.

10.1 mi **EXCELSIOR PARK** has a fine beach and bathhouse. With all the people milling about you'll want to be doing your best breaststroke as you round the point.

12.8 mi Watch your directions coming through Excelsior as you head to **CRESCENT BEACH**. This tiny beach

holds a panoramic view. Sunsets must be great here but time's a wasting.

14.7 mi **TONKA BAY BEACH** (alias Wekota Beach Park) is hidden back amidst the big houses. Float awhile as you consider what it would be like to be wealthy.

19.4 mi Stop and smell the roses at **NOERENBERG MEMORIAL PARK.** Fred Noerenberg came here from Berlin in the 1880s and established the brewery that became Grain Belt. Today 10,000 flowers are planted here each year, including some bulbs from the original European stock.

24.6 mi You are almost certainly ready for a swim by now. **WAYZATA BAY BEACH** is a first-class operation with changing rooms and showers. Show off the sidestroke you've been practicing.

29.2 mi **BACK TO** *GO!* Take McGinty Road or the shortcut across Minnehaha Creek. I'm sure you'll want to towel off and head to **DAIRY QUEEN**, about a mile east of City Hall on Minnetonka Boulevard.

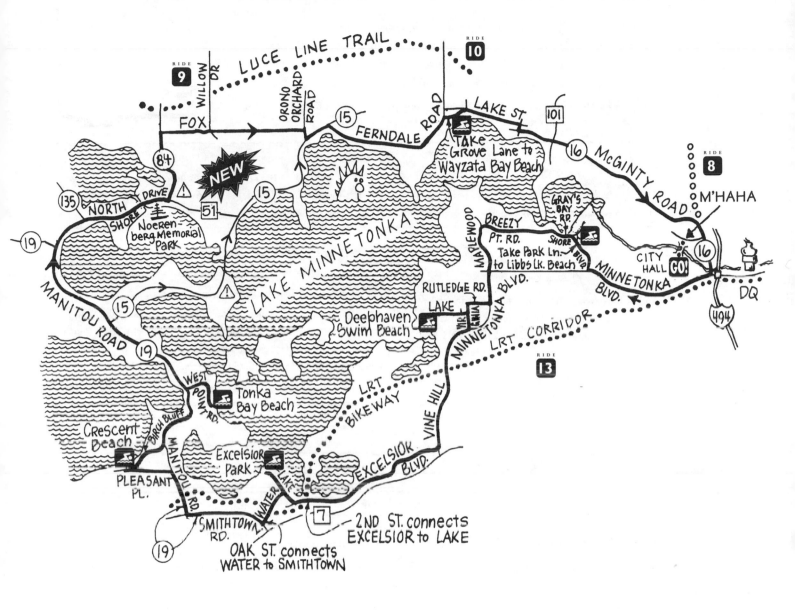

SWIM ROUND LAKE MINNETONKA

RIDE 12

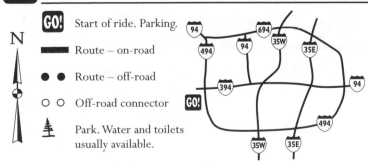

N

GO! Start of ride. Parking.

—— Route – on-road

• • Route – off-road

○ ○ Off-road connector

🌲 Park. Water and toilets usually available.

© 1999 by Richard Arey. Have fun. Take care. Ride at your own risk.

RIDE 13 LRT TRAIL NORTH

Hennepin and Carver County. Connects with Rides 5, 8, 12, and 14

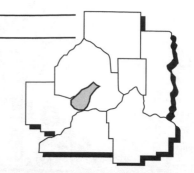

LENGTH
RATING

- 🚲 16.0 miles – One way as described to Victoria
- 🚲 8.5 miles – Additional paved path in Carver Park Reserve
- 〽️ 37.4 miles – Loop using County Road 11 and LRT South

Path is packed limestone. Trail is open 5 a.m. to sunset.

CAUTION   Be careful crossing all roads along path and on County Road 11 if connecting with LRT Trail South.

This is a very attractive and popular off-road path. LRT Trail North follows the abandoned railroad bed of the Chicago and North Western Railway and traverses beautiful woodlands, skirts the shores of Lake Minnetonka and goes by some very nice real estate before delivering you to Carver Park Reserve (Phone 612-472-4911). Carver has plenty of biking and other diversions so some folks may wish to drive out and spend the day here.

GO!   Start in downtown **HOPKINS**. The trail begins at 8th Avenue just north of Main Street.

2.4 mi   Follow the paved path through the quiet backyards of residential Hopkins. Cross over Highway 7 and into a more natural setting. **DAIRY QUEEN** is across the street at 12940 Minnetonka Boulevard.

3.6 mi   The Minnetonka **CIVIC CENTER** has parking and washrooms available on weekdays.

9.5 mi   A couple short but tasty stretches of lakeside path take you to the bustling village of **EXCELSIOR**.

14.5 mi   **CARVER PARK RESERVE** contains 3,300 acres, 8.5 miles of bike paths and six lakes (Lake Auburn has camping and a swimming beach). These abundant natural resources are the focus of programming at the **LOWRY NATURE CENTER**.

16.0 mi   Or, continue on through the town of Victoria to the **DQ** at the corner of County Roads 5 and 11.

RIDE 14 LRT TRAIL SOUTH

Hennepin and Carver County. Connects with RIDES 5, 11, 13, 15, 16 and 17

LENGTH & RATING   🚲 11.5 miles – One way off-road limestone path

CAUTION   Follow the marked signs as you zig-zag across 62nd Street and Highway 5. There is a 5-foot shoulder and traffic on Highway 212 going <u>into</u> Chaska but shoulder is not continuous coming back.

Dedicated on June 3, 1995, this is the latest — and one of the greatest — rail-to-trail conversions in Minnesota. Employing the old rail bed of the C&NW Railway, this limestone path provides safe and scenic passage from Hopkins to Chaska. Those with a mountain bike and a yen for adventure can bike through Chaska (RIDE 15) and on to the Minnesota Valley State Trail (RIDE 16) that goes all the way to Belle Plaine, a 39.2 mile (one way) off-road trip! Hennepin Parks Trail Hotline is 612-559-6778.

GO!   Start at the **PARK AND RIDE** lot at Excelsior and 8th Avenue in Hopkins, (just west of Highway 169).

6.0 mi   The trail winds past a series of lakes and wetlands before taking you up, over and under the bridge at Highway 62. Soon you reach **EDENVALE PARK** at Valley View Road.

8.5 mi   The shores of **LAKE RILEY** make a nice rest stop, though there are no facilities.

9.5 mi   **A SWEEPING PANORAMA** of the Minnesota River Valley is gained from the overlook marking the trail's long gradual descent to the valley floor.

10.5 mi   **BLUFF CREEK RAVINE** is located just past Highway 101. Car parking is available where the trail intersects Bluff Creek Drive.

12.2 mi   The path traverses a wide marsh before reaching Highway 212 and **TRAIL'S END**. There is a path or shoulder on 212 that goes into Chaska.

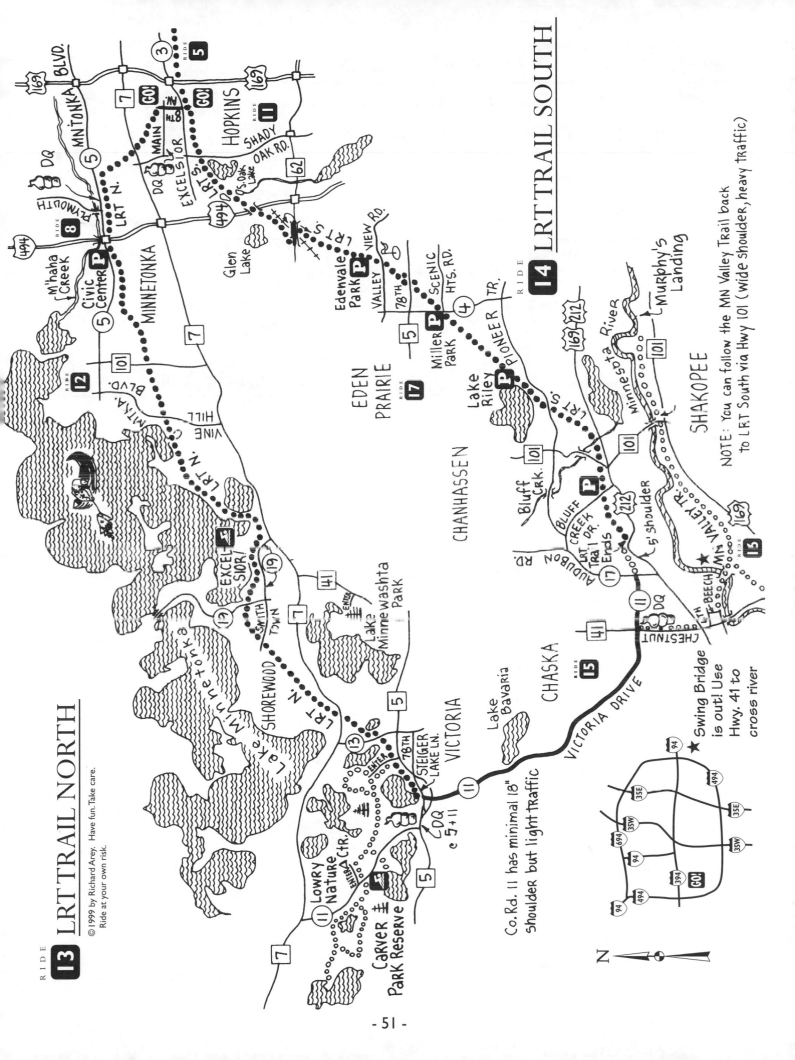

LRT TRAIL NORTH

RIDE **13**

© 1999 by Richard Arey. Have fun. Take care. Ride at your own risk.

LRT TRAIL SOUTH

RIDE **14**

NOTE: You can follow the MN Valley Trail back to LRT South via Hwy 101 (wide shoulder, heavy traffic)

★ Swing Bridge is out! Use Hwy. 41 to cross river

Co. Rd. 11 has minimal 18" shoulder but light traffic

RIDE 15

CHASKA CHASER

Carver County. Connects with RIDES 14 and 16.

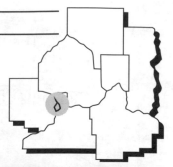

LENGTH	13.2 miles – Route as described below (mostly gravel)
RATING	25 miles – Total miles of path shown on map
	⚫ All trails are rated easier but there are some hills.
CAUTION	Watch out for pedestrians along the paths and cars at road crossings.
PHONE	City of Chaska, 612-448-2851.

These are some of the prettiest off-road city paths in the metro area and well worth a visit even if you live as far away as St. Paul. The paved path from Shakopee (See RIDE 16) glides over the vast wetlands of the Minnesota River and an ancient iron swing bridge before cruising into Chaska. The rest of the trails fan north through the old river town, up wooded ravines, past lakes and into the new town of Jonathan. Along the way, there are songbirds and soybeans, modern architecture and monkey bars. There is a bit of everything along these trails that can easily take the better part of a day to explore. Be courteous while sharing the trail and then head for a DQ with a view. That's right. The Dairy Queen at 1095 Chestnut Street North is perched on a bluff with a vista that just doesn't quit. There are several other choices for food and refreshments in downtown Chaska.

GO!   Start your tour at the **CITY SQUARE** in downtown Chaska on the corner of Walnut and 4th Street. The old fashioned square looks one step removed from the set of *The Music Man* and also features a couple of ancient **INDIAN MOUNDS**. Chaska comes from the Dakota name that was generally given to a first born son.

0.6 mi   Cross over Highway 212 and find the trail going east (right) along the lake. This will take you to the start of the **WOODED RAVINE**.

1.4 mi   **LIONS PARK** is a short way up the path and has ballfields, tennis courts, toilets and a picnic shelter. The **SMALL BROOK** running through the ravine looks innocent enough, but my last trip here in 1992 was shortly after the engorged stream had tossed footbridges around like matchbooks. Exit the ravine up the paved path to the south near the school. Turn right and go north along Highway 41 past the top of the ravine you were just in.

3.4 mi   Carefully cross **HIGHWAY 41** and look for the connecting path about 50 yards to the north. Continue up the ravine.

4.2 mi   Cross under Hundertmark Road and enter **JONATHAN**. While Chaska is the quintessential river town with roots going back to the mid-1800s, Jonathan is the original new town, developed as a **MODEL COMMUNITY** back in the late 1960s. This brainchild of State Senator Henry McKnight

has fallen far short of its original goal for a town of 50,000, but the modern architecture, separated path system and lakeside community center are a testament to his dream. Jonathan was named after Jonathan Carver, who journeyed up the Minnesota River in 1766–67 in search of a route to the **PACIFIC OCEAN**.

4.7 mi   **JONATHAN BEACH** is located on the southeast corner of Lake Grace. Swimming is allowed on summer afternoons, and there are changing rooms, toilets, a volleyball court and picnic facilities.

5.5 mi   Follow the **CHAIN OF LAKES** north to McKnight Park. Parking and picnicking are located here. Continue north along the lakes by walking your bike across the railroad tracks.

7.7 mi   The **TRAIL ENDS** at 82nd Street just shy of the Minnesota Landscape Arboretum.

12.4 mi   Retrace your path back to Highway 41 and then follow the paved path along the west side of 41 to **DAIRY QUEEN**. You know what's good for you.

13.2 mi   Coast on **BACK TO** *GO!* Add 8 miles for round trip to Shakopee.

15 CHASKA CHASER

© 1999 by Richard Arey. Have fun. Take care. Ride at your own risk.

ENTER

82nd St.

Minnesota Landscape Arboretum

Co. Rd. 18 and 19 paths 1999-2000

CO. RD. 18

Hazeltine Lake

Chaska Par 30 Golf Course

Hazeltine Nat'l Golf Course (Private)

McKnight Road

Lake Bavaria

100 Acre Park

McKnight Park

JONATHAN

Lake Grace

Pioneer Trail

Paved Shoulder

Bavaria Road

Hundertmark Road

Community Park

Friendship Park

Underpass at Hwy 41

Chaska East Creek

Wooded Ravine

RIDE 14

HWY. 212

School Campus

Engler Blvd.

5'-0" PAVED SHOULDER

Co. Rd. 11

Bavaria Rd.

Meadow Park

Lions Park

Chaska Creek

Co. Rd. 10

Victoria Drive

Crosstown

DQ

Minnesota River

Schimelpfenig

Chaska East Creek

Minnesota Valley National Wildlife Refuge

CHASKA PARKS AND TRAILS

N

Firemen's Park

Co. Rd. 140

5TH ST

CHASKA

Walnut St.

4th St.

Beech St.

City Square

Swing Bridge

3 Miles to Shakopee (Paved Trail)

CITY PARKS AND OPEN SPACE

EXISTING TRAILS

PROPOSED TRAILS

P PARKING AND TRAILHEAD

PICNIC SHELTER

PUBLIC SWIMMING

★ Swing Bridge is out! Use Hwy. 41 to cross river

Winkel Park

HWY. 212

Athletic Park

Chaska Lake

HWY. 41

MN. River Valley Trail

RIDE 16

20 Miles to Belle Plaine (Gravel/Dirt Trail)

HWY. 41

94 | 694 | 35W | 35E
494 | 94 | 35W | 35E
394 | 94
494
35W | 35E

GO!

CO. RD. 18

HWY. 41

Co. Rd. 19

Co. Rd. 17

MINNESOTA VALLEY STATE TRAIL

Scott and Carver County. Connects with RIDES 15 and G.

LENGTH
RATING

25 miles (one way) – Belle Plaine to Shakopee. Mountain bike ride.

10.0 miles (round trip) – Shakopee to Minnesota River. Paved, easier

6.1 miles mountain bike loop at the Lawrence Unit.

CAUTION

This route is long, isolated, and sometimes under water. Mountain bikes work best on the flat dirt and sand trail. Bring extra water and a friend. Mosquitoes are bad in summer. Phone Trail Headquarters (612-492-6400) in advance to check on trail conditions.

NEW

A new bike-pedestrian bridge is being built next to Highway 41 in 1999 to replace the old swing bridge. A mile long, paved path connecting it to the Shakopee Trail will also be built.

I know this isn't Montana, but I've always thought of the Minnesota River Valley as Big Sky Country. Certainly it is an immense valley — over 3 miles from bluff to bluff — carved by the powerful, glacial River Warren some 10,000 years ago. It is only when the Minnesota River is in a major flood, like the summer of 1993, that you get a hint of the River Warren's size. Floods like this were the impetus for creating the Minnesota Valley National Wildlife Refuge in 1976. It is one of only a handful of urban wildlife refuges in the country. A place where wild coyotes, bald eagles, badgers and beavers live comfortably within minutes of 2 million people.

The Refuge consists of several units strung along the river from Fort Snelling to Belle Plain. Eventually a 75-mile trail will join them all together and extend up the river to Le Sueur. Stop by the Visitor Center (3815 E. 80th Street in Bloomington, or phone 612-854-5900) for an excellent overview of the Refuge and scheduled activities. RIDES 19, 30, 31 and M visit parts of the Refuge not discussed below.

GO! The paved path starts in Shakopee. It goes four miles west to the Minnesota River and one mile east to Memorial Park. There is parking next to the trail one block east of Hwy. 101 in Shakopee.

GO! The following route description begins in Belle Plaine. Start where the trail intersects State Highway 25. You will need to park on a side street in **BELLE PLAINE** as there is no trailhead. See map and description for other trailheads.

4.3 mi **LAWRENCE UNIT** is a **TRAILHEAD** and campground with parking, toilets and picnic facilities.

6.6 mi The 1859 **STAGECOACH STOP** (0.2 miles up from the river) is about all that remains of the pioneer settlement of St. Lawrence.

7.9 mi A small canoe campsite across from **BEVENS CREEK** is the site of a steamboat landing that operated here in the 1850s. This is the trail's most remote section and the path is occasionally sandy, but the opportunity to enjoy a wilderness setting so close to home offsets any drawbacks.

9.7 mi The trail is lifted high above the river to an **OVERLOOK** on a sandy dune.

10.8 mi **THOMPSON FERRY** operated until the 1930s and was the key link between Chaska and Jordan when it began during Minnesota's territorial days. Today, there is a **TRAILHEAD** here with parking.

13.8 mi The **LOUISVILLE SWAMP** area has a **TRAILHEAD** and several miles of mountain bike trails that are described in RIDE G. Take the right fork to enter this area.

16.4 mi Louisville Swamp trails connect again with the Minnesota Valley Trail at the mouth of **SAND CREEK**.

17.5 mi Shortly after crossing under the railroad tracks the **TRAIL FORKS**. The expansive wetlands impart a feeling of great openness here. In early spring the trail following the river is your best bet, but in drier times the route past Gifford Lake is 1.7 miles shorter and just as scenic.

22 mi The two trails converge, and about a quarter mile later you reach the **PAVED PATH** to Shakopee. The 1870 Swing Bridge that crossed the Minnesota River just west of here was damaged by floods and removed in 1996.

24.5 mi The path winds through some woods and then breaks into the open where a **GRAND PANORAMA** of the valley unfolds.

25.0 mi Shakopee is named for the great Dakota Chief Shakopee (SA-KPE), meaning six in Dakota, whose village was here.

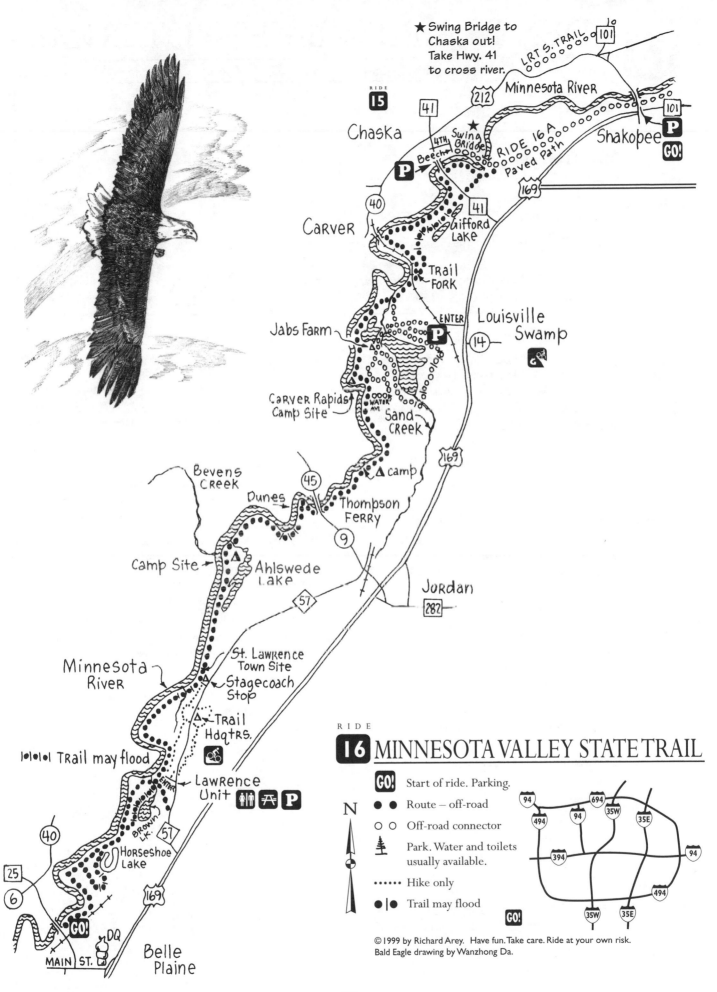

★ Swing Bridge to Chaska out! Take Hwy. 41 to cross river.

LRT S. TRAIL

Minnesota River

101

RIDE 15

41 212

Chaska

4TH Beech Swing Bridge

RIDE 16 A Paved Path

Shakopee

101 P GO!

40

Carver

Gifford Lake

41

Trail FORK

169

Jabs Farm

ENTER P

Louisville Swamp

14

Carver Rapids Camp Site

WATER Avl.

Sand Creek

169

△ camp

Bevens Creek

45

Dunes

Thompson Ferry

9

Camp Site △ Ahlswede Lake

Jordan

57

282

St. Lawrence Town Site

△ Stagecoach Stop

Minnesota River

△ Trail Hdqtrs.

Trail may flood

Lawrence Unit

40

BROWN LK.

51

25

Horseshoe Lake

6

GO!

DQ

MAIN ST.

Belle Plaine

169

RIDE
16 MINNESOTA VALLEY STATE TRAIL

GO! Start of ride. Parking.

● ● Route – off-road

○ ○ Off-road connector

🌲 Park. Water and toilets usually available.

····· Hike only

●|● Trail may flood

N

94 694

494 94 35W 35E

394 94

35W 35E 494

GO!

© 1999 by Richard Arey. Have fun. Take care. Ride at your own risk.
Bald Eagle drawing by Wanzhong Da.

17 EDEN PRAIRIE – BIKES NOT BOMBS

Hennepin County. Connects with RIDES 11 and 14.

LENGTH
RATING

⚡ 20.8 miles – Full loop as described

🎾 2.4 miles – One lap around Staring Lake

🎾 11.1 miles – Short loop, cut across on Anderson Lakes Parkway

CAUTION Eden Prairie has an excellent map showing their entire park and bike-way system. Phone 612-949-8300 for information.

The Planes of Fame Air Museum used to be the marque billing for this route but went down in flames — nevertheless, the city of Eden Prairie has done an excellent job in providing a network of paths that connect neighborhoods, lakes and office parks. The trail around Staring Lake Park is especially nice as are the views out across the Minnesota River Valley and Anderson Lakes. Eden Prairie was named in 1853 by Mrs. Elizabeth Eliot, an eastern journalist who proclaimed the area a "garden of Eden."

GO! Start at **STARING LAKE PARK**. Park is on the north side of Pioneer Trail one mile west of Highway 169. A solid hour or two can be spent doing a couple of laps around Staring Lake and then sliding, swinging and climbing your way around the creative play area. Enjoy the view. **PIONEER TRAIL** follows the track of a major Indian trail later used as a military road from Fort Snelling.

3.4 mi **RIVER VIEW ROAD** marks the beginning of the major stretch of on-road bicycling. When the leaves are down you can sneak some major views across the Minnesota River Valley. This huge valley was formed over 10,000 years ago when the mighty Glacial River Warren flowed through here.

5.5 mi Enjoy the wooded Purgatory Creek ravine before heading up into the land of big houses. Watch closely for **CANADIAN LANDING** to connect with Franlo Road.

8.1 mi **ANDERSON LAKES** are a reminder of how this area looked before the suburbs crept in. You can take the shortcut back to Staring Lake Park by continuing across on Anderson Lakes Parkway.

Prairie Center Drive and Valley View Road have paved paths to usher you through the car-centered corporate world. Count the number of **EDENs** en route and decide if Joni Mitchell was correct when she sang, "they paved paradise and put up a parking lot."

12.7 mi Hennepin County's **LRT TRAIL CORRIDOR** crosses Valley View Road and offers another short-cut. Save about 2.4 miles if you take it.

13.9 mi **ROUND LAKE PARK** has a swimming beach and other diversions. A combined path circles the lake.

16.4 mi You will cross the LRT Trail just before reaching **SCENIC HEIGHTS ROAD**. Take a left and watch your step until you reach the paved path. There is a nice run down Anderson Lake Parkway before reaching the turnoff back to Staring Lake.

20.8 mi You may want to stop at the **OUTDOOR CENTER** or do an extra lap around the lake before heading **BACK TO GO!**

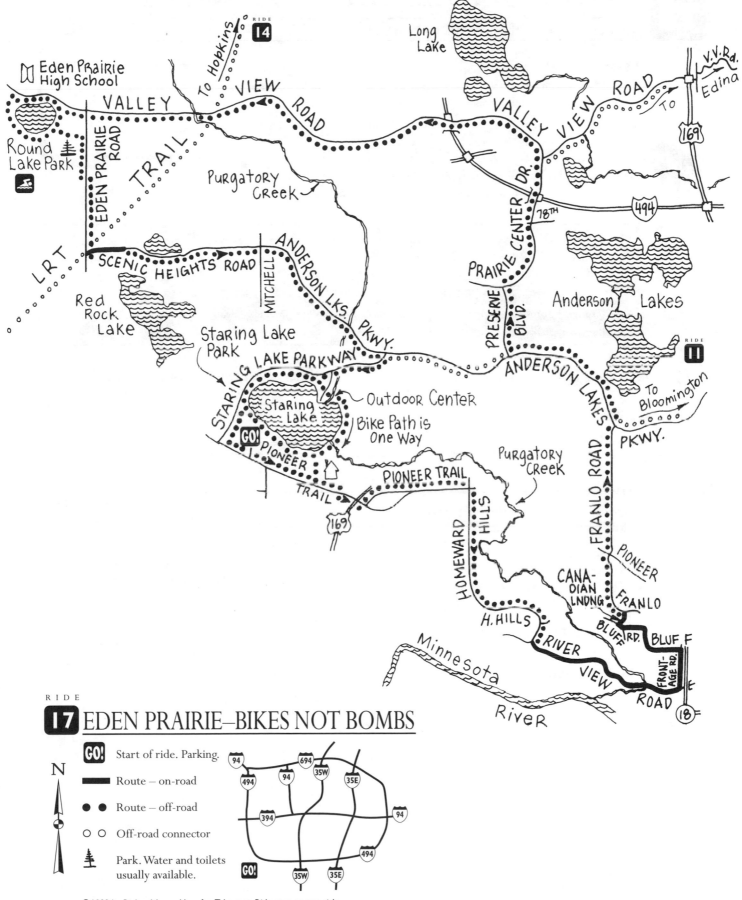

RIDE

17 EDEN PRAIRIE–BIKES NOT BOMBS

N

GO! Start of ride. Parking.

── Route – on-road

●● Route – off-road

○○ Off-road connector

🌲 Park. Water and toilets usually available.

© 1999 by Richard Arey. Have fun. Take care. Ride at your own risk.

BURNSVILLE BIKE BYWAYS

Scott County. Connects with RIDES 19, 31, D, E and F.

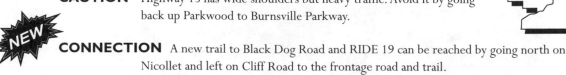

LENGTH   18.4 mile loop

RATING   Intermediate – most of route off-road or on shoulders. There are many hills on this route.

CAUTION   Highway 13 has wide shoulders but heavy traffic. Avoid it by going back up Parkwood to Burnsville Parkway.

NEW

CONNECTION A new trail to Black Dog Road and RIDE 19 can be reached by going north on Nicollet and left on Cliff Road to the frontage road and trail.

*T*his route circumnavigates the bike-friendly streets and paths of Burnsville. It connects the major parks, winds around beautiful Crystal Lake and directs you to three of the best mountain bike trails in the metro area. (Always call before using. See separate descriptions in the Mountain Biking chapter.) Burnsville has made excellent strides in creating a bicycle-friendly community. Only a portion of their routes are shown on this map. Phone the Burnsville Parks and Recreation Department at 612-895-4500 to obtain a copy of their map "Going Places — Burnsville Bikeways."

GO!   Start at **TERRACE OAKS WEST PARK**. Park is reached by exiting I-35E at County Road 11 and heading north. Go 1 mile and take a right (east) on Burnsville Parkway to entrance on right at Kennelly Road. This is also the starting point for the mountain bike trail. See RIDE D.

3.6 mi   **ALIMAGNET PARK** sits above its beautiful namesake lake. There are picnic facilities here complete with bocce ball courts.

5.5 mi   Head west (right) at Bluebill Bay Road and watch the street signs closely as you bike through the neighborhood south of **CRYSTAL LAKE**.

7.2 mi   The off-road path on the west end of Crystal Lake is the prettiest stretch on this route. Savor it slowly.

8.7 mi   Buck Hill Road is the turnoff for the **BUCK HILL MOUNTAIN BIKE AREA**. See RIDE E.

11.8 mi Good bike lanes on 150th Street and Judicial Road take you through the suburban office parks and over to **SUNSET PARK**. Add 1.7 miles to your total if you do the loop here.

Head South on Burnsville Parkway (It becomes Hanrehan Lake Boulevard and has a 7 foot shoulder most of the way. Turn left on Murphy Lake Road.) about 2 miles to reach **MURPHY-HANREHAN REGIONAL PARK**. See RIDE F.

14.3 mi Burnsville Parkway has a 2 foot shoulder and goes past some nice parks and many homes. Enjoy the **PANORAMIC VIEW TO DOWNTOWN** from Travelers Trail West.

16.3 mi Be bold. Slide down to Highway 13 and order a Nutty Double Fudge at **DAIRY QUEEN**. That burst of sugar will come in handy as you head back up the hill to Terrace Oaks Park.

18.4 mi BACK TO *GO!*

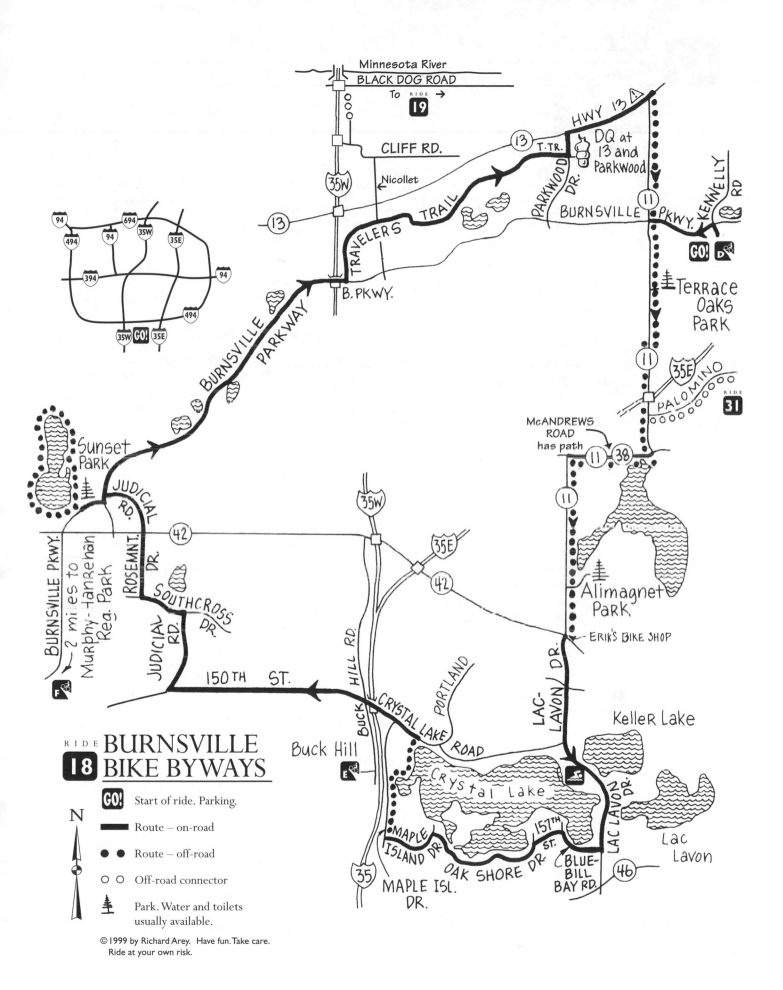

Minnesota River
BLACK DOG ROAD
To RIDE 19 →

CLIFF RD.

Nicollet

HWY 13
DQ at 13 and Parkwood

TRAVELERS TRAIL

BURNSVILLE PKWY.
KENNELLY RD

GO!

Terrace Oaks Park

PALOMINO
35E
RIDE 31

McANDREWS ROAD has path

BURNSVILLE PARKWAY

Sunset Park

JUDICIAL RD.

ROSEMNT. DR.

SOUTHCROSS DR.

JUDICIAL RD.

42

35W

35E

42

Alimagnet Park

Erik's Bike Shop

Keller Lake

LAC-LAVON DR.

150TH ST.

Burnsville Pkwy. 2 miles to Murphy-Hanrehan Reg. Park

F

BUCK HILL RD.

CRYSTAL LAKE ROAD

PORTLAND

Crystal Lake

LAC LAVON DR.

Lac Lavon

Buck Hill
E

MAPLE ISLAND DR.

OAK SHORE DR.

157TH ST.

BLUE-BILL BAY RD.

46

MAPLE ISL. DR.

35

RIDE 18 BURNSVILLE BIKE BYWAYS

GO! Start of ride. Parking.

— Route – on-road

•• Route – off-road

○○ Off-road connector

🌲 Park. Water and toilets usually available.

N

© 1999 by Richard Arey. Have fun. Take care.
Ride at your own risk.

BIKING FOR THE BIRDS

19

Hennepin and Dakota County. Connects with RIDES 4, 18, 20, 31 and C.

LENGTH   36.8 miles – Full tour as described with mountain bike trail
RATING   11.4 miles – Round trip on mountain bike trail only
CAUTION   Two of the places shown can be biked to, but NOT within. Bring a lock and
walking shoes. Be very careful along Lyndale Av. to Lakeshore Drive (take the
sidewalk or a side street.)

The dirt trail along the Minnesota River (it is part of Fort Snelling Park) is
one of the best local introductions to mountain biking for beginners. And, as would be expected, you can
see some excellent birds. I saw a bald eagle for instance. These trails can be accessed just below the historic
1836 Sibley House at 55 D Street in Mendota (651-452-1596) or at the parking lot on Silver Bell Road.

Located at the crossroads of three major biomes (northern coniferous forest, eastern deciduous forest, and western tallgrass prairie), and blessed with three major river valleys, the Twin Cities provides plentiful habitat for some of the best birdwatching (birding!) in the Midwest. Over 340 species of birds (out of the 800 possible in North America) have been seen in the seven county area, and this ride takes you to some of the best local places. Bring your binoculars for best results. The best birding is along the Minnesota River so more serious birders will park at the Cedar Avenue Bridge and go from there.

Birding is seasonal. Migrants pass through in April (waterfowl, hawks) and May (warblers, shorebirds). Many species are found here all summer and winter. Biking birders in winter will often be rewarded by rarities found on open water near the NSP power plant. Join the Minnesota Ornithologists Union, a local Audubon Society, or call the MOU Birding Hotline (612-780-8890) for more specific information and trips.

GO!   Start at the parking lot on the north end of **LAKE NOKOMIS** (612-661-4800) or along the parkway. I once spotted a greenbacked heron wading in some shade on Minnehaha Creek. Hint: Those silver winged creatures flying over the south end of the lake are NOT Canada geese. Go around the lake and take 12th Avenue to 60th Street to Bloomington Avenue south.

7.0 mi   At 73rd cut over to **WOOD LAKE NATURE CENTER** (612-861-9365) and lock up your bike. Wood Lake is one of the premier birding spots in the state. A migratory hot spot, 21 species of warblers were seen during a single day in early May of 1988. During the summer, check around the boardwalk for rails (sora and yellow) and least bitterns. When you're finished backtrack to 73rd. Biking on Lyndale is definitely "for the birds!"

11.8 mi   This next stretch is a bit boring and a little hectic in places. But consider how much you're helping the environment by bicycling rather than driving to these spots. The **BASS PONDS** are reached by walking your bike down the hill at the end of 86th Street. Look for waterfowl and warblers in the spring.

13.7 mi   A mountain bike trail (shared with hikers!) will take you to the **OLD CEDAR AVENUE BRIDGE**. You can also get there via the sidewalk along Old Shakopee Road. The off-road paths west of the parking lot are closed to bikers but patience rewards viewing from the bridge. Bitterns, rails and heron are just some of the species that may be observed.

15.6 mi   Continue south and cross over the Minnesota River on the bike/walk bridge. Head upstream on Black Dog Road toward the **NSP POWER PLANT**. Open water in November and December makes this area particularly productive for hardy winter hikers and bikers. Grebes, goldeneyes, gulls and eagles may be spotted along the quiet road.

MOUNTAIN BIKING the dirt trail along the Minnesota River is great fun and can be productive for birding if you take it slow. This adds almost 12 miles to the tour.

24.9 mi   You won't even need binoculars to pick out the **DAIRY QUEEN** on Cedar Avenue.

25.4 mi   BACK TO *GO!* If you did the Fort Snelling dirt bike trip your mileage is closer to 36.8.

19 BIKING FOR THE BIRDS

© 1999 by Richard Arey. Have fun. Take care. Ride at your own risk.

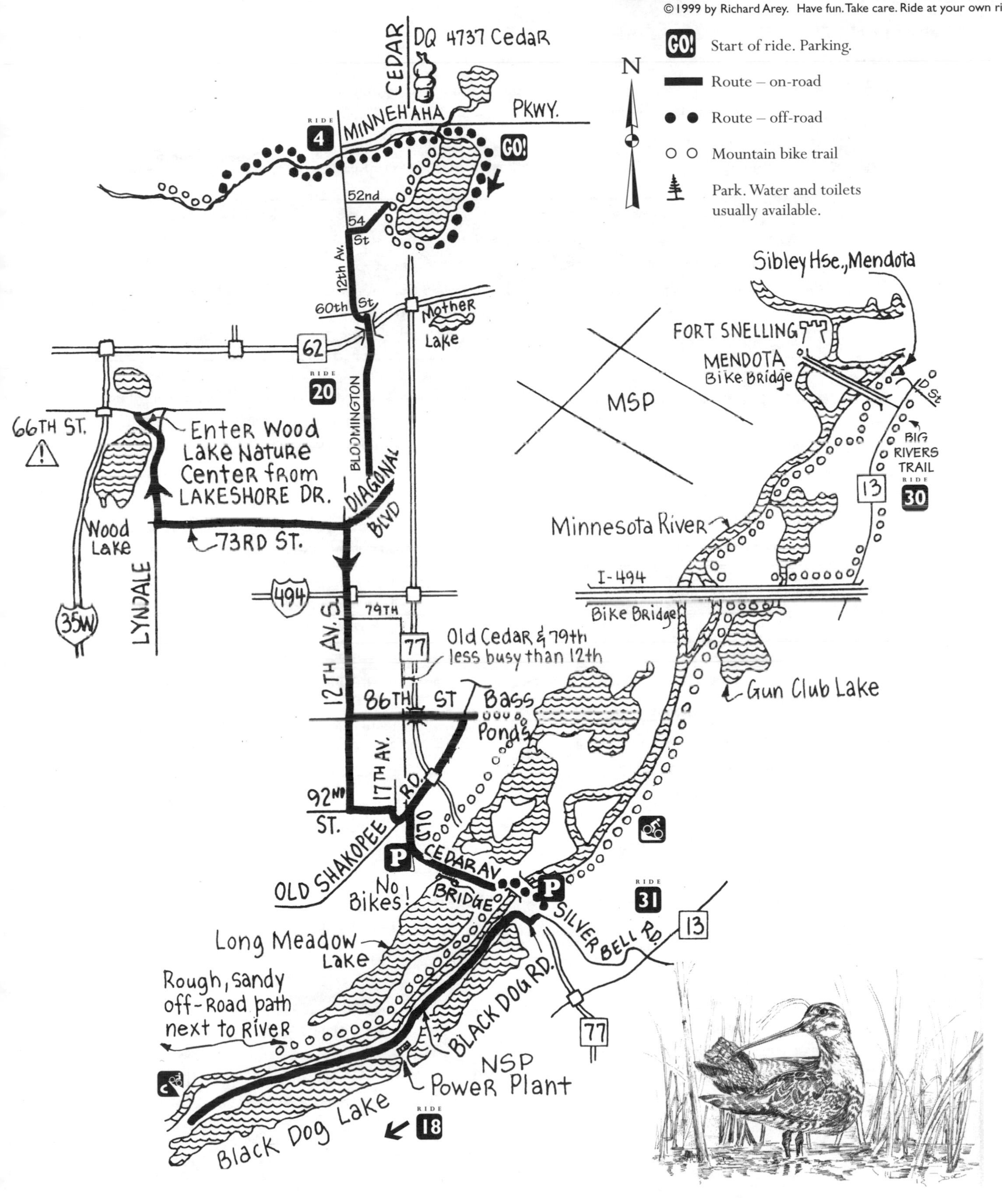

GO! Start of ride. Parking.

▬▬▬ Route – on-road

•• •• Route – off-road

○ ○ Mountain bike trail

🌲 Park. Water and toilets usually available.

N

CEDAR

DQ 4737 Cedar

MINNEHAHA PKWY.

RIDE 4

52nd

54 St

12th Av.

60th St

Mother Lake

62

RIDE 20

BLOOMINGTON

DIAGONAL BLVD

GO!

66TH ST. ⚠

Enter Wood Lake Nature Center from LAKESHORE DR.

Wood Lake

73RD ST.

LYNDALE

35W

494

12TH AV. S.

79TH

77

Old Cedar & 79th less busy than 12th

86TH ST   Bass Ponds

17TH AV.

92ND ST.

OLD CEDAR RD.

P

OLD SHAKOPEE

No Bikes!

CEDAR BRIDGE

P

Long Meadow Lake

Rough, sandy off-Road path next to River

🚲

NSP Power Plant

Black Dog Lake

RIDE 18

Sibley Hse., Mendota

FORT SNELLING

MENDOTA Bike Bridge

MSP

D St.

BIG RIVERS TRAIL

RIDE 30

13

Minnesota River

I-494

Bike Bridge

Gun Club Lake

🚲

SILVER BELL RD.

RIDE 31

13

BLACK DOG RD.

77

PLANES, TRAINS & AUTOMOBILES

Hennepin County. Connects with RIDES 4, 19, 27, 28, 30, 39 and 49.

LENGTH 〰 17 miles — Loop as described

RATING Intermediate, but often used as a training run for racers.

CAUTION Low flying planes. There is a fair amount of traffic and no longer a shoulder on 34th Avenue.

Recent airport expansion swallowed Standish Avenue so Cedar Frontage Road to Bloomington to 66th is the quickest reroute.

*This route circles the MSP International Airport. A primary attraction for training is the long stretches of road unencumbered by traffic signals or stop signs on a route that is readily accessible to so many people. The scenic attractions are found between Fort Snelling and Lake Nokomis. The paved path perched above the river on the bluff south of 54th Street is as pretty as you will find anywhere. It runs along an old **TRAIN** line. The **PLANES** are best seen along Post Road and the rush of **AUTOMOBILES** is hard to miss on the Interstate 494 frontage road. Bike safely — you will also be passing the Fort Snelling National Cemetery.*

GO! Start at **MINNEHAHA PARK** (612-661-4800). A parking sticker is now required for cars. Minnehaha Park has been a tourist destination for over 150 years thanks to the falls that were immortalized in Henry Longfellow's popular poem, *The Song of Hiawatha*. The name **MI-NI** (water) **HA-HA** (noise of waterfalls or rapids) comes from the Dakota who knew of this place for centuries. The geologic history goes back another 10,000 years and is told on the bronze plaques that are found near the falls. The replica **LONGFELLOW HOUSE** has been relocated into the park and is being renovated for use as a trail center.

Cross Hiawatha and follow **MINNEHAHA PARKWAY**. The Dakota knew Minnehaha Creek as **WA-KPA** (river) **CI-STIN-NA** (small). The parkway was opened in 1893 and follows an old wagon trail. Today, it is especially pretty in the spring when thousands of daffodils are in bloom and the crab apple trees are bursting with color.

2.1 mi **LAKE NOKOMIS** has good biking on either the path or adjacent parkway. A small recreation center on the north end of the lake has water and washrooms.

3.5 mi At Cedar and Nokomis Parkway go left and hang right so you stay on the frontage road. This will take you down to 60th Street and you can cross Highway 62 on Bloomington. At 66th go left to Longfellow and than right.

10 mi This next stretch is where you can pump it up as you race along the perimeter of the airport, eventually delivering you to **POST ROAD**.

11.8 mi **FORT SNELLING STATE PARK** (612-725-2390) has a swimming beach, picnic facilities, boat launches, an interpretive center and more. Biking is allowed everywhere <u>except</u> on Pike Island

13.8 mi Follow the paved path until it starts to climb the bluff along the Mississippi. Rising above you is **HISTORIC FORT SNELLING**. Colonel Josiah Snelling took command of this post in 1820 and the locally quarried limestone walls began to rise in the wilderness. Minnesota did not become a state for 38 more years. The fort was never fired upon and the soldiers were more involved with mediating the fighting between the Dakota and Ojibway than between settlers and Indians until the 1862 Dakota conflict. Duing the winter of 1862 some 1,600 Dakota were confined here and at least 130 died during the long internment.

15.0 mi There are some informal dirt paths where **MOUNTAIN BIKING** is allowed on the right (east) side of the paved path just before 54th Street. Be mindful of hikers and paths closed to prevent erosion.

Follow the trail and service road along the bluff and past the **JOHN H. STEVENS HOUSE** (1849, oldest in Minneapolis) and **PRINCESS DEPOT** (1875) to your real destination — **DAIRY QUEEN**. Forget this training stuff and order a large, dipped ice cream cone.

17 mi BACK TO *GO!*

20 PLANES, TRAINS & AUTOMOBILES

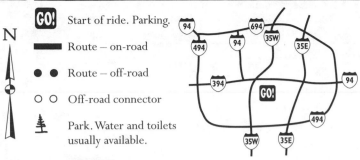

GO! Start of ride. Parking.

▬▬▬ Route – on-road

● ● Route – off-road

○ ○ Off-road connector

🌲 Park. Water and toilets usually available.

N

© 1999 by Richard Arey. Have fun. Take care. Ride at your own risk.

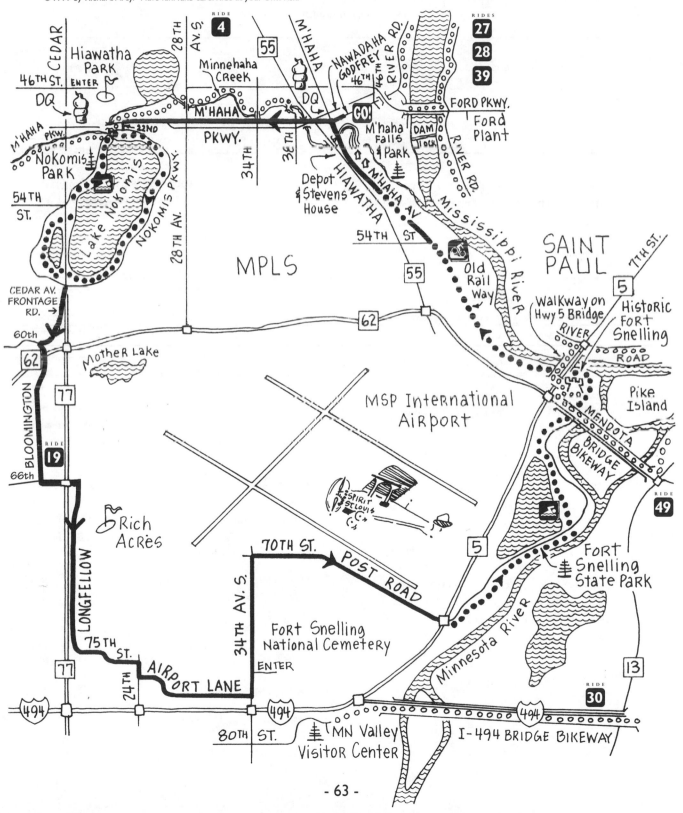

21 SCANDIA SOJOURN

Washington County. Connects with RIDE 23, 42, 43 and 44.

LENGTH
RATING

28.8 miles – Full loop using Scandia Trail

8 miles – William O'Brien to Marine off-road, round trip

19.1 miles – Ostrum Trail loop if County Road 3 is closed.

Olinda Trail (County Road 3) is being rebuilt with 8 foot shoulders in 1999-2000 and may be closed for construction.

CAUTION Norell, Olinda and Scandia Trail have light traffic but no shoulders. Washington Parks parking sticker required at Pine Point.

This is some of the best bicycling to be found in the metro area if you are comfortable on country roads. The oak woods, lakes, marsh and rolling farmland blend harmoniously. The little villages of Scandia and Marine are a delight. This is a landscape — a way of life, really — that has almost disappeared in the Twin Cities area. And to top it off, this ride visits Gammelgarden (site of the first Swedish settlement in Minnesota), beautiful William O'Brien State Park, and the swimming beach on crystal clear Square Lake. Need I mention the award-winning desserts at Crabtree's Kitchen or the Village Scoop?

GO! Start at the parking lot in the **PINE POINT COUNTY PARK** (651-731-3851) at the end of the Gateway State Trail. Take County Road 55 (Norell Avenue) 3 miles north from County Highway 96 to Pine Point parking lot.

4.1 mi **WARNER NATURE CENTER** (651-433-2427) is owned and operated by the Science Museum (651-221-9444) and has a variety of programs available. Habitats for wildlife are exciting and varied and include a beautiful peat bog. Call first to make reservations for programs.

6.2 mi Intersection of County Road 3 and **OSTRUM TRAIL NORTH**. This is a good shortcut over to Marine.

9.1 mi The **HAY LAKE SCHOOL** (1899) and **JOHANNES ERICKSON LOG HOUSE** (1868) anchor this historic corner. An excellent guided tour is available weekend afternoons from 1:30 to 4:30 p.m. for just one dollar.

10.9 mi **SCANDIA**, the oldest Swedish Settlement in Minnesota, began in 1850 when three Swedish lads built a log cabin on Hay Lake. **GAMMELGARDEN** houses six structures built between 1850 and 1880 and is open for guided tours (fee charged) on weekend afternoons.

15.1 mi Stop in at **CRABTREE'S KITCHEN** and discover why they won *Mpls. St. Paul* magazine's award for "Best Old-Fashioned Desserts." Try the strawberry shortcake, "made from scratch and as light, sweet and delectable as a summer romance."

15.8 mi **WILLIAM O'BRIEN STATE PARK** offers all the amenities and you can glide on down to the river on the park road. Watch for hawks soaring above the bluffs. Save a couple miles and a 100-foot climb if you do not go down to the river.

20.1 mi Take the off-road paved path down into **MARINE ON ST. CROIX**. Platted in 1839, the downtown is a National Register Historic District. Minnesota's logging era began here and the 1888 Marine Village Hall is still the place for lively weekend dances. Satisfy your ice cream fix at the **VILLAGE SCOOP**.

24.3 mi **SQUARE LAKE PARK** is renowned for the clarity of its water and a dip here is hard to beat on a hot summer day. Those black shiny heads you see are scuba divers, not seals, surfacing. A bath house and picnic facilities overlook the lake.

28.8 mi BACK TO *GO!*

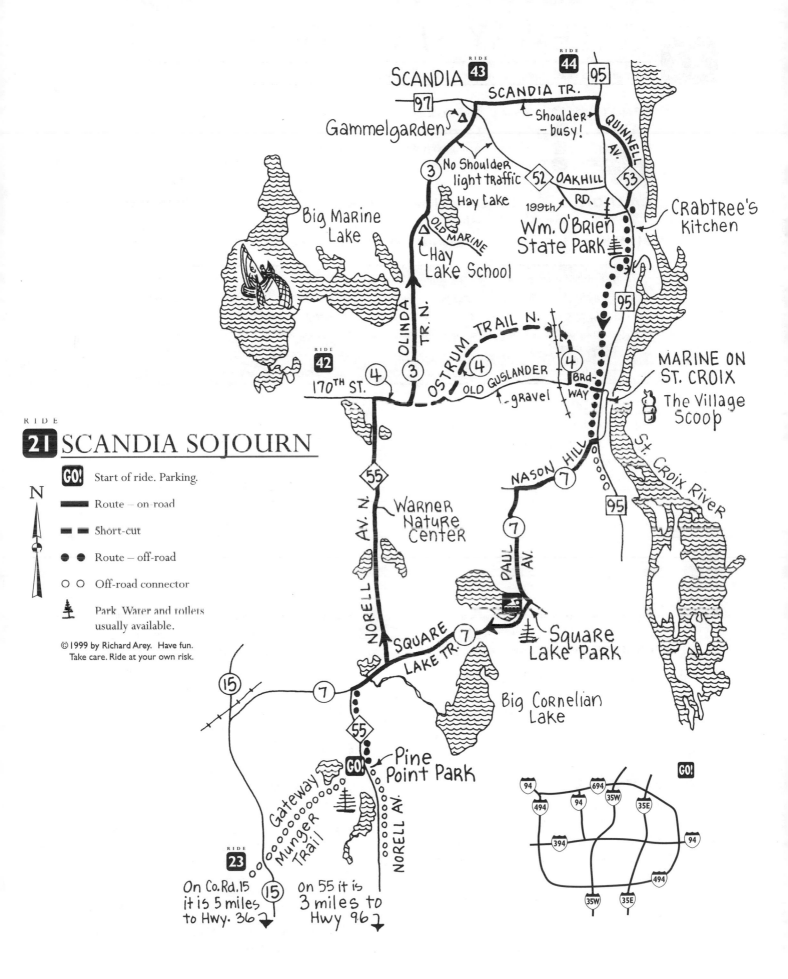

RIDE 21 SCANDIA SOJOURN

N

GO!   Start of ride. Parking.

───   Route – on-road

– – –   Short-cut

●●●   Route – off-road

○○○   Off-road connector

🌲   Park. Water and toilets usually available.

© 1999 by Richard Arey. Have fun.
Take care. Ride at your own risk.

SCANDIA — RIDE 43 — RIDE 44 — 95

SCANDIA TR.

97 — ← Shoulder – busy!

Gammelgarden ▲

3 — No Shoulder light traffic — 52 — OAKHILL — 53 — QUINNELL AV.

Big Marine Lake

Hay Lake

199th

RD.

▲ OLD MARINE

↑ Hay Lake School

Wm. O'Brien State Park 🌲

Crabtree's Kitchen

95

RIDE 42

170TH ST. — 4 — 3

OLINDA TR. N.

OSTRUM TRAIL N. — 4 — 4 — BRd-WAY

OLD GUSLANDER — ↑ gravel

MARINE ON ST. CROIX

The Village Scoop

St. Croix River

95

55

NORELL AV. N.

Warner Nature Center

NASON HILL — 7

7

PAUL AV.

SQUARE LAKE TR. — 7 — 7 🌲 Square Lake Park

Big Cornelian Lake

15 — 7

55

Gateway Munger Trail

RIDE 23

GO! Pine Point Park

NORELL AV.

15

On Co.Rd.15 it is 5 miles to Hwy. 36 ⤵

On 55 it is 3 miles to Hwy 96 ⤵

94 — 694 — GO!
494 — 94 — 35W — 35E
394 — 94
494
35W — 35E

GATEWAY STATE TRAIL

Ramsey and Washington Counties. Connects with RIDES 23, 26, 27, 28 and 40.

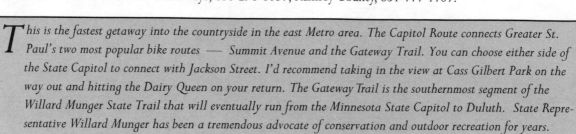

LENGTH
RATING

NEW

33.8 miles – Entire **Gateway State Trail**, round trip

21.8 miles – Cathedral to I-694, round trip

14.4 miles – Arlington trailhead to I-694, round trip

4 miles – **Trout Brook Trail** (1.2 miles long) makes a nifty connection to the 1.7 mile loop around McCarron's Lake.

CAUTION   There are hills and traffic between the Cathedral and Oakland Cemetery. Sidewalk may be preferable on Rice Street.

PHONE   DNR Trails and Waterways, 651-296-6157, Ramsey County, 651-777-1707.

This is the fastest getaway into the countryside in the east Metro area. The Capitol Route connects Greater St. Paul's two most popular bike routes — Summit Avenue and the Gateway Trail. You can choose either side of the State Capitol to connect with Jackson Street. I'd recommend taking in the view at Cass Gilbert Park on the way out and hitting the Dairy Queen on your return. The Gateway Trail is the southernmost segment of the Willard Munger State Trail that will eventually run from the Minnesota State Capitol to Duluth. State Representative Willard Munger has been a tremendous advocate of conservation and outdoor recreation for years.

GO!   Park on Summit Avenue near the **SAINT PAUL CATHEDRAL.** The trip begins with a long downhill coast on John Ireland Boulevard, named after the Archbishop who was the force behind the Cathedral's construction (1906-1915).

0.5 mi   Cass Gilbert's impressive **MINNESOTA STATE CAPITOL** was built between 1893 and 1904. Gilbert, a St. Paul native, had originally designed the Capitol's mall to tumble down to the river. Stop back for a free tour some day.

0.8 mi   Go around the right (east) side of the Capitol and up Cedar Street to the fine lookout at **CASS GILBERT MEMORIAL PARK.**

1.8 mi   The historic **OAKLAND CEMETERY** was designed by H. W. S. Cleveland, the godfather of all Twin Cities parks. Famous Minnesotans, including U.S. Senators and St. Paul madams, have come to rest here.

TROUT BROOK TRAIL

In 1999 a trail will be built off of the Gateway just south of Arlington. It follows Trout Brook, mostly culverted now but open to daylight here for a short stretch. The creek originally flowed to the Mississippi and the Lower Landing where St. Paul was born.

GATEWAY STATE TRAIL

3.7 mi   Begin the Gateway State Trail at the **ARLINGTON TRAILHEAD** located just east of I-35E. (Exit I-35E at either Wheelock Parkway or Maryland Avenue and take side streets to trailhead.) The first 2 miles are paved with asphalt mixed with 3,300 used tires. This is a very pretty introduction to the trail. The trail also goes <u>south</u> two miles to Cayuga Street.

5.3 mi   **PHALEN PARK.** Take a 3.2 mile lap around the lake if you wish (not included in mileage listed). Just past the park you will cross the unmarked 45th parallel of latitude. You are now halfway between the North Pole and the equator.

7.2 mi   The **GOODRICH GOLF COURSE** is a pleasant interlude as you traverse the suburban landscape.

9.1 mi   The stretch of trail adjacent to Highway 36 is the least appealing, though you will get a kick out of the **GIANT SNOWMAN.** Use great care while crossing the streets.

9.4 mi   Take a break from the traffic with a Dilly Bar at **DAIRY QUEEN** (located at the northwest corner of Highway 36 and 120).

10.9 mi   Trail goes under I-694. See RIDE 23 for map and description of the rest of the **GATEWAY TRAIL.**

21.8 mi   At the I-694 underpass it's time to turn around and head **BACK TO GO!**

RIDE
22 GATEWAY STATE TRAIL

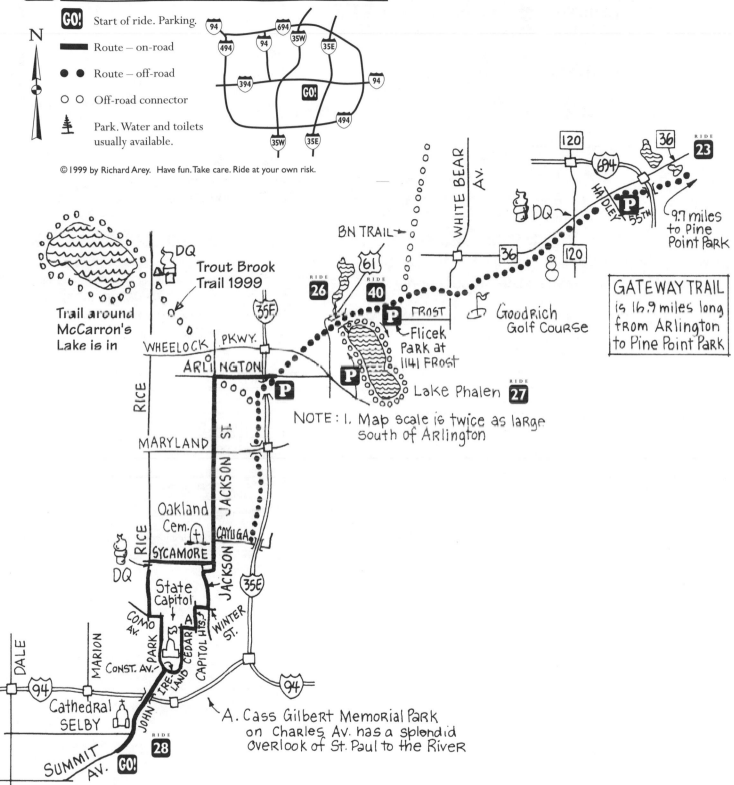

GO! Start of ride. Parking.

━━━ Route – on-road

•••• Route – off-road

○ ○ Off-road connector

🌲 Park. Water and toilets usually available.

© 1999 by Richard Arey. Have fun. Take care. Ride at your own risk.

Trail around McCarron's Lake is in

DQ

Trout Brook Trail 1999

BN TRAIL →

WHITE BEAR AV.

DQ

Hadley 55TH P

RIDE 23

9.7 miles to Pine Point Park

GATEWAY TRAIL is 16.9 miles long from Arlington to Pine Point Park

RIDE 26

RIDE 40

P FROST

Flicek Park at 1141 Frost

Goodrich Golf Course

WHEELOCK PKWY.

ARLINGTON

P

Lake Phalen

RIDE 27

NOTE: 1. Map scale is twice as large south of Arlington

RICE

MARYLAND

JACKSON ST.

Oakland Cem.

CAYUGA

RICE

DQ

SYCAMORE

State Capitol

COMO AV.

JOHN IRE. LAND CEDAR

CAPITOL HTS.

WINTER ST.

CONST. AV.

DALE

94

MARION

Cathedral SELBY

RIDE 28

SUMMIT AV. GO!

A. Cass Gilbert Memorial Park on Charles Av. has a splendid overlook of St. Paul to the River

GATEWAY TRAIL TO STILLWATER

Washington County. Connects with 21, 22, 24, 35 and 44.

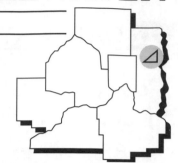

LENGTH 🎾 19.5 miles – Full loop to Pioneer Park
RATING 🎾 15 miles to Pine Point Park and back

Big fun for everyone

CAUTION Big hill and traffic if you go down into Stillwater. Lots of folks on the Gateway Trail.

PHONE DNR Trails and Waterways, 651-296-6157.

*I*t's hard to imagine a better introduction to the scenic wonders of Washington County. This is the prettiest stretch of the Gateway Trail and the view of the St. Croix River from Pioneer Park is as good as it gets in the Midwest. The entire route is off-road or on the broad shoulders of County Road 55. Check out the Outing Lodge at Pine Point or cruise down into Stillwater for lunch and a little antiquing. I have seen deer on more than one occasion leaping across the trail.

GO! Start at the **MAHTOMEDI HIGH SCHOOL** parking lot. Exit I-694 on Highway 120 and go north 1 mile to Highway 244. Turn right (east) on 244 and go 1.5 miles to Highway 12. Go right (east) on Highway 12 just over half a mile to the high school lot on your left. A paved off-road path leads to the Munger Trail.

0.6 mi **GATEWAY MUNGER STATE TRAIL** intersects the paved path along Highway 12.

2.8 mi Rest stop at **MASTERMAN LAKE**. There is parking and a portable toilet here.

6.7 mi The **OUTING LODGE** is reached from a separate entrance road off County Road 61, about one block north of the trail. The Outing Lodge at Pine Point is well worth a return visit for an overnight getaway

or a special dinner (Phone 651-439-9747). Built in 1924 as the county poor farm, the brick building has been reborn as a handsome country inn with warm wood paneling and a huge fireplace topped with a ten-foot limestone mantel.

7.5 mi **PINE POINT COUNTY PARK** is a beauty with maturing pine plantations and ponds filled with the choruses of frogs in spring.

8.7 mi The off-road path ends but County Road 55 has wide bike-friendly shoulders.

12.5 mi Laurel Avenue leads to **PIONEER PARK** and a spectacular vista of the St. Croix River Valley. This is a fine place for a picnic.

19.5 mi Bike the wide shoulders or off-road path on County Highway 12, **BACK TO** *GO!*

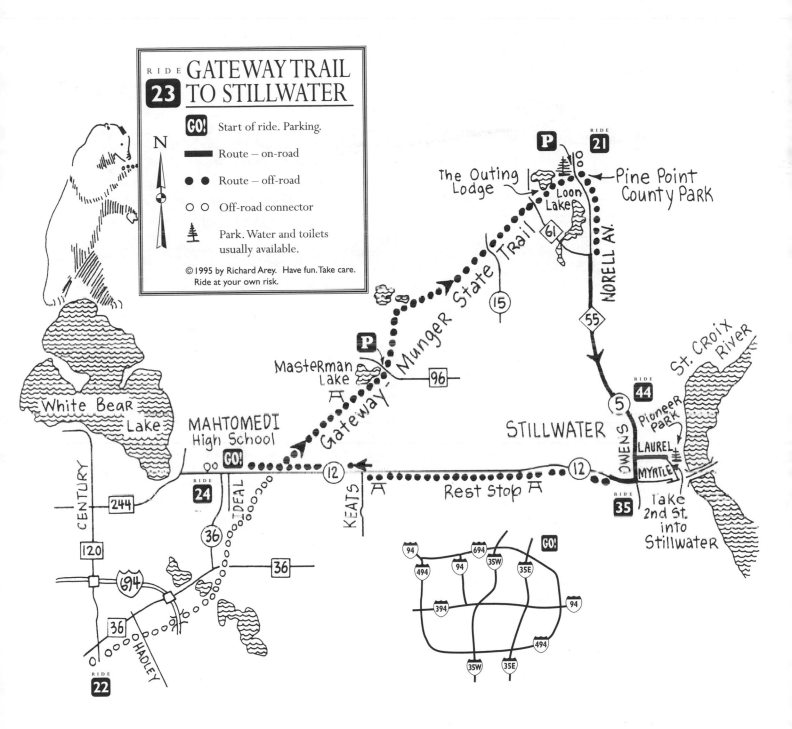

RIDE 23 GATEWAY TRAIL TO STILLWATER

GO! Start of ride. Parking.

▬▬▬ Route – on-road

●●● Route – off-road

○○ Off-road connector

🌲 Park. Water and toilets usually available.

© 1995 by Richard Arey. Have fun. Take care. Ride at your own risk.

N

Pine Point County Park

RIDE 21

The Outing Lodge

Loon Lake

NORELL AV.

61

15

55

St. Croix River

Masterman Lake

P

96

Gateway-Munger State Trail

STILLWATER

RIDE 44

Pioneer Park

5

OWENS

LAUREL

MYRTLE

MAHTOMEDI High School

GO!

White Bear Lake

CENTURY

244

RIDE 24

120

694

36

HADLEY

RIDE 22

IDEAL

36

36

KEATS

12

Rest Stop

12

RIDE 35

Take 2nd St. into Stillwater

94

694

GO!

494

94

35W

35E

394

94

35W

35E

494

24 JERRY'S RIDE

Ramsey and Washington County. Connects with RIDES 22, 23, 25 and 42.

LENGTH
RATING

〰 27 miles – Full loop as described

⬤ 15.6 miles – Bald Eagle Lake loop and back

The Bald Eagle Lake loop (recently repaved!) is easier and the rest not much more difficult, as traffic is light.

CAUTION There are stretches with only narrow shoulders. Use a mirror. Take the Beach Road to Cedar Street cut-off if you prefer serenity to stopping at Dairy Queen. County Highway 244 (Wildwood Road) is very busy.

*T*his is the Big Lakes ride. White Bear Lake was a resort town for years and has attracted a number of characters in its time — Ma Barker and Machine Gun Kelly, Zelda and F. Scott Fitzgerald, Mark Twain and...my old buddy Jer. As in Jerry Hass. He accompanied me on many of the rides in this book and helped power my first century ride. If you see a couple of funny-looking guys on an old green tandem tooling around Bald Eagle Lake, wave! — that's us. Good views of the lakes, some bona fide historic sites, wide-open spaces (for now) and a Dairy Queen to sweeten the deal are yours for the taking on this ride. And lest we forget. Another Gerry, Gerry Spiess, christened his tiny 10-foot sailboat, Yankee Girl, on White Bear Lake before his World Record (shortest boat) solo voyage across the Atlantic in 1979. But now, let's go biking!

GO! Start your ride at **BELLAIRE PARK** (651-429-5827). Exit I-694 on Highway 120 and go north one mile, turning left (west) on Highway 244. Go one mile to Bellaire Avenue and take a right (north) on Bellaire to park entrance.

Bellaire Park was originally a streetcar stop on the way to the old Wildwood Amusement Park which ran from 1899 to the mid-1930s.

1.3 mi **JOHNSON BOAT WORKS** is where Iver Johnson designed his class X sailboats, one of which is in the Smithsonian Institute in Washington, D.C. Lake Avenue is one of the bike routes shown on the 1899 St. Paul Cycle Path Association map.

2 mi The wonderfully picturesque **FILLEBROWN HOUSE** sits at Lake and Moorhead. Built in 1879, it is a classic example of Stick Style architecture. It has been restored with Victorian furnishings and is open for tours on summer Sunday afternoons.

3.3 mi Take the paved path, just past the OPTIMIST'S CLUB, that leads to the **WHITE BEAR LAKE COUNTY PARK**. There is a swimming beach, picnic facilities and a boat launch here.

4.1 mi Make a short sprint on Highway 96 and a careful left onto Northwest Avenue. Cross Highway 61 on Buffalo and you will soon be cruising around **BALD EAGLE LAKE**.

10 mi The scenic loop around the lake brings you back to the Highway 61 crossing at 120th Street. Take Hugo back to Buffalo for the **SHORT LOOP**.

16.4 mi The **WITHROW BALLROOM** is a landmark that still holds Saturday night dances. From here you can take County Road 68 to Lansing if you want to bike a longer stretch of the Gateway Trail. Or take County Road 9 back to 12.

22.3 mi Intersection of County Highway 12 and the **GATEWAY TRAIL**. Taking 12 to Beach Road to Cedar Street is the more scenic, lower traffic recommendation.

25.1 mi If you simply cannot wait, take the heavily travelled Highway 244 (it does have a good shoulder) to **DAIRY QUEEN**. After boosting your blood sugar level, continue west on County Road E and north on Bellaire.

27 mi **BACK TO GO!** On a hot day you'll wish you had your swimsuit. There is a nice **SWIMMING BEACH** at Bellaire Park.

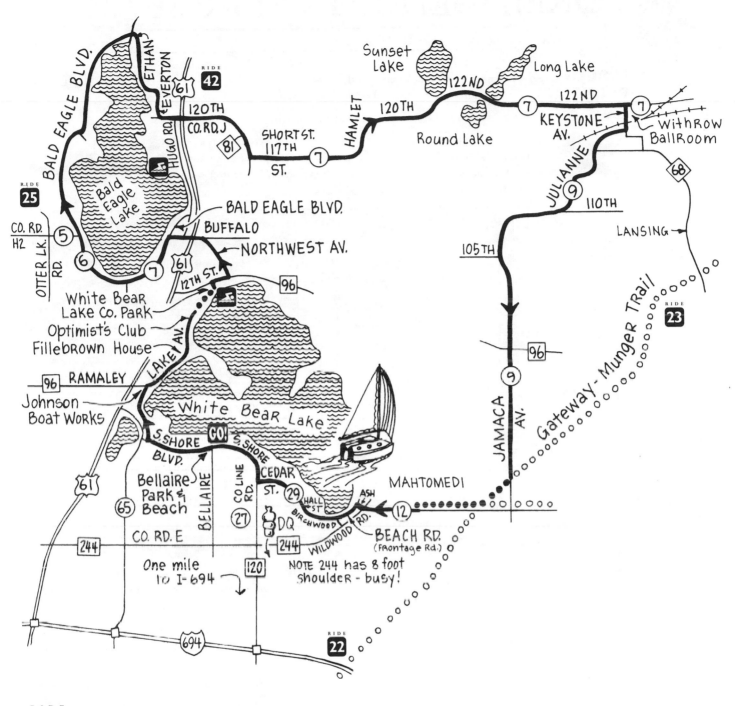

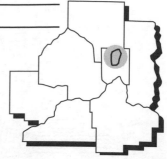

LENGTH ∿ 24.1 miles – Full loop as described

RATING Intermediate, most of route has shoulders, no big hills

CAUTION A ¾ mile stretch on Otter Lake Road has no shoulder.

By late 1999 an off-road path will circle Birch Lake and continue north to Tamarack Nature Center. In addition, a 10' paved path is being built along the south side of Highway 96 across the entire county. It will be complete in 2001 but some stretches are done now.

This is a beautiful countryside ride. Surprisingly rural in places, the road through Lake Vadnais will take you (mentally) far up into the north woods. Ponder the potential of the Arsenal property (being decommissioned) and enjoy the fall colors of the numerous stands of maple-basswood forest. It is, in fact, possible for outsiders to enter the "forbidden city" of North Oaks. All you need to do is get permission from each and every homeowner, as property lines extend to the middle of the street. That done, you will enjoy the off-road trail circling Pleasant Lake. Take some time to enjoy Snail Lake Park and the Tamarack Nature Center.

GO! A small parking lot is found at **VADNAIS LAKE PARK** (651-766-4150) at the SW corner of Edgerton Road and Vadnais Boulevard. Larger groups may want to start at the big parking lot at Tamarack Nature Center (651-777-1707). To reach Vadnais Lake Park exit I-694 at Rice Street (Highway 49) and go north, taking the first right onto Vadnais Boulevard. Proceed 1.5 miles to park on right.

1.3 mi Turn right onto Vadnais Lake Road that runs between **LAKE VADNAIS**. This is the last of the chain of lakes that supplies St. Paul's drinking water. Refresh in the pine scented air.

2.8 mi Take a left on County Road F, cross the railroad tracks and take the first right on the unmarked road to **SUCKER LAKE**.

For a 2 mile shorter loop continue west on County Road F to Rice Street. At the end of F is a pretty path through **SNAIL LAKE PARK**. Follow the map.

4.3 mi The palace guard stands watch at the gatehouse into the **FORBIDDEN CITY**. North Oaks was once the rural retreat and experimental farm of railroad baron James J. Hill. He raised livestock here that he would then donate to farmers along his Great

Northern Railroad line. Three original farm buildings are being renovated. Buy a home here (average cost is $250,000) and you not only get a set of golden keys but the possibility of having someone like Walter Mondale or Kevin McHale as your neighbor.

6.1 mi **GRASS LAKE PARK** is a large wetlands along the south side of Gramsie Road.

10.1 mi A small public park is set into the huge open landscape of the federally owned **ARSENAL**. Public debate will help determine the fate of this land.

14.3 mi Turn right (east) on Ash Street. **FARMS**, marsh and stands of hardwood trees dominate the view — for now, at least.

18.7 mi **TAMARACK NATURE CENTER** (651-429-7787) is a good place to stretch. Walk over to the interpretive center and spend a little time looking at the natural history exhibits and live animal room. A large tamarack bog once covered this land. Tamarack trees are prized for being rot resistant and this area was clear-cut in 1917 for log home construction.

21.1 mi The last ¾ mile of Otter Lake Road has only a gravel shoulder. Turn right on Goose Lake Road and you pass **GEM LAKE HILLS** golf course.

24.1 mi BACK TO *GO!*

RIDE
25 FORBIDDEN CITY CIRCLE

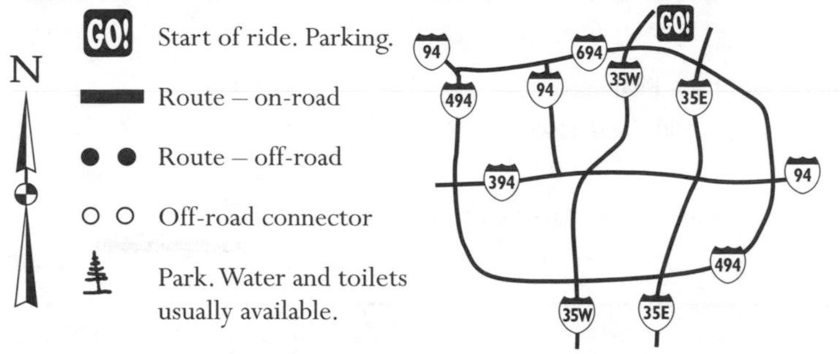

GO! Start of ride. Parking.

— Route – on-road

●● Route – off-road

○○ Off-road connector

🌲 Park. Water and toilets usually available.

© 1995 by Richard Arey. Have fun. Take care. Ride at your own risk.

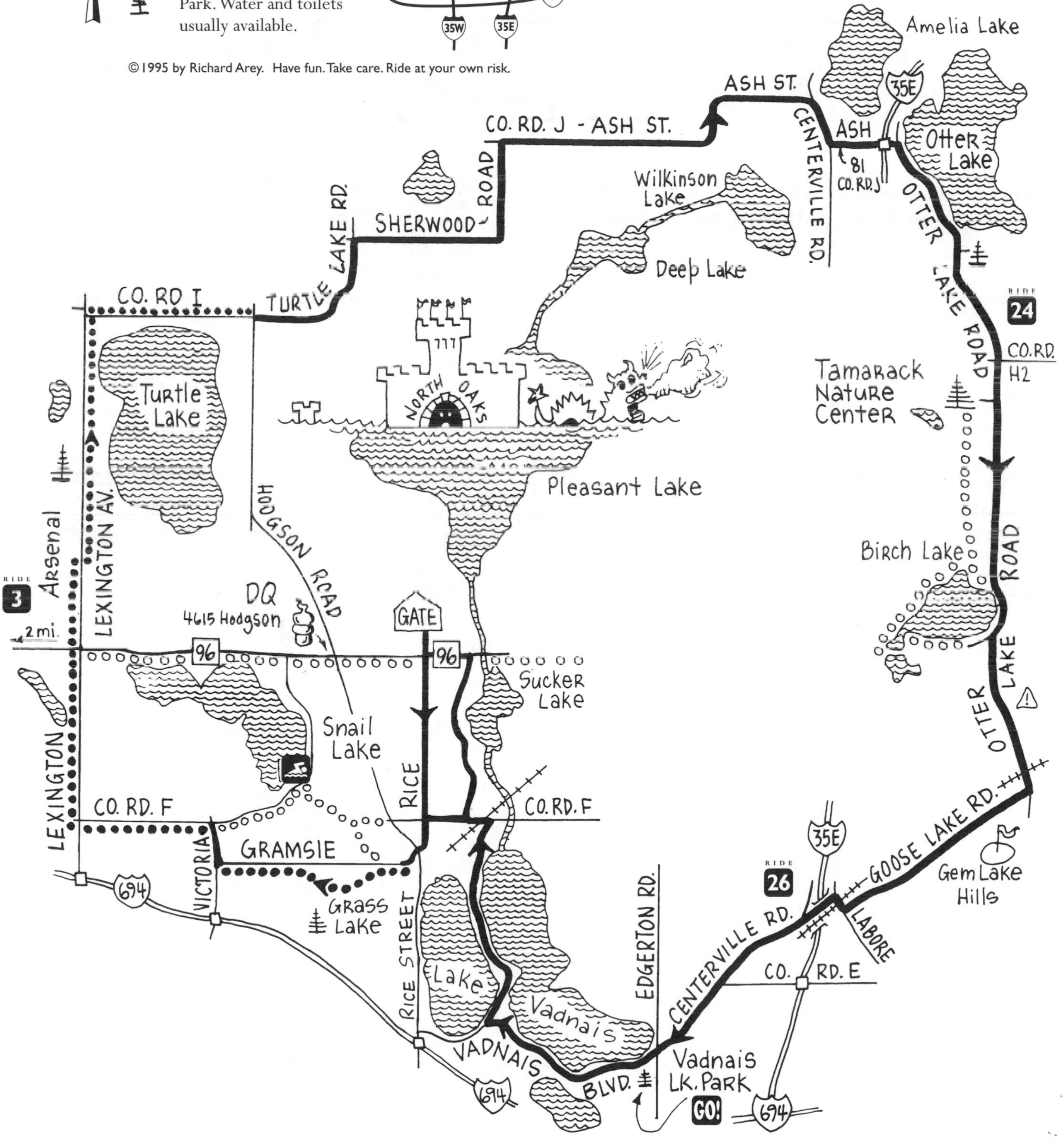

N

Map labels:

GO! 94 694 35W 35E GO!
494 94 494
394 94
35W 35E
494
35W 35E

Amelia Lake

ASH ST.

CO. RD. J - ASH ST.

ASH
81
CO. RD. J

35E

Otter Lake

Wilkinson Lake

CENTERVILLE RD.

SHERWOOD ROAD

TURTLE LAKE RD.

Deep Lake

RIDE 24

CO. RD. H2

CO. RD. I

Turtle Lake

NORTH OAKS

Pleasant Lake

Tamarack Nature Center

OTTER LAKE ROAD

Birch Lake

Arsenal

LEXINGTON AV.

RIDE 3

2 mi.

HODGSON ROAD

DQ 4615 Hodgson

GATE

96

96

Sucker Lake

Snail Lake

Rice

LEXINGTON

CO. RD. F

CO. RD. F

GRAMSIE

Victoria

694

Grass Lake

Rice Street

Lake

Vadnais

EDGERTON RD.

35E

RIDE 26

CENTERVILLE RD.

LABORE

CO. RD. E

GOOSE LAKE RD.

Gem Lake Hills

VADNAIS

BLVD.

Vadnais Lk. Park

GO! 694

694

- 73 -

LAND OF LAKES

Ramsey County. Connects with RIDES 22, 25, 27, 28 and 40.

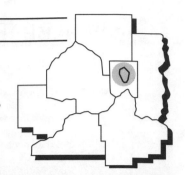

LENGTH
RATING

22 miles – Full loop as described

4.7 miles – Paved path around Lake Phalen and Round Lake

10 miles – Short loop around Gervais Lake plus Lake Phalen loop

17 miles – Medium loop around Lake Owasso

CAUTION Careful crossing Highway 36 and I-694 on Rice Street. The sidewalk along Rice Street may be preferable.

This is a country cousin to the old AYH favorite Lotsa Lakes route. A great summertime ride with plenty of opportunities to cool off at one of the four swimming beaches. The multitude of lake views are a treat in any season. Geology fans will note that these lakes mark the ancient path of the Glacial Mississippi River.

GO! Start at one of the parking lots on the west side of Lake Phalen. **PHALEN REGIONAL PARK** (651-266-6400) has a swimming beach, oak shaded picnic grounds and small craft for rent. To reach Phalen Park take the Wheelock Parkway exit on I-35E and go east about 2 miles to park entrance on left.

3.2 mi This is one full lap around Lake Phalen.

1.6 mi This is the distance if you go up the west side of Lake Phalen and continue along the creek up and over to the corner of **ARCADE AND ROSELAWN.** Watch for egrets along the creek.

2.8 mi Corner of Keller Parkway (Little Canada) and Edgerton. Go left (south) if you are doing the **SHORT LOOP**.

5.7 mi You've reached the entrance to the **ST. PAUL WATER WORKS**. Beautiful pine groves line the narrow drive between the lakes. Shore fishing along here is excellent. Continue east on Vadnais Boulevard to Rice Street if you are doing the **MEDIUM LOOP**. (Enjoy a swim at Lake Owasso before heading home.)

8.4 mi Another gorgeous stretch along **SUCKER LAKE** takes you to Highway 96.

10.1 mi **SNAIL LAKE REGIONAL PARK** has swimming, boating, picnicking and a great little trail in the woods to the east.

13.6 mi It's hot. It's sunny. It's time for a Misty Freeze at **DAIRY QUEEN**. Or make the scene at **LAKE JOSEPHINE** where you find another beach.

14.8 mi You won't mistake Roseville for New York City but enjoy the ride through **CENTRAL PARK**. Like its big city namesake, you can play a round of bocce ball or feed the ducks on Lake Bennett.

15.9 mi **HARRIET ALEXANDER NATURE CENTER** has a few live amphibians on display and a nice view over a marsh. Phone 651-415-2161 for program information.

16.9 mi An unmarked trail leads to and through wooded **MATERION PARK**.

20.6 mi After making it across Highway 36 on Rice Street you will have an uphill climb on County Road B followed by a couple nice glides on Edgerton to **WHEELOCK PARKWAY**.

22 mi BACK TO *GO!*

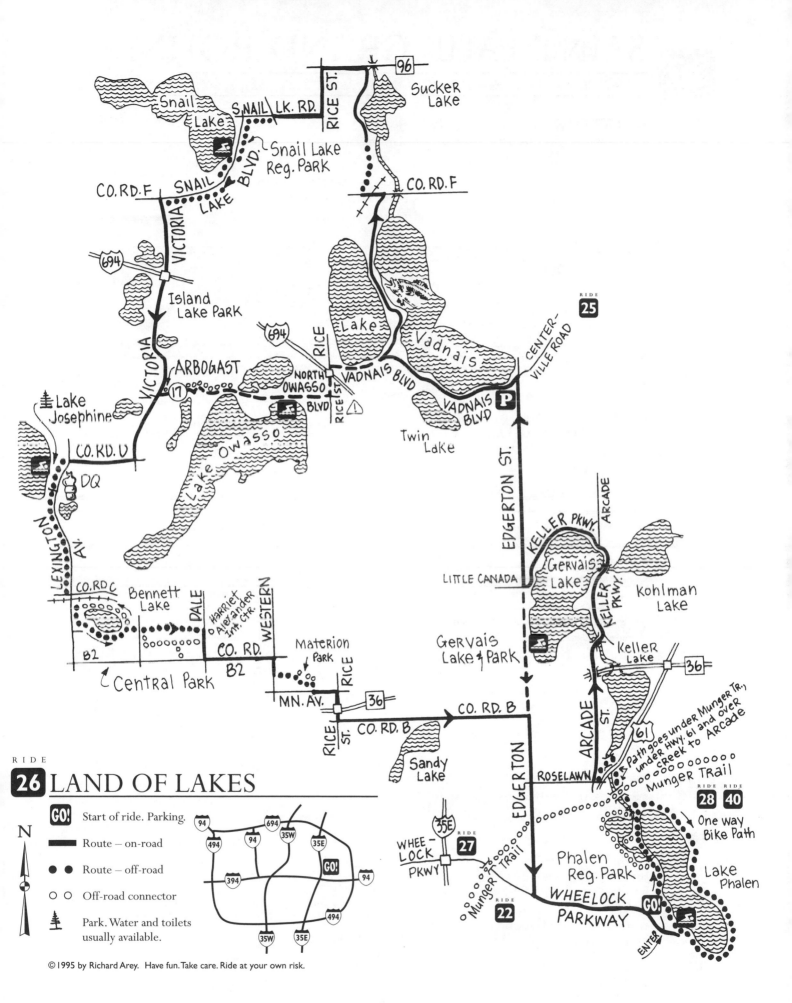

Snail Lake

SNAIL LK. RD.

RICE ST.

96

Sucker Lake

Snail Lake Reg. Park

CO. RD. F

CO. RD. F

SNAIL LAKE BLVD.

VICTORIA

694

Island Lake Park

694

RICE

Lake Vadnais

RIDE
25

CENTERVILLE ROAD

VICTORIA

ARBOGAST

17

NORTH OWASSO

VADNAIS BLVD

P

VADNAIS BLVD

Lake Josephine

CO. RD. V

DQ

BLVD

RICE ST.

Twin Lake

Lake Owasso

EDGERTON ST.

KELLER PKWY.

ARCADE

LEXINGTON AV.

CO. RD. C

Bennett Lake

DALE

Harriet Alexander Int. Ctr.

WESTERN

LITTLE CANADA

Gervais Lake

Kohlman Lake

KELLER PKWY.

Keller Lake

36

B2

Central Park

CO. RD. B2

Materion Park

RICE

Gervais Lake & Park

Keller St.

ARCADE ST.

61

Path goes under Munger Tr., under Hwy. 61 and over creek to Arcade

MN. AV.

36

CO. RD. B

RICE ST. CO. RD. B

Sandy Lake

EDGERTON

ROSELAWN

Munger Trail

RIDE 28   RIDE 40

One way Bike Path

26 LAND OF LAKES

RIDE

GO! Start of ride. Parking.

N

——— Route – on-road

•• Route – off-road

○○ Off-road connector

🌲 Park. Water and toilets usually available.

94   694

494   94   35W   35E

394   GO!

94

35W   35E

494

35W   35E

WHEELOCK PKWY

35E

RIDE 27

Munger Trail

RIDE 22

Phalen Reg. Park

WHEELOCK PARKWAY

Lake Phalen

GO!

ENTER

©1995 by Richard Arey. Have fun. Take care. Ride at your own risk.

SAINT PAUL GRAND ROUND

Ramsey County. Connects with RIDES 4, 20, 23, 26, 28, 29, 30, 32, 33, 39, 40, 49.

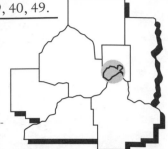

LENGTH   28.2 miles – Full loop as described
RATING   10.8 miles – Mississippi River Boulevard path, round trip
               4.1 miles – Como Park paved paths

CAUTION   Raymond north of Energy Park Drive is very tight. Use sidewalk as necessary. Shepard and Warner Road bikeway is scheduled for completion in 2000, the sidewalk on the south side is recommended.

*T*his "Grand Round" of St. Paul was conceived and promoted over a century ago by park visionaries such as Horace William Shaler Cleveland and Joseph Wheelock. Today it is nearly complete. The St. Paul Grand Round connects all five of the city's regional parks and features 14 miles of biking along the Mississippi River.

An annual citizen's tour — the Saint Paul Classic Bike Tour — is one of the Midwest's largest. The ride takes place on the Sunday after Labor Day each year. Phone 612-372-3424 for details.

GO!   Start at the overlook where Summit Avenue intersects Mississippi River Boulevard. Enjoy the view over **MISSISSIPPI GORGE REGIONAL PARK**. Head south. Faster bicyclists should use the parkway. Families may prefer the off-road combined path.

2.5 mi   Enter **HIDDEN FALLS REGIONAL PARK** (at Magoffin Avenue). Careful on the steep downhill. NOTE: While this park is really quite safe, single bicyclists may prefer to stay on the blufftop path that parallels Mississippi River Boulevard and then Shepard Road. (Saves 0.6 miles).

The riverside paved path enjoys some of the sweetest views of the Mississippi to be found anywhere. Wildlife is abundant and a short stop at the **CROSBY FARM NATURE CENTER** (just past the marina) is worthwhile. Marvel at the immense cottonwoods and take care if a "state endangered" Blanding's turtle should cross your path.

6.3 mi   Exit **CROSBY FARM** and head northeast (right) on the paved path along Shepard.

8.1 mi   Bike path ends at Randolph. Follow the road and use the sidewalk as necessary to where the new bike path begins.

11.2 mi   Follow the bike path along Warner Road. Enjoy the great vista over the river toward the white sandstone cliffs below Indian Mounds Park. The Dakota name for the St. Paul area is **I-MNI-ZA** (ledge) **SKA** (white), or white rocks. Just past Fish Hatchery Road a pedestrian bridge crosses Warner Road and takes you up the bluff.

13.9 mi   **JOHNSON PARKWAY** begins. It is definitely worth a short detour over to **INDIAN MOUNDS**

PARK to enjoy the spectacular panorama and the sacred mounds (add 0.8 miles). Johnson Parkway has a wide paved shoulder and was named after Minnesota Governor John Johnson (1905–1909).

16.3 mi   **PHALEN REGIONAL PARK** was acquired in 1899 and named after Edward Phalen. Ed distinguished himself by being accused of the city's first murder and later fleeing town. Take a short swim or enjoy a lakeside picnic. A complete loop of Lake Phalen adds 3.2 miles.

WHEELOCK PARKWAY skirts the southern end of Lake Phalen and heads west. It is named after Joseph Wheelock, founder of the St. Paul Pioneer Press (1861) and president of the St. Paul Park Board (1893–1906). Nobody fought harder for establishing St. Paul's parks and a connected parkway system than Wheelock.

21.7 mi   Lake Como comes into view and you enter **COMO REGIONAL PARK**. Minnesota's oldest and St. Paul's finest park began as a potato patch farmed by Charles Perry who named the lake after his birthplace, Como, Italy. Enjoy the FREE Zoo, the historic conservatory, Como Pool or a lap around Como Lake (add 1.5 miles).

23.5 mi   Take **MIDWAY PARKWAY** to the **STATE FAIR GROUNDS**. NOTE: Como Avenue is the alternative when the fair is in session.

24.6 mi   Take a left on Raymond. HEADS UP! This next stretch is busy.

27.1 mi   Pelham Boulevard returns you to the **MISSISSIPPI RIVER BOULEVARD**.

28.2 mi   BACK TO *GO!*

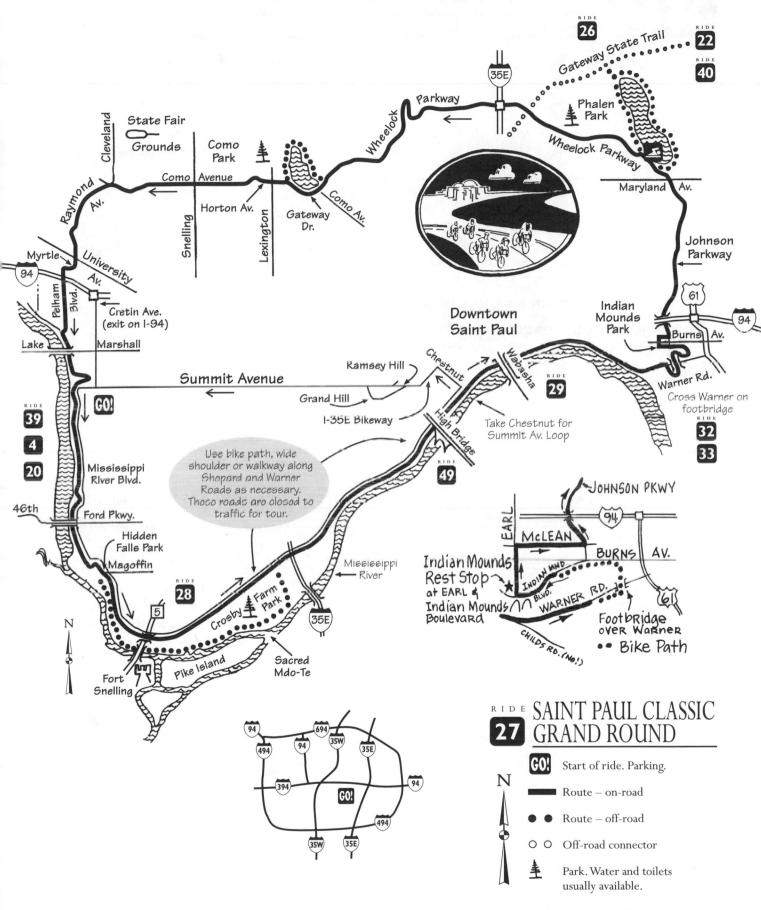

State Fair Grounds

Como Park

Como Avenue

Gateway Dr.

Como Av.

Wheelock Parkway

Parkway

Phalen Park

Maryland Av.

Cleveland

Raymond Av.

Snelling

Horton Av.

Lexington

Johnson Parkway

Myrtle

University Av.

Pelham Blvd.

Cretin Ave. (exit on I-94)

Indian Mounds Park

Burns Av.

Lake

Marshall

Downtown Saint Paul

Warner Rd.

Cross Warner on footbridge

Summit Avenue

Ramsey Hill

Chestnut

Grand Hill

I-35E Bikeway

High Bridge

Wabasha

Take Chestnut for Summit Av. Loop

GO!

RIDE **39**

RIDE **4**

RIDE **20**

RIDE **29**

RIDE **32**

RIDE **33**

RIDE **49**

Use bike path, wide shoulder or walkway along Shepard and Warner Roads as necessary. These roads are closed to traffic for tour.

Mississippi River Blvd.

46th

Ford Pkwy.

Hidden Falls Park

Magoffin

Mississippi River

RIDE **28**

Crosby Farm Park

Fort Snelling

Pike Island

Sacred Mdo-Te

N

RIDE **26**

RIDE **22**

RIDE **40**

Gateway State Trail

35E

JOHNSON PKWY

EARL

McLEAN

94

BURNS AV.

Indian Mounds Rest Stop at EARL & Indian Mounds Boulevard

INDIAN MND. BLVD.

WARNER RD.

61

Footbridge over Warner

CHILDS RD. (NO!)

•• Bike Path

SAINT PAUL CLASSIC GRAND ROUND

RIDE **27**

94   694

494   94   35W   35E

394   94

GO!

35W   35E   494

N

GO! Start of ride. Parking.

Route — on-road

•• Route — off-road

○ ○ Off-road connector

Park. Water and toilets usually available.

SAINT PAUL SAMPLERS

RIDE
28

Ramsey County. Connects with RIDES 4, 22, 26, 27, 30, 32, 39 and 40.

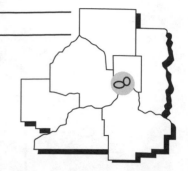

**LENGTH
RATING**

〰 32.5 miles – Both loops, as described

🬉 9.0 miles to Cathedral and back. Flat with bike lanes.

〰 21.9 miles – **Gateway Trail – Indian Mounds Loop**.

〰 14.6 miles – **Mississippi River - I-35E Bikeway Loop**.

● 8.0 miles – Hidden Falls-Crosby Farm Park, paved path

CAUTION   The Kellogg – West 7th – Grand Avenue area is very busy.

> *S*ummit Avenue is St. Paul's show street and is featured on both of these loop rides. More experienced cyclists are sure to enjoy the Gateway Trail – Indian Mounds Loop, which includes a cruise along Lake Phalen, the eye-popping panorama from Indian Mounds Park and the exhilarating downhill run on Kellogg into downtown St. Paul. A shorter sampler, the Mississippi River–I-35E Bikeway Loop, goes south along the Mississippi and through beautiful Hidden Falls Park before returning you along the I-35E Bikeway to Summit Avenue.

GATEWAY TRAIL – INDIAN MOUNDS LOOP

GO!   Start at **SUMMIT AVENUE** and Mississippi River Blvd. Take Summit east toward the Cathedral.

2.7 mi   The Governor's mansion is at **1006 SUMMIT AVENUE**. F. Scott Fitzgerald once referred to Summit Avenue as a "museum of American architectural failures," but the fact remains that Summit Avenue is the best preserved monumental residential boulevard in America.

599 Summit • F. Scott Fitzgerald completed *This Side of Paradise* on the 3rd floor and danced in the street when it was accepted by his publisher.

432 Summit • Burbank House (1862)

240 Summit • J. J. Hill House (1887), take a tour.

4.5 mi   The **ST. PAUL CATHEDRAL** crowns the top of the bluff. Designed by Emmanuel Masqueray and built between 1906 and 1941, the cathedral is a monument to the vision of Archbishop John Ireland.

5.2 mi   Coast to a stop in front of St. Paul native Cass Gilbert's finest effort — the **STATE CAPITOL**. This beautiful Beaux Arts pile (1893-1904) features four gold-gilded horsemen high above the entrance.

8.0 mi   Start of **GATEWAY MUNGER TRAIL** at Cayuga Street just east of Jackson.

9.8 mi   Watch the left-hand exit and cloverleaf to take you into **PHALEN REGIONAL PARK**.

11.6 mi   Enjoy the lakeside ride, then head south on **JOHNSON PARKWAY**.

14.4 mi   **INDIAN MOUNDS PARK** commands a spectacular view atop historic Carver's Cave and is used by Native Americans in sunrise tobacco ceremonies.

16.7 mi   Whistle into downtown St. Paul and take a peek inside beautifully restored **CITY HALL** (15 Kellogg Boulevard). The 55-ton, 36-foot high God of Peace rules magnificent Memorial Hall.

17.5 mi   Take care as you wind through downtown toward either the **DAIRY QUEEN** (280 W. 7th Street) or **GRAND OLE CREAMERY** (up the hill at 750 Grand Avenue).

21.9 mi   BACK TO *GO*.

MISSISSIPPI RIVER – I-35 BIKEWAY LOOP

GO!   Start at Summit Avenue and **MISSISSIPPI RIVER BOULEVARD**. Head south on Mississippi River Boulevard toward Ford Parkway.

2.5 mi   The waterfall in **HIDDEN FALLS REGIONAL PARK** can be seen from above on the path just past the overlook. Around the bend is the park entrance at Magoffin Avenue. The path along the river is beautiful, with sheer limestone cliffs rising next to you in spots.

4.8 mi   Just past the marina you enter **CROSBY FARM PARK**. This area has an abundance of wildlife and the Nature Center is worth a short visit. I watched a black-billed cuckoo here one fine spring day. The cottonwood trees are huge.

6.9 mi   Exit the park and head up Elway Street. Cross 7th Street on Albion and pick up the **I-35E BIKEWAY**.

10 mi   Follow the I-35E Bikeway back to **GRAND AVENUE**. Depending on how you are feeling take the Ramsey Street hill (very steep) or Grand Avenue hill (moderate) back to Summit Avenue.

14.6 mi   BACK TO *GO!*

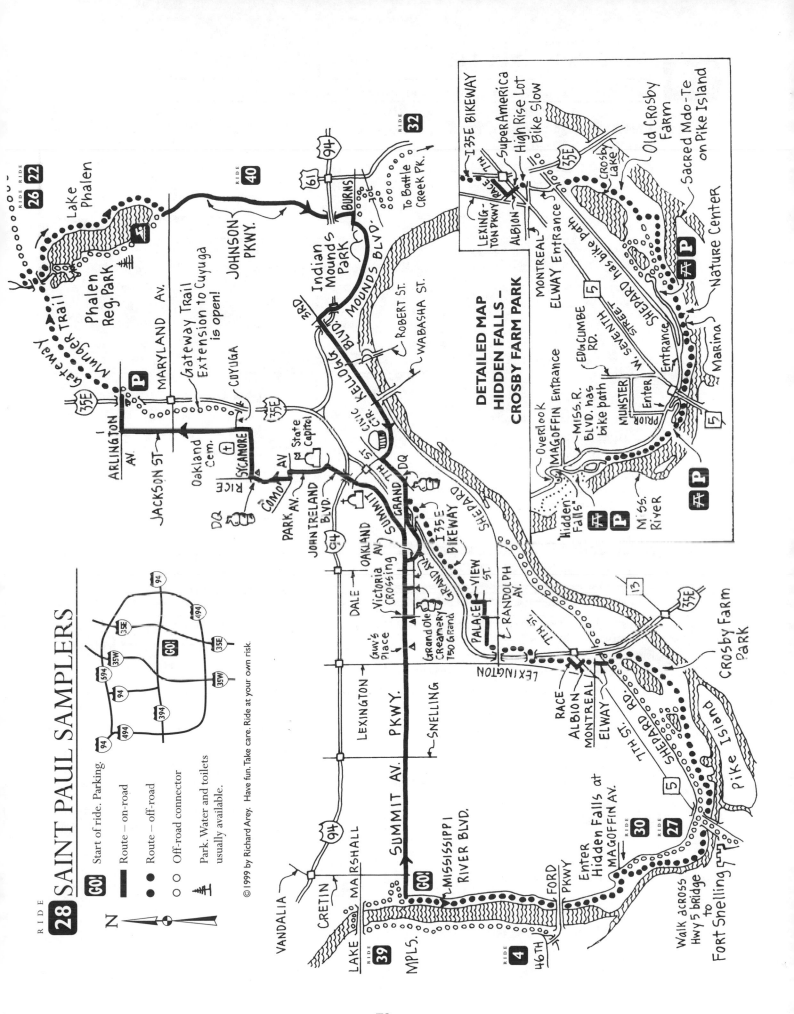

SAINT PAUL SAMPLERS

RIDE **28**

N

GO! Start of ride. Parking.
■ Route – on-road
•• Route – off-road
○○ Off-road connector
⛺ Park. Water and toilets usually available.

© 1999 by Richard Arey. Have fun. Take care. Ride at your own risk.

**DETAILED MAP
HIDDEN FALLS –
CROSBY FARM PARK**

RIDE 29

WEST SIDE WINDER

Ramsey and Dakota County. Connects with RIDES 30, 31, 32 and 49.

LENGTH 🏔 10.8 miles – Full loop as described

RATING 🎾 6.0 miles – Round trip Harriet Island to Lilydale, paved path

CONNECTION The Big Rivers Regional Trail connects Lilydale Regional Park to the Mendota Bridge and Fort Snelling (see RIDE 30 and 31).

*B*e the first on your block to test drive the new bike path through Lilydale Park. Check out the fancy new pier at Harriet Island. Ponder the possibilities of outdoor baseball on the riverfront. For those folks who have a hard enough time locating St. Paul, let alone the West Side of the Capitol City, here is a chance to do some exploring. But first, a quick geography primer so you can get your bearings. The West Side is actually on the south side of St. Paul, but the west side of the Mississippi River if you are coming into town on a steamboat. The town of West St. Paul is south of the West Side and South St. Paul is east of West St. Paul. Western Avenue, of course, plows right up through the middle of the city. OK, let's go biking!

GO!

Start at **HARRIET ISLAND** in the main parking area near the marina. A good breakfast at the **NO WAKE CAFE** (651-292-1411) is an excellent way to gear up. The No Wake Cafe is located on the 1946 towboat, *The Covington*, a unique floating bed and breakfast establishment. You'll like it so much you will want to call up Tom Welna and book a couple nights on the Mississippi. Phone 651-292-1411.

0.2 mi As you head up along the river you quickly reach the **HARRIET ISLAND PICNIC PAVILION**. This distinctive moderne-style building was designed by St. Paul's first black architect, Charles Wigington. It has survived three major river floods since its construction in the 1940s, and the Kasota limestone walls were actually salvaged from the 1886 Industrial Exposition Building. Take a left at the intersection just before you reach the pavilion.

HARRIET BISHOP CREATIVE PLAY AREA. Harriet Bishop came to town on a canoe in 1854 and was St. Paul's first teacher. Since you may still be reeling from your recent geography lesson, you will be glad to know that Harriet Island is no longer an island but is solidly attached to the south bank of the river. A **MAJOR RENOVATION** of the park featuring a music pavilion designed by Minnesota artist Siah Armajani is underway.

1.0 mi Find the start of the newly separated paved bike path heading southwest. The city disappears as you cross under the High Bridge and into **LILYDALE REGIONAL PARK**. This is a great place for

wildlife. I've seen herds of deer, kingfishers, pileated woodpeckers and indigo buntings. In early April, scoot over to spring-fed Pickerel Lake and look for migrating loons and other waterfowl.

3.5 mi The **POOL AND YACHT CLUB** marks the end of Lilydale Park and the start of a major uphill ride.

3.8 mi Watch for an unmarked bike path on the south side of the road just below Highway 13. Take it and enter **SCENIC VALLEY PARK**. The paved path through here follows a tiny bubbling brook. The city is still nowhere to be seen, and if it wasn't for the light hum of traffic from I-35E, you would bet you are far out in the countryside.

4.8 mi The underpass at **MARIA AVENUE** is located at the southwest corner of the tennis courts.

5.7 mi The final stretch of path skirts a large wetlands before delivering you back to civilization at **DODD ROAD**.

7.2 mi Ride the broad shoulders of Dodd Road past **SOMERSET COUNTRY CLUB** and back into town.

9.5 mi South side, west side, any side, anytime is good for **DAIRY QUEEN**. Located at Stryker and George Streets.

10.8 mi Take George Street and than the flying curves of Wabasha Street back to Harriet Island and **BACK TO GO!**

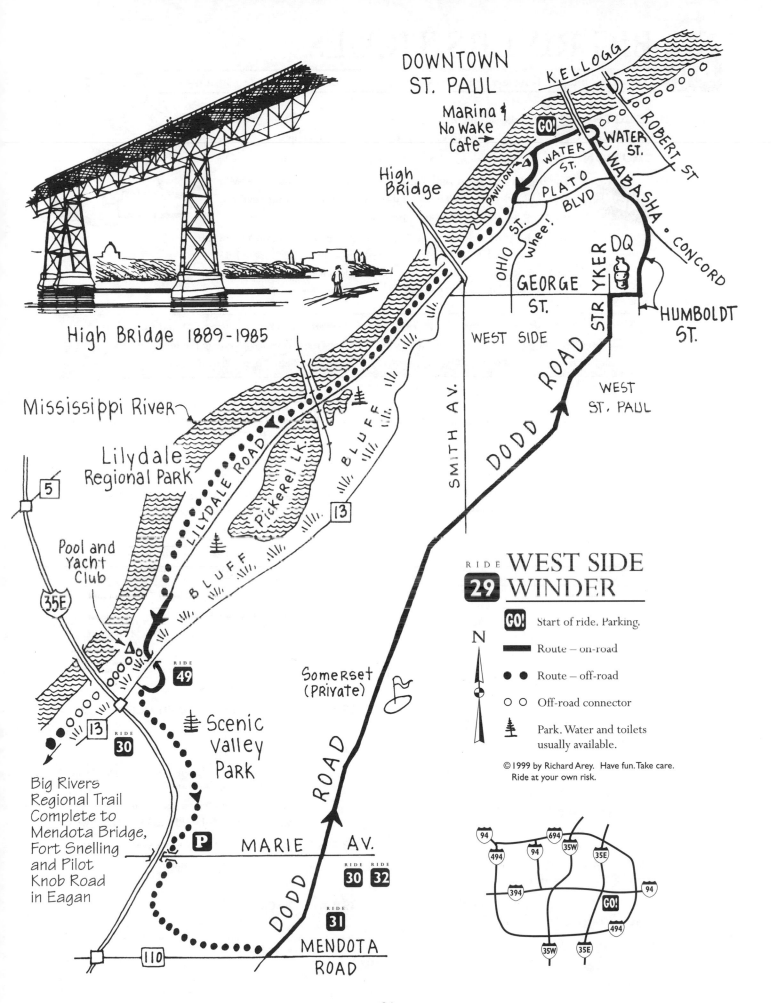

High Bridge 1889-1985

DOWNTOWN ST. PAUL

Marina & No Wake Cafe →

High Bridge

Mississippi River →

Lilydale Regional Park

Pool and Yacht Club

Big Rivers Regional Trail Complete to Mendota Bridge, Fort Snelling and Pilot Knob Road in Eagan

Scenic Valley Park

Somerset (Private)

WEST SIDE

WEST ST. PAUL

KELLOGG

WATER ST.
PLATO BLVD
GEORGE ST.

STRYKER ROAD

DODD ROAD

SMITH AV.

BLUFF
Pickerel Lk.
BLUFF

MARIE AV.

MENDOTA ROAD

DQ

WABASHA
ROBERT ST.
CONCORD
HUMBOLDT ST.

OHIO ST.
Whee!
PAVILION

GO!

RIDE 29 **WEST SIDE WINDER**

GO! Start of ride. Parking.

⸺ Route – on-road

•• Route – off-road

○○ Off-road connector

🌲 Park. Water and toilets usually available.

© 1999 by Richard Arey. Have fun. Take care. Ride at your own risk.

N

RIDE 49

RIDE 30

RIDE 30 RIDE 32

RIDE 31

94 | 694
494 | 94 | 35W | 35E
394 | 94
GO!
35W | 35E | 494

BIG RIVERS TRAILS

30

Dakota, Hennepin, Ramsey. Connects with RIDES 4, 20, 27, 28, 29, 31, 39 and 49.

LENGTH 〰 29.3 miles – Full loop as described
RATING ⬤ 7.8 miles – **Big Rivers Regional Trail**, round trip.
CAUTION Be careful biking along 34th Avenue and Highway 13. Big hills.

The **Big Rivers Regional Trail** glides above the Mississippi and Minnesota Rivers with views so sweet that this became one of the region's most popular trails as soon as it opened.

The trail is at the heart of this ride and can be accessed from the Yacht Club (bottom of Lilydale Road cloverleaf off of Highway 13, just east of I-35E), the WPA Scenic Overlook (west end of Mendota Heights Road at Highway 13) and from Fort Snelling via the Mendota Bridge Bikeway. Enjoy!

The Mississippi, Minnesota and St. Croix Rivers provide the main drama in the metro area landscape. This route celebrates two of these great rivers and includes my favorite downhill (since giving up the luge), the High Bridge highball that screams across the Mississippi with St. Paul and the State Capitol looming in the distance.

GO! Start at the parking lot for **LOCK AND DAM NO. 1** (612-724-2971) located in Minneapolis just below the Ford Bridge: See inset map. A self-guided walking tour (keep your bikes locked) of the lock and dam gives an excellent introduction to these working rivers. The visitor promenade offers a bird's-eye view of boats going through the locks.

0.6 mi Bike down Godfrey Parkway and follow the signs to **MINNEHAHA FALLS**. The falls were immortalized when Alex Hesler took a couple daguerreotypes of the falls in 1852. He brought them back home to Illinois, gave one to a buddy visiting from out East, who in turn showed it to Henry Wadsworth Longfellow. You know the rest.

0.8 mi Or skip the falls and have a cone at **DAIRY QUEEN** (corner of Minnehaha and Nawadaha).

1.9 mi Head south on Minnehaha Parkway past the Princess Depot and on to the start of the **MINNEHAHA TRAIL** at 54th Street. You're rolling gently downhill on an old railroad grade and soon reach **FORT SNELLING**. The center of white settlement after its erection in the 1820s, this area is also sacred to the Dakota, who called this place **MDO-TE MI-NI-SO-TA**. MDO-TE refers to the confluence of the Minnesota and Mississippi Rivers and the name was adapted by the town of Mendota.

4.4 mi Follow the paved path over to the **SWIMMING BEACH** in Fort Snelling State Park.

6.1 mi Take the long uphill road out of the State Park and onto **POST ROAD**. Gawk at the planes awhile.

9.1 mi Be careful on 34th Avenue and 80th Street before reaching the **MINNESOTA VALLEY NATIONAL WILDLIFE REFUGE VISITORS CENTER** (612-854-5900) There are superior interpretive displays and program information for future visits.

11.4 mi Cross over the Minnesota River and up to **PILOT KNOB ROAD** where you turn left.

18.7 mi A quick right on Mendota Heights Road will take you over to Dodd Road, which has a wide shoulder. At Smith Street take a left and head on down or if you want an extra climb on this route, take Wentworth (left), Wachtler (right) and head up Highway 13 to the High Bridge.

19.9 mi Coast to a stop at the **DAIRY QUEEN** (280 W. 7th Street) for a Misty Kiss.

26.3 mi Follow the I-35E Bikeway to Jefferson and up to Edgcumbe Road. Edgcumbe is a scenic, hilly romp through Highland Park. After another fun downhill, take the right on Munster, the left on Prior and you will intersect **MISSISSIPPI RIVER BOULEVARD**.

28.3 mi Take this to the **FORD PARKWAY BRIDGE**. Stop at one of the beautiful river overlooks along the way.

29.3 mi BACK TO *GO!*

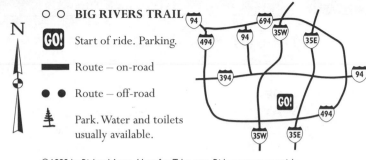

○ ○ **BIG RIVERS TRAIL**

GO! Start of ride. Parking.

—— Route – on-road

••• Route – off-road

🌲 Park. Water and toilets usually available.

©1999 by Richard Arey. Have fun. Take care. Ride at your own risk.

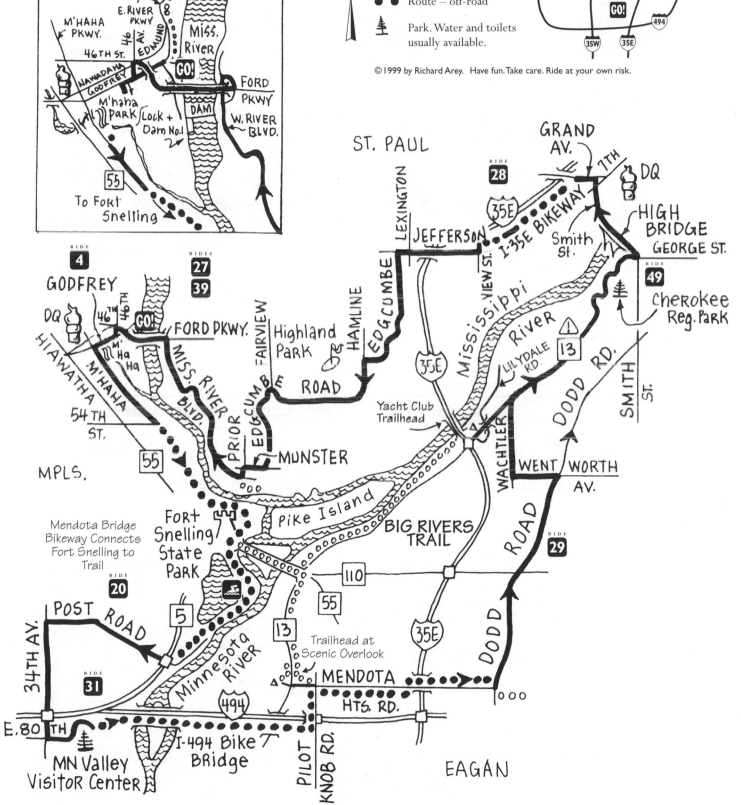

BIKE TO THE ZOO

Dakota County. Connects with RIDES 18, 19, 20, 29, 30, 32, 49, D and J.

LENGTH	12.0 miles – from Fort Snelling
TO THE	12.5 miles – from Marie Avenue and Dodd Road
ZOO	11.1 miles – from Minnesota Valley Visitor Center
ONE	8.5 miles – from Old Shakopee Road
WAY	6.4 miles – from Dairy Queen on Highway 13
	6.1 miles – from Patrick Eagan Park
RATING	Virtually every route is on an off-road paved path suitable for all levels of cyclists.
CAUTION	Be careful at all intersections. Most routes are hilly.

*T*he Minnesota Zoo (612-432-9000) is nationally acclaimed for balancing conservation efforts with family enter-
tainment. Why not take this environmental and recreational approach one step further and bike to the zoo! Yes,
this is the best place to view wildlife in the Twin Cities. The zoo features over 1,700 animals in specially designed
habitats so they feel at home. The Siberian tigers, musk oxen and Tropics Trail are personal favorites. And don't
miss the World of Birds show. Biking is not allowed within the zoo, so bring a lock and some cash to visit.

GO! Since many of the routes overlap, the following
descriptions are capsule summaries from each starting point. The mileage listed above uses the most
direct route.

FORT SNELLING (612-725-2389)

Start at the gate of the old stone fort. The path to the
MENDOTA BRIDGE is about 100 yards due west
of here. The bikeway on the bridge is complete and
offers a grand panorama that includes both down-
towns. Cross the bridge and hop onto the **BIG
RIVERS REGIONAL TRAIL**. The short (50') connection will be paved soon. Proceed to the scenic
overlook at the end of Mendota Heights Road.

MARIE AVENUE

Dodd Road has a wide shoulder that takes you to
the path along Mendota Heights Road. Head south
on the rolling hills of Pilot Knob Road. The highest
point of land was a landmark known by riverboat
pilots as **PILOT HILL**.

MINNESOTA VALLEY VISITOR CENTER

(612-854-5900)

This striking contemporary structure is the headquarters for the Minnesota River Valley National
Wildlife Refuge. Interactive displays, exhibits and
handouts introduce you to this incredible resource.

See RIDE 16. The **I-494 BIKE BRIDGE** spans the
huge valley carved by the Glacial River Warren.

OLD SHAKOPEE ROAD

Take the Old Cedar Avenue Bridge across the Minnesota River (watch for yellow-headed blackbirds)
and up to Silver Bell Road. The **HIGHLINE
TRAIL** is quite scenic.

DAIRY QUEEN ON HIGHWAY 13

Stoke up on some **STRAWBERRY SHORTCAKE**.
Palomino Road is pretty, wooded and steep in spots.

PATRICK EAGAN PARK (651-681-4660)

A gem of a city park, it is named after the town-
ship's first chairman who came here from Tipperary,
Ireland, in 1853. Stop in at the privately owned
CAPONI ART PARK if it is open. **THOMAS
LAKE PARK** features a 12-acre native prairie and a
picnic pavilion overlooking the lake.

LEBANON HILLS REGIONAL PARK is the premier natural preserve in the area. A beautiful swimming beach and excellent hiking trails are available.
There is ample opportunity to find seclusion within
the 2,000 acres of lakes, hills and woods, but bicycling is only allowed at the designated mountain
bike area west of Johnny Cake Road. See RIDE J.

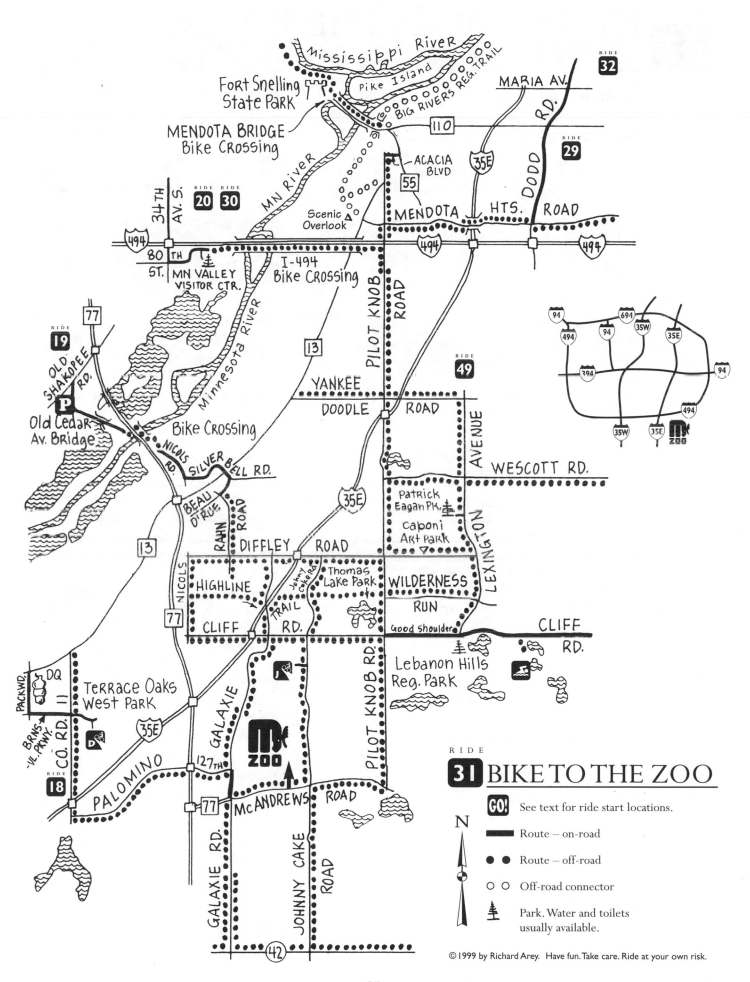

Mississippi River

Pike Island

Fort Snelling
State Park

MENDOTA BRIDGE
Bike Crossing

BIG RIVERS REG. TRAIL

MARIA AV.

RIDE **32**

110

MN River

ACACIA BLVD

35E

DODD RD.

RIDE **29**

34TH AV. S.

RIDE **20** RIDE **30**

55

MENDOTA   HTS.   ROAD

Scenic
Overlook

494

494

494

80TH ST.

I-494
Bike Crossing

MN VALLEY
VISITOR CTR.

13

PILOT KNOB ROAD

77

RIDE **19**

OLD SHAKOPEE RD.

94

494   94   35W   35E

694

P

Old Cedar
Av. Bridge

Bike Crossing

NICOLS RD.

SILVER BELL RD.

13

YANKEE

DOODLE   ROAD

RIDE **49**

394

94

35W   35E

AVENUE

WESCOTT RD.

35W   35E

M ZOO

BEAU D'RUE

RAHN ROAD

35E

Patrick
Eagan Pk.

caponi
Art Park

LEXINGTON

13

Nicols

77

DIFFLEY   ROAD

HIGHLINE

John's Cake Rd.

Thomas
Lake Park

WILDERNESS

RUN

CLIFF

TRAIL RD.

Good shoulder

CLIFF RD.

Lebanon Hills
Reg. Park

PACKWD.

DQ

Terrace Oaks
West Park

GALAXIE

PILOT KNOB RD.

BRNS. VL. PKWY.

CO. RD. 11

35E

127TH

M ZOO

77

RIDE **18**

PALOMINO

GALAXIE RD.

McANDREWS   ROAD

JOHNNY CAKE ROAD

42

RIDE **31** BIKE TO THE ZOO

GO! See text for ride start locations.

N

Route — on-road

• • • Route — off-road

○ ○ Off-road connector

Park. Water and toilets
usually available.

© 1999 by Richard Arey. Have fun. Take care. Ride at your own risk.

- 85 -

PATTI ROCKS THE RIVER

RIDE 32

Ramsey, Washington & Dakota County. Connects with RIDES 27, 28, 29, 30, 33 and 40.

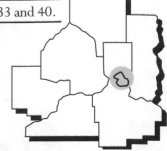

**LENGTH
RATING**

⬧ 25.5 miles – Full loop as described

⬧ 5.0 miles – Indian Mounds through Battle Creek, round trip

CAUTION Three major climbs and heavy traffic on Kellogg and Babcock at rush hour. Toll Bridge is open for bicyclists May through October and a 30-cent fee is charged per bicyclist. Bridge phone is 651-450-0757 and it is worth a call to make sure it's open before riding.

> *This is a fascinating route that has it all — great scenic vistas, quiet backwoods roads, a bustling downtown (well, St. Paul anyway), a Dairy Queen and a historic 1895 double decker swing bridge. The 1988 movie PATTI ROCKS had a scene featuring this historic toll bridge.*

GO! Start at **INDIAN MOUNDS PARK** (651-266-6400). To reach the park from the west, take the Mounds exit off I-94 and go right (southeast) on Mounds Boulevard. From the east, exit I-94 at Highway 61, go south to Burns Avenue, and right (west) on Burns, forking left on Mounds Boulevard to the park.

Indian Mounds Park offers an unsurpassed view of downtown St. Paul and the Mississippi River. There were 18 mounds when the site was originally surveyed by Edward Neill in 1856. These six mounds are some of the last remaining in Minnesota, where 10,000 had been tallied at the turn of the century. The sacred burial mounds are still used for worship by Native Americans in sunrise tobacco ceremonies. The Dakota knew this place as **WA-KAN TI-PI**, or sacred habitation, referring to Carver's Cave directly below. Picnic areas and restrooms are nearby.

2.5 mi An off-road paved path leads to **BATTLE CREEK REGIONAL PARK**. The entrance is framed by two sandstone cliffs. A creek bubbles out under the white sculpted rocks and if time permits a very scenic side trip can be made on a paved path up the wooded ravine.

8.6 mi Pay your money and bike across the double decker **TOLL BRIDGE**. Imagine a train going overhead. Make a note to rent the video *Patti Rocks* but be sure your kids are in bed as the language is definitely salty.

9.9 mi It is a long uphill climb on 66th Street to reach **SKYVIEW PARK** where you can refill your water bottles and look out over the valley.

11.2 mi Take 70th Street to Cahill if you would like to refuel at **DAIRY QUEEN**. Cahill Avenue and 55th Street now have off-road bike paths.

13.1 mi A couple more hills on 55th Street will take you to the **SALEM METHODIST CHURCH** — a brick landmark since 1854.

15.7 mi Babcock and Oakdale take you to Maria and a modern landmark — the **WATER TOWER**. It is all downhill from here.

18.2 mi Enter scenic **VALLEY PARK** and take the paved path heading north. This will lead you to a curving road exiting the park (go right) headed down toward the river.

19.5 mi Follow Lilydale Road downstream along the Mississippi River and you will soon enter **LILYDALE REGIONAL PARK**. Though you are rapidly approaching a major downtown it feels more like a backwoods road in the bayou. Birdwatching is excellent. Look for wood ducks, kingbirds and common goldeneyes in spring. A new paved path along the river starts at the boat ramp access road. The path (or Lilydale Road) takes you to **PLATO BOULEVARD.**

22.8 mi The **ROBERT STREET BRIDGE** crosses over the Mississippi and provides a dramatic entry into downtown St. Paul. Completed in 1926, the beautiful 264-foot-long rainbow arch was recently refurbished to its original glory. If you prefer, the **WABASHA BRIDGE**, completed in 1998, has striped bike lanes.

25.4 mi A long uphill march on Kellogg Boulevard takes you **BACK TO GO!** Enjoy the great view along the way.

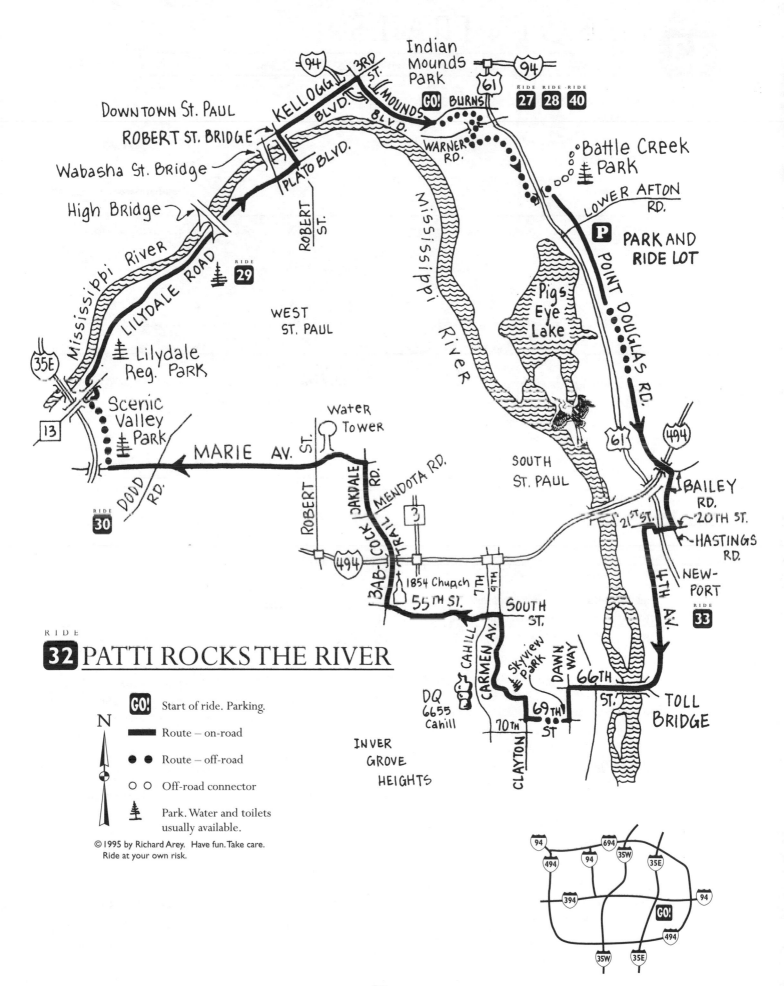

32 PATTI ROCKS THE RIVER

RIDE

GO! Start of ride. Parking.

——— Route – on-road

•• • Route – off-road

○ ○ Off-road connector

♠ Park. Water and toilets usually available.

© 1995 by Richard Arey. Have fun. Take care.
Ride at your own risk.

RIDE
33 DAKOTA TRAILS

Ramsey & Washington County. Connects with RIDES 27, 28, 32, 34 and 40.

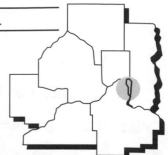

LENGTH ❖ 39.4 miles – Full loop as described
RATING ◐ 21.2 miles – Toll bridge, Red Rock and return
◐ 5.0 miles – Battle Creek Park trails

CAUTION Light traffic, except at rush hour, but no shoulder on Grey Cloud Island Drive and Bailey Road. Big hills over I-494, on 70th Street and Bailey Road.

*T*he place names of the Dakota Indians echo across Minnesota. This tour brings together archaeological sites and features that have been revered for centuries. Red Rock, Indian Mounds Park, Battle Creek and Grey Cloud Island all resonate with storied pasts. The trip begins with a spectacular view over the Mississippi River from Indian Mounds Park. It includes half a dozen more river views along the way. The southern half of the ride is surprisingly rural for now but bicycling over to the Dairy Queen on 80th Street gives an indication of what may lie ahead. Grey Cloud Island is destined to be a tremendous addition to the metropolitan park system. Tell your influential friends and politicians.

GO! Start at **INDIAN MOUNDS PARK** (651-266-6400). To reach the park from the west, exit I-94 at Mounds Boulevard and go right (southeast) on Mounds. From the east, exit I-94 at Highway 61, go south to Burns Avenue, then right (west) on Burns, forking left on Mounds Boulevard to the park.

Indian Mounds Park, dating back to 1893, is not simply one of the oldest parks in the region — it is a living link with a time and people that fades into prehistory. The mounds were built as burial sites by various Native American nations commencing with the Hopewell culture some 2,000 years ago. The mounds remain sacred for Indians who honor the dead with sunrise tobacco ceremonies. Picnic grounds with restrooms are located nearby.

2.5 mi Two large shoulders of sandstone guard the entrance to **BATTLE CREEK REGIONAL PARK**. From this ravine in June, 1842, Ojibway Indians attacked the Dakota village of Kaposia across the river. A paved bike path follows the creek up this beautiful wooded ravine and adds about 3 miles to the trip. Otherwise, continue along Bob Dylan's famous Highway 61 — the Point Douglas Bike Route.

4.8 mi **FISH CREEK OPEN SPACE** lies hidden just past Carver Avenue. Take a short walk to a tiny waterfall.

8.6 mi If it is still open, pay your money and bike across the historic **1895 TOLL BRIDGE**. This double decker swing bridge was featured in the 1988 movie *Patti Rocks*. The bridge phone is 651-450-0757.

13.9 mi Cross the bridge onto **GREY CLOUD ISLAND**. If good sense prevails this will eventually be one of the gems of the Mississippi National River and Recreation Area. The 1,400-acre park reserve will include trails, camping and an interpretive center. There is certainly a wealth of material to interpret. There are ancient habitation sites here that date back long before the time of the Dakota woman, **MA-HPI-YA** (clouds) **HO-TA** (grey) **WIN** (woman), for whom the island is named.

16.0 mi **END OF THE ROAD.**

21.5 mi Take Hadley Avenue and Grange to the **DAIRY QUEEN** at 7175 S. 80th Street. Stoke up for the big hill on 70th Street.

27.4 mi Cross Highway 61 twice more and head up 11th Avenue to the Newport United Methodist Church and the historic **RED ROCK**. The rock is smaller than expected and was moved here from its original location on the banks of the Mississippi River. Known by the Dakota as **IN-YAN** (stone) **SA** (red), it has been revered for generations and painted red stripes are still barely visible.

33.5 mi If traffic is light and you have the energy, take Bailey Road up the big bluff and then over on Sterling and Carver to McKnight Road. Enter **BATTLE CREEK PARK** from Lower Afton Road and take a lap before heading over to glide down through beautiful Battle Creek Ravine.

39.4 mi One more hill and it is **BACK TO** *GO!*

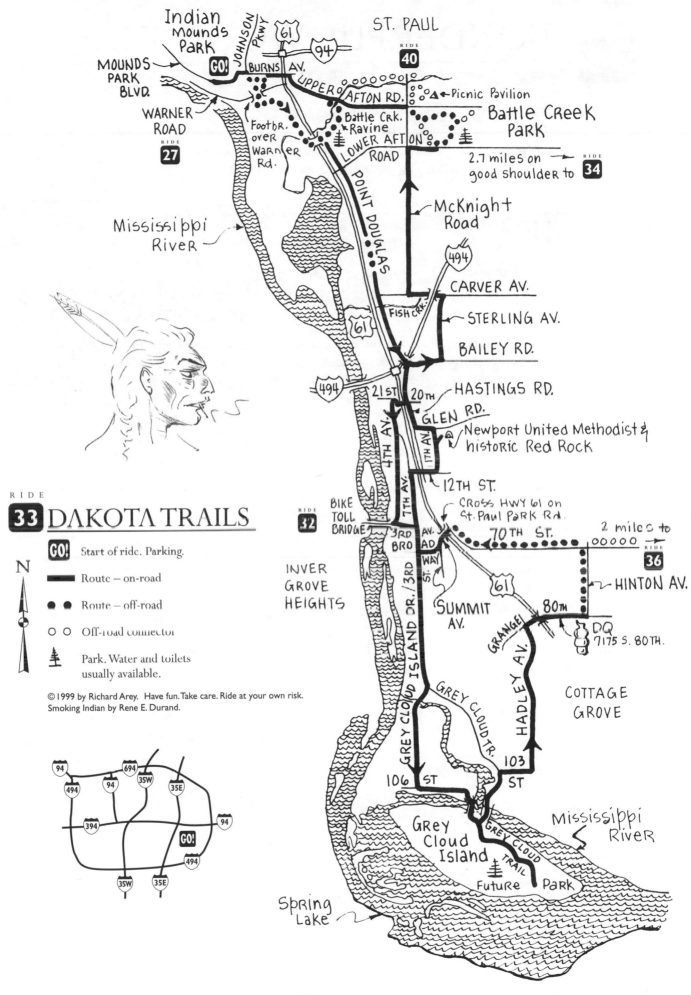

Indian Mounds Park

ST. PAUL

MOUNDS PARK BLVD.

JOHNSON PKWY

61

94

RIDE 40

BURNS AV.

UPPER AFTON RD.

WARNER ROAD

RIDE 27

Footbr. over Warner Rd.

Battle Crk. Ravine

LOWER AFTON ROAD

Picnic Pavilion

Battle Creek Park

2.7 miles on good shoulder to RIDE 34

Mississippi River

POINT DOUGLAS

McKnight Road

494

CARVER AV.

FISH CRK.

STERLING AV.

BAILEY RD.

61

494

21ST 20TH

HASTINGS RD.

4TH AV.

11TH AV.

GLEN RD.

Newport United Methodist & historic Red Rock

7TH AV.

12TH ST.

CROSS HWY 61 on St. Paul Park Rd.

RIDE 33 DAKOTA TRAILS

GO! Start of ride. Parking.

N

——— Route – on-road

•• Route – off-road

○ ○ Off-road connector

🌲 Park. Water and toilets usually available.

© 1999 by Richard Arey. Have fun. Take care. Ride at your own risk.
Smoking Indian by Rene E. Durand.

RIDE 32

BIKE TOLL BRIDGE

3RD BRO

AV. AD

WAY ST.

GRAY CLOUD ISLAND DR./3RD

INVER GROVE HEIGHTS

70TH ST.

2 miles to ○○○○○ RIDE 36

HINTON AV.

SUMMIT AV.

61

80TH

GRANGE

HADLEY AV.

DQ 7175 S. 80TH.

COTTAGE GROVE

GREY CLOUD TR.

103 ST

106 ST

Grey Cloud Island

GREY CLOUD TRAIL

Future Park

Mississippi River

Spring Lake

94   694

494   94   35W   35E

394

94

GO!

494

35W   35E

WONDERFUL WOODBURY

Washington County. Connects with RIDES 32, 33, 35, 36, H and I.

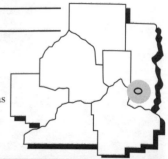

LENGTH	⬤ 14.2 miles - Full loop as described
RATING	⬤ 10.0 miles - Half loop
CAUTION	Route is tricky to navigate the first time. Woodbury (651-739-5972) has an excellent map of its parks and bikeway system.

Woodbury township was named in honor of Judge Levi Woodbury in 1858 — the same year Minnesota became a state. Levi was a New Hampshire resident and an old buddy of the local chair of the county commission. It is not known if Woodbury ever even visited here, but if you're in the neighborhood, definitely stop by. This route bends and twists to capture every inch of natural beauty it can muster. Colby and Wilmes Lakes are treats. Get off your bike to explore a bit of the Tamarack Nature Preserve. Here is a wild chunk of the far north settled in the suburbs.

The key to Woodbury's beautiful trail system is the city's farsighted public policy that requires developers to dedicate 150-foot-wide strips of land around their lakes for public trails. This policy is unique in Minnesota and bodes well for future trail development as the progressive community continues to grow.

GO! Start your tour in **OJIBWAY PARK**, Woodbury's recreational hub. The park entrance is reached by exiting I-494 at Valley Creek Road and heading east. Take the first right (south) on Woodlane Drive to Courtly Road. Go left (east) on Courtly and right on Ojibway Drive one block to entrance.

Water, washrooms, play areas and a host of other recreational opportunities are available.

Take the path directly east of the recreation center for 0.4 miles.

0.4 mi Take the right fork at the "T" intersection and proceed along the creek 0.4 miles to Tower Drive.

3.0 mi **COLBY LAKE** is the centerpiece of the town's biggest park. It is a beauty. Follow the paved path north up the short chain of lakes.

5.4 mi A thin wooded ravine follows a tiny creek up to **SEASONS PARK**. Check out the action on the soccer fields.

6.3 mi Exit the ravine, cross a street and proceed past the parking lot and along the creek.

6.6 mi Take the left fork in the path at the pond.

6.7 mi Take a sharp left toward the tennis courts after passing the baseball fields.

7.8 mi After negotiating the small residential maze take the bike paths along Radio Drive and Valley Creek Road to **TAMARACK NATURE PRESERVE**. This is a bog, not for bikes, but worth the short walk in. Tamaracks (larch trees) have soft needle-like leaves that turn golden yellow in fall. Tamarack bogs are much more comfortable in the wilds of central Canada. They are growing here at the southern edge of their range.

9.0 mi One block north of Valley Creek Road on Bielenberg Drive is — you guessed it — a **DAIRY QUEEN**.

9.5 mi Wind your way over to the historic limestone **BISCHOSLICHE METHODISTEN CHURCH** built in 1868. On Steeple View Road, you know.

10.0 mi Head south, back into Ojibway Park and soon you will **PASS GO!** Collect $200 and head for Carver Lake.

11.8 mi Uh oh! **CARVER LAKE** has a resort hotel on it, pay $300. Enjoy the view before heading......

14.2 mi BACK TO *GO!*

34 WONDERFUL WOODBURY

GO! Start of ride. Parking.

N

—— Route – on-road

• • Route – off-road

○ ○ Off-road connector

🌲 Park. Water and toilets usually available.

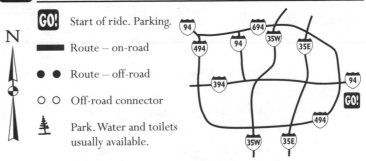

© 1995 by Richard Arey. Have fun. Take care. Ride at your own risk.

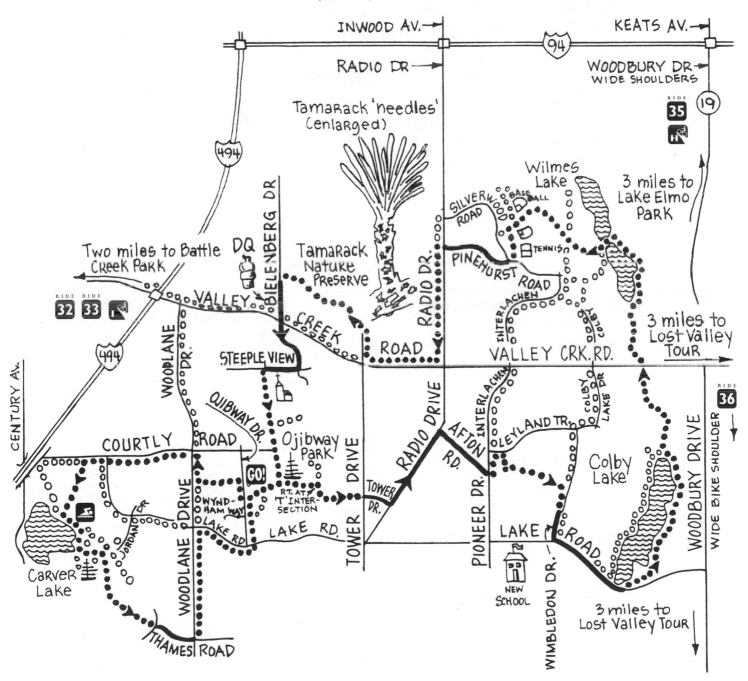

INWOOD AV. →

KEATS AV. →

RADIO DR →

WOODBURY DR WIDE SHOULDERS

94

19

RIDE 35 H

Tamarack 'needles' (enlarged)

Wilmes Lake

3 miles to Lake Elmo Park

494

BIELENBERG DR.

Two miles to Battle Creek Park

DQ

SILVERWOOD ROAD

BASE BALL

TENNIS

Tamarack Nature Preserve

VALLEY

CREEK

PINEHURST ROAD

RIDE 32 RIDE 33

WOODLANE DR.

STEEPLE VIEW

RADIO DR.

ROAD

INTERLACHEN

VALLEY CRK. RD.

3 miles to Lost Valley Tour

494

OJIBWAY DR.

Ojibway Park

RADIO DRIVE

AFTON RD.

INTERLACHEN

LEYLAND TR.

COLBY LAKE DR.

RIDE 36

CENTURY AV.

COURTLY ROAD

GO!

R.T. AT 'T' INTER-SECTION

TOWER DRIVE

Colby Lake

WOODBURY DRIVE

WIDE BIKE SHOULDER

WYND-HAM WAY

TOWER DR.

PIONEER DR.

LAKE RD.

WOODLANE DRIVE

JORDANA DR.

LAKE RD.

LAKE RD.

WIMBLEDON DR.

ROAD

NEW SCHOOL

Carver Lake

THAMES ROAD

3 miles to Lost Valley Tour

STAGECOACH TO STILLWATER

Washington County. Connects with RIDES 23, 36, 44 and H.

LENGTH RATING

- 43.9 miles – Longest loop as described
- 5.5 miles – Lake Elmo Park Reserve paved path
- 25.4 miles – Shortest loop to Stillwater
- 30.4 miles – Afton and Hudson (but not Stillwater) and back

CAUTION Car parking fee at Lake Elmo (free with Washington Parks sticker). Stagecoach Trail has no shoulder south of Hudson Road. Big hills and traffic in Stillwater.

*S*teamboating the scenic St. Croix rivertowns would be a good subtitle for this ride. Afton, Hudson, Lake Elmo and Stillwater are all quite charming. You may wish you had brought a trailer along if you enjoy antiquing. Stop in one of the excellent used book stores in Hudson or Stillwater for a more portable treasure. If nothing else, you're sure to return with some memorable images of quaint villages, unspoiled countryside and the wide pristine waters of the St. Croix River.

GO! Start at **LAKE ELMO PARK RESERVE** (651-731-3851). Take Keats Avenue (County Road 19) north 1 mile from I-94 to park entrance. Lake Elmo offers 3½ square miles of recreational opportunities. As a *Park Reserve*, 80 percent of the land will remain in a natural state. Besides the paved paths there is an 8-mile mountain bike course (See RIDE H) and horseback riding. Boating, camping, picnicking and a wonderful 2-acre swimming pond are all part of the mix.

3.8 mi Follow County Roads 10 and 15 to the **HUDSON ROAD BIKE ROUTE.** (An off-road path along County Road 19 also leads there but is less scenic.)

NOTE: Another interesting way to get to Afton is to cross I-94 at County Road 71 and take Hudson Boulevard east to **INDIAN TRAIL.** This leads you down to Stagecoach Trail.

6.0 mi **ST. CROIX TRAVEL INFORMATION CENTER** has all the requisite traveler's needs and is the geographic center of I-94. A paved path behind the rest area leads to a secluded overlook of the farmstead site where three generations of the Splinter family tended the land from 1883 to 1976.

7.4 mi Intersection of I-94 and **STAGECOACH TRAIL.** You will save 14.1 miles if you skip the side trips to Afton and Hudson.

11.6 mi Scenic Stagecoach Trail winds down to **AFTON.** Pick up an ice cream cone at **SELMA'S** and stroll down to the river.

15.4 mi An off-road paved path leads up to 8th Street (I-94 and 95).

17.6 mi Follow 8th Street until it ends and goes below the I-94 bridge. A ramp on the north side takes you to the bikeway over the St. Croix River and into **HUDSON.** Time for a **DAIRY QUEEN.**

21.5 mi Back to I-94 and Stagecoach Trail. Head north on the broad shoulders of this historic route.

29.5 mi A long fast downhill on 3rd Street takes you into the heart of **STILLWATER.** It is just a couple blocks down Chestnut or Myrtle to the main business district or the river. Climb the 2nd Street hill up to **PIONEER PARK** and a wonderful vista.

30.4 mi Owens and Myrtle Street. Decision time. The quickest way back is to continue two more blocks to Olive Street and take Highway 5. This busy route has a wide shoulder and saves 4.5 miles. But before you go too far, stop at **NELSON'S DRIVE INN** (corner of Olive and Greeley Streets) for a huge scoop of Brown's Ice Cream. Highway 5 is one of the oldest travel routes in Minnesota and even appeared on the 1899 St. Paul Cycle Path Association Route Map of the Twin Cities.

39.5 mi Take the paved path or wide shoulder of Highway 12 to Keats Avenue and head south into the town of **LAKE ELMO.** The stamped metal siding of the Lake Elmo mill is striking on a sunny day.

43.9 mi Enjoy the beautiful stretch of County Road 17 along Lake Elmo before heading **BACK TO GO!**

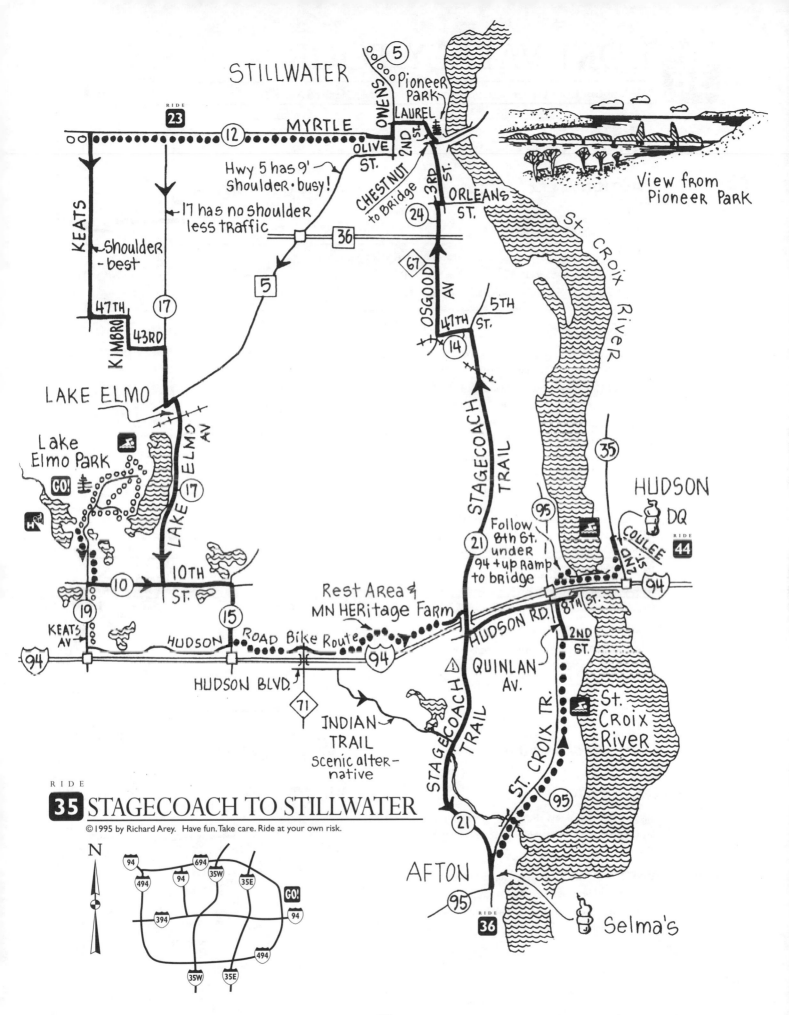

STILLWATER

View from Pioneer Park

Hwy 5 has 9' shoulder·busy!

17 has no shoulder less traffic

Shoulder -best

LAKE ELMO

Lake Elmo Park

GO!

Rest Area & MN HERitage Farm

Road Bike Route

Follow 8th St. under I 94 + up Ramp to bridge

HUDSON DQ

RIDE 44

St. Croix River

HUDSON BLVD.

INDIAN TRAIL scenic alter- native

QUINLAN AV.

HUDSON RD.

STAGECOACH TRAIL

St. Croix River

KEATS AV.

RIDE 35 STAGECOACH TO STILLWATER

AFTON

Selma's

RIDE 36

N

GO!

LOST VALLEY TOUR

Washington County. Connects with RIDES 33, 34, 35, 50 AND K.

LENGTH   ⚡ 41.1 miles – Full loop as described below
RATING   ⚡ 32.7 miles – Valley Creek Cutoff, without Afton Park
             ⚡ 19.6 miles – Half Lost Loop using Co. Hwy. 20 shortcut
CAUTION Co. Rd. 21 and Co. Rd. 71 have no shoulder and growing traffic. Hilly!

*T*his delightful tour of Southern Washington County features ice cream at Selma's (try the chocolate chip waffle cones!) and views of the distinctive Bissell Mound. Scenic solitude can be found on the gravel Trading Post Trail. And if you have the time (and energy), the trip down into Afton State Park is well worth it.

GO!

Start at **COTTAGE GROVE RAVINE REGIONAL PARK** (651-731-3851). Watch for the County Road 19 (Chemolite Road) exit off Highway 61, south of Cottage Grove. Parks sticker or fee required. Cottage Grove Ravine is a handsome park centered around a picturesque pond. There are some great hiking and skiing trails in the 4-mile-long ravine but these are closed to bicyclists. The ravine is believed to have been carved by a former channel of the Glacial St. Croix River.

5.3 mi   **LOST VALLEY PRAIRIE, STATE NATURAL AREA** is a ½ mile detour up Nyberg. Rare prairie plants can be found (with the help of a naturalist) on the rocky hilltops.

10.3 mi   **AFTON STATE PARK** (651-436-5391) is classified a "natural" park to preserve and perpetuate presettlement landscape features of the St. Croix River Valley. A scenic 3.2 mile (one way, 300-foot drop) paved bike path winds down through restored prairie, a wooded ravine and along the St. Croix River. Stop at the Interpretive Center to see the excellent displays. A secluded swimming beach and picnic area is found on the river.

15.3 mi   **SELMA'S ICE CREAM PARLOR** in downtown Afton is a must, then stroll on down to the river.

VALLEY CREEK CUTOFF

Take a left from County Road 21 directly on to Valley Creek Trail and then another left on Trading Post Trail to Oakgren.

19 mi   **BISSELL MOUND** is a natural formation that looks like either a miniature Midwestern volcano or an ancient Native American Indian Mound. Use your imagination.

19.7 mi   The scenic, hilly, gravel **TRADING POST TRAIL** is a fine getaway. Neal Avenue is a paved (without shoulders) alternative that shortens the trip 3 miles.

27.3 mi   County Highway 20 (70th Street) has a paved shoulder.

34.7 mi   BACK TO *GO!*

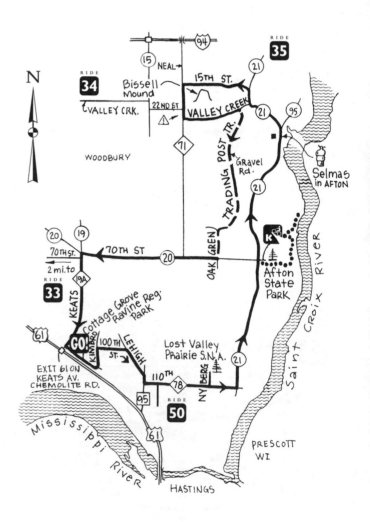

Dakota County. Connects with RIDES 38 and 50.

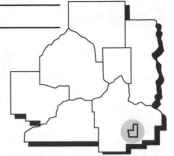

LENGTH 24 miles

RATING Not too tough a mountain bike, gravel road route.

CAUTION There is almost no traffic except near Miesville and a short dash on 61. This is one of the most rural rides in this book and I did notice a rather large dog on 210th Street. It did not give chase.

This route is for all you folks that have been riding your mountain bikes on city streets and paved paths. Here's a chance to get out into the country and eat up some gravel roads. Your bike is ready — are you?

Chimney Rock Ramble explores a small corner of the Twin Cities metropolitan area that was never scoured by the last glacial advance. Proof lies in the 25-foot high pillar called Chimney Rock. This sandstone kingpin would certainly have been bowled over had the huge sheets of ice pushed through here. The southeast leg of this ride passes through the rugged undeveloped Miesville Ravine Park Reserve. Then it's back to civilization and the little town of Miesville.

GO! Start at **MARSHAN TOWN HALL**. There is a small parking lot at 205th Street on the west side of Highway 61. (See inset map.)

2.8 mi At the top of a wooded hill, **CHIMNEY ROCK** rises above the surrounding farmscape. It is on private land so admire it from the road.

6.3 mi Go straight across Highway 50 and onto the **MINIMUM MAINTENANCE ROAD**. The sign says, "Travel at your own risk," but you are on your mountain bike, so no problem.

14.2 mi You haven't entered an Appalachian hollow but you are in the "driftless area." **MIESVILLE RAVINE REGIONAL PARK** was never filled with glacial drift (rock material deposited as a result of glaciation). Instead the ravine has enlarged and deepened over time. Park Reserve development is still a number of years off.

18 mi If you time your trip just right you'll be able to catch the **MIESVILLE MUDHENS** in action at Jack Ruhr Field. These boys play a solid brand of town ball that has earned them state championships in 1978, 1989, 1992 and 1993. You can always pick up a schedule, a King burger and a cold cola at **KING'S PLACE** across the street.

22.2 mi You bike past a **STATE GAME REFUGE** and the **BELLWOOD OAKS** golf course on 210th Street East. Check out which place has the most birdies.

24 mi A half mile dash on Highway 61 takes you **BACK TO GO!** Traffic can be heavy but there is a wide shoulder.

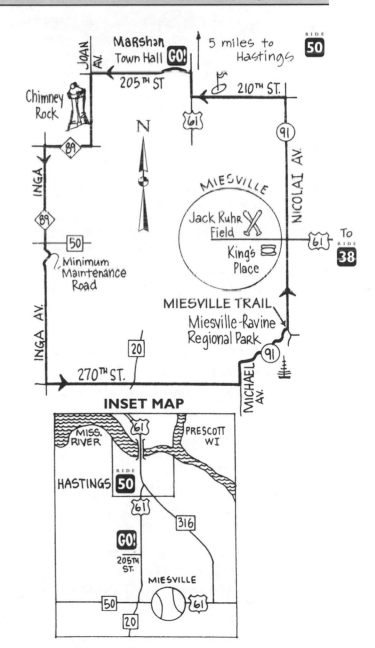

INSET MAP

38 CANNON VALLEY TRAIL

Goodhue County. Connects with RIDE 37, 47, 50 and K.

LENGTH · 20 miles – **Cannon Valley Trail**, one-way, 8 foot wide paved trail

RATING · 19 miles – Welch to Cannon Falls, round trip (best intro)

NEW → 19.5 miles – Poetry Circle · 34.8 miles – King Vasa Tour

FEE Wheel Pass is $2/day or $10/year · **PHONE** 507-263-3954

FUTURE · 6.5 miles – **Goodhue Pioneer Trail**, 10 foot wide paved by year 2000.

The Cannon Valley Trail runs through secluded and spectacular scenery on a former Chicago North Western Railroad line. This rail trail was named one of the best in the country by Bicycle magazine and it is easy to see why. The landscape, history, wildlife and natural features are outstanding and unique.

While most of the Twin Cities area was scoured flat by glaciers, the Cannon River Valley is part of the "driftless area." Rugged, almost Appalachian in feel, this valley was never filled with glacial drift (rock material) and has enlarged and deepened over time. Fragile sandstone peaks crown the surrounding bluffs in many places. The Dakota knew the Cannon River as IN-YAN BO-SDA-TA WA-KPA or "River-of-the-standing-rock." Human activity in the valley dates back to nearly the time of the glaciers — the oldest documented sites of people living in Minnesota are here. Today, the trail undulates gently as it follows the state designated "Wild and Scenic" Cannon River. Anchored by the picturesque towns of Red Wing and Cannon Falls, the trail offers bicyclists three seasons of fun.

GO! Start at the trail in downtown **CANNON FALLS** on Highway 19 one block west of the stoplight.

1.6 mi **PRAIRIE REMNANT** with pasque flowers, monarda, kittentails and big bluestem.

2.6 to 3.4 mi. Trail hugs a rockcut high above the river, with a **SCENIC OVERLOOK**, ferns and rare plants.

3.8 mi The **ANDERSON MEMORIAL REST AREA** has picnicking, a trout stream and a half-mile walk.

6.1 mi The **CANNON VALLEY INTERPRETIVE TRAIL** is 1.5 miles long and makes a good quick mountain bike run. We saw turkeys too.

6.4 mi The rough-cut granite block displayed here is from a **1912 TRAIN WRECK**. The 500-pound block has only been stolen once.

9.5 mi **HIDDEN VALLEY CAMPGROUND** is privately owned and can get loud on weekends.

10.0 mi Water, portable toilets, picnic tables and parking are found at **WELCH STATION**. The tiny town of Welch is just a few blocks north and presents the difficult choice of beers or hand-scooped ice cream.

11.5 mi A 150-foot-long bridge crosses **BELLE CREEK**. Look for warblers, woodpeckers and deer here.

15.4 mi The historic 1856 Mendota to Wabasha **MILITARY ROAD** crosses the trail. This well-preserved 3,200 foot section is a worthy side trip.

16.2 mi Red Wing **ARCHAEOLOGICAL PRESERVE.** A steep path leads to a 1,000-year-old village site. About as many people lived in the valley then as now.

19.7 mi The trail ends near historic **RED WING POTTERY** and a signed bike route will take you to Bay Point Park overlooking the Mississippi.

POETRY CIRCLE Start this tour in Red Wing.

> *It is difficult   to get the news from poems*
> *yet men die miserably every day*
> *for lack   of what is found there.*
>
> William Carlos Williams

There may be a closer connection between farming and poetry than first meets the eye. In 1983 Massachusetts's environmental artist Mark Mendel created *Four Seasons* and put these poems in huge sentences on the barns along this route. They're starting to fade and "Winter" is partially covered with a new addition but they are surprisingly good. Here's the missing poem.

> *Wind walking after the storm   tracks filling with moonlight*
> *stars in a mare's silhouette   fenced snow waits for dawn.*

KING VASA TOUR This route starts in Welch and continues on to Red Wing with an on-road route past the historic Swedish settlement of Vasa. This tiny village was founded in 1853 and named for King Gustav Vasa. The huge brick Lutheran church looms over town like a judgment. There is a big climb out of the valley and these country roads have no shoulder, but traffic is generally low and skilled cyclists will find this a rewarding route.

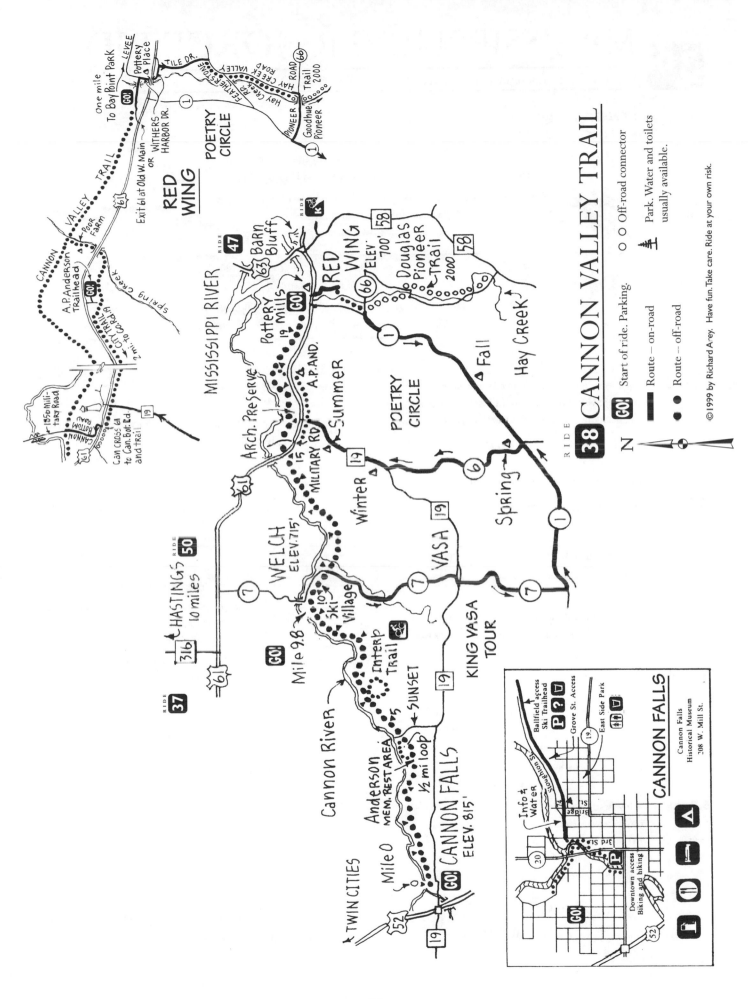

RIDE **38** CANNON VALLEY TRAIL

N

© 1999 by Richard A. Arey. Have fun. Take care. Ride at your own risk.

GO! Start of ride. Parking.

○ ○ Off-road connector

━━━ Route — on-road

•••• Route -- off-road

⚲ Park. Water and toilets usually available.

CANNON FALLS

Cannon Falls Historical Museum 208 W. Mill St.

MISSISSIPPI RIVER GORGE RIDE

Ramsey and Hennepin County. Connects with RIDES 4, 5, 20, 27, 28 and 30.

LENGTH 〰 19.4 miles – Full loop as described

RATING ● 8.5 miles – Ford Parkway to Washington Avenue Loop

CAUTION Bring a lock as you will need to walk to some of the falls. Cross the Mississippi on the Ford Bridge or use the stairs on Highway 5.

West River Road is now complete. This links St. Anthony Falls to Minnehaha Falls with a beautiful off-road route. The on-road route from the University through downtown Minneapolis is optional.

A beautiful loop around the mighty Mississippi. This ride features the legendary St. Anthony and Minnehaha Falls as well as lesser known cascades such as Hidden Falls, Shadow Falls and Bridal Veil Falls. Early spring, or after a heavy rain, is the best time to visit these ephemeral beauties. Spring (or later in fall) is also best because much of the river gorge becomes obscured once the trees have leafed out.

GO! Start your tour where Summit Avenue intersects **MISSISSIPPI RIVER BOULEVARD**. There is a small parking lot or use the street. Head south.

1.8 mi **LOCK AND DAM NO. 1 FALLS** can be observed from the overlook just south of the Ford Parkway Bridge (cross here for the short loop).

2.4 mi Just down the road a piece is a nice overlook of the Mississippi. Park your bike and take the stone staircase down into the ravine. Admire the beautiful WPA-era stonework, and in short order, **HIDDEN FALLS** will be revealed.

3.75 mi Continue south on Mississippi River Boulevard and watch for the **HIGHWAY 5 BRIDGE** down below. Find the unmarked stairway that leads to a walkway on the bridge across the river.

3.9 mi Walking up the stairs on the Minneapolis side of the river takes you right into **FORT SNELLING STATE PARK**. Proceed counterclockwise around the old stone fort. On the south side of the fort take the long ramp down until you intersect the paved path and take this left, heading upstream, under the Highway 5 Bridge you just crossed.

6.9 mi A lovely stretch of trail hugs the bluff and provides some nice river views, eventually taking you to **MINNEHAHA FALLS**. There are concessions, washrooms, picnic facilities and, of course, the laughing, leaping waters. Take the time to read the geological markers that point out an **ABAN-DONED WATERFALL**.

11.6 mi Godfrey Parkway becomes West River Parkway as you head north. Just north of Franklin Avenue (cross the Mississippi here for the short loop) the path and road make a long exciting descent to the river. The **ICE FALLS** on the cliffs last into April.

12.9 mi Save a mile and the on-street hassle by using **WEST RIVER ROAD** into downtown, or take 4th Street out of the river valley. Jog over to 6th Street and you will soon see **THE DOME** looming ahead. It was here on the night of October 25, 1987, that the Minnesota Twins beat the St. Louis Cardinals to become World Champions. A brilliant, defining moment in Minnesota history.

14 mi Follow the striped bike lanes to another Minnesota landmark. The James J. Hill **STONE ARCH BRIDGE** (1883) is an engineering masterpiece that echoes the great roman aqueducts. The new walking and biking paths lead to a terrific view of **ST. ANTHONY FALLS**, "the most abrupt drop in the 2,200 mile course of the Mississippi River." The Ojibway called this cataract **KITCHI KAK-ABIKA**, "The Great Severed Rock."

15.3 mi Second Street curves up to the bike lane on University Avenue. Take a right where the sign says 14th Avenue SE and you will be on **EAST RIVER ROAD.** Just after you cross under the Washington Avenue Bridge take a right into East River Flats Park. Follow the new paved path along the river one mile to **BRIDAL VEIL FALLS**. Continue on and the path climbs back up to the blufftop.

19 mi **SHADOW FALLS** Lock your bike at the top of the ravine near Cretin and follow the tiny walking path down for a view of this delicate, moss-covered drop.

19.4 mi BACK TO *GO!*

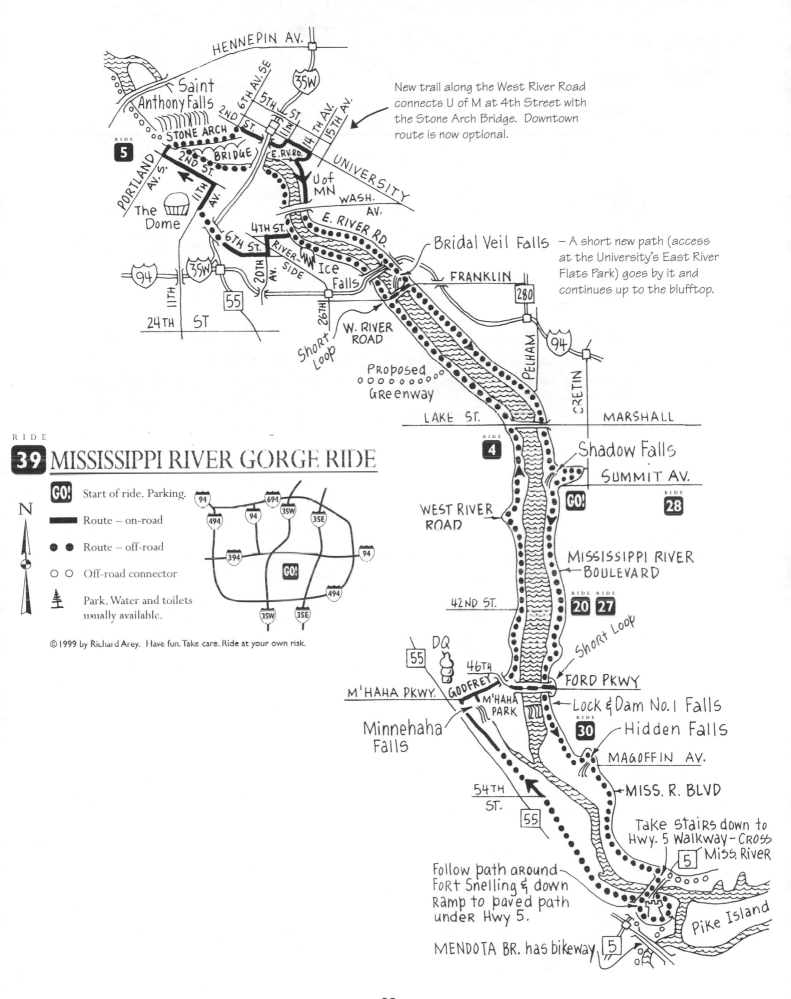

New trail along the West River Road connects U of M at 4th Street with the Stone Arch Bridge. Downtown route is now optional.

Bridal Veil Falls — A short new path (access at the University's East River Flats Park) goes by it and continues up to the blufftop.

RIDE 39 MISSISSIPPI RIVER GORGE RIDE

GO! Start of ride. Parking.

N

— Route — on-road

• • Route — off-road

○ ○ Off-road connector

🌲 Park. Water and toilets usually available.

© 1999 by Richard Arey. Have fun. Take care. Ride at your own risk.

Take stairs down to Hwy. 5 Walkway - Cross Miss. River

Follow path around Fort Snelling & down Ramp to paved path under Hwy 5.

MENDOTA BR. has bikeway

RAGS TO RICHES RIDE

Ramsey County. Connects with RIDES 22, 26, 27, 28, 32, 33 and I.

LENGTH ≈ 22.8 miles – Full loop as described
RATING ● 14.4 miles – Short loop around Silver Lake
CAUTION Hilly in spots. Mounds Boulevard - 7th Street connection to Swede Hollow has heavy traffic.

The paved **Battle Creek Ravine Trail** from McKnight Road to Highway 61 is finally complete.

For over a century the shanty town of Swede Hollow welcomed the poorest newcomers to St. Paul. In 1850 it was home to the Swedes, followed by the Irish, Poles, Italians, and finally, Mexican Americans, before the shacks were razed in the 1950s. Not so far, but a world away, McKnight Road is named after William McKnight, who began his tenure at 3M as an assistant bookkeeper. Rising through the ranks, McKnight led the Minnesota Mining and Manufacturing Company to the top of the heap as an international business concern. The gleaming 3M corporate campus you pass on McKnight Road is a far cry from the 18th century industrial relics along upper Swede Hollow.

This ride capitalizes on the recently built Swede Hollow Trail and Burlington Northern (BN) Regional Trail. A less than stellar path along Beam Avenue leads to a pleasant circuit of Silver Lake and the always difficult summertime choices of ice cream or a cool swim. Beaver Lake is a fine addition to the crowd pleasing paths along Battle Creek, Indian Mounds and Lake Phalen.

GO! **LAKE PHALEN REGIONAL PARK** (651-266-6400). To reach Phalen Park exit I-35E at Wheelock Parkway and head east 1.7 miles to park entrance on left. Phalen is a wonderful full-service facility with a swimming beach, picnicking, washrooms, boat rental and golf course. Many folks remember the magical ice palace built here in 1986.

1.4 mi The **GATEWAY STATE TRAIL** is reached via a short ramp just past the stone arch underpass north of Lake Phalen. Head east. In about one mile you reach the **BURLINGTON NORTHERN REGIONAL TRAIL**. This makes a beeline north.

4.8 mi If you always wanted to bicycle to **MAPLEWOOD MALL** you can now check that off your list. The paved path only gets you so close. You will still need to cross a vast moat of cars.

7.8 mi **SILVER LAKE** is a delight with three parks sprinkled around the perimeter. Take a right on 20th Street to the swimming beach, picnic area and small playground.

7.7 mi Or, continue south on County Highway 120 to **DAIRY QUEEN**. The Banana Supreme always works for me.

8.3 mi Either route returns you to the Gateway Trail and the **BIG SNOWMAN**.

9.2 mi **McKNIGHT ROAD** is the next decision point. After crossing the long steel bridge you can con-

tinue along the Gateway Trail back to Lake Phalen. This is the **SHORT LOOP**. Or cloverleaf off the Gateway and head south on McKnight.

13.3 mi Just past **3M** is the potentially dangerous I-94 underpass. You may opt for crossing to the west side of McKnight at the stoplight and using the sidewalk until you can cross safely back to the path.

13.9 mi **BATTLE CREEK REGIONAL PARK** (651-777-1707) has a modern picnic pavilion and trails that will all be connected in 1996 via a ravine trail.

17.9 mi Follow Upper Afton Road or the new paved path through Battle Creek Ravine and up the Highway 61 path to **INDIAN MOUNDS PARK**. Break out a picnic and enjoy the spectacular view over the Mississippi River and downtown St. Paul.

19.6 mi The **SWEDE HOLLOW TRAIL** is a little tough to connect with. It begins at the busy 7th Street-Payne Avenue intersection. Your reward for persevering is an impressive stone arch underpass leading to a most unexpected scene. The wooded hollow is cool and green. And dancing down a limestone stairway is **PHALEN CREEK**. Mostly buried now, it makes the most of its brief moment in the sun.

22.8 mi Follow the trail to Lake Phalen and **BACK TO** *GO!*

40 RAGS TO RICHES RIDE

© 1995 by Richard Arey. Have fun. Take care. Ride at your own risk.

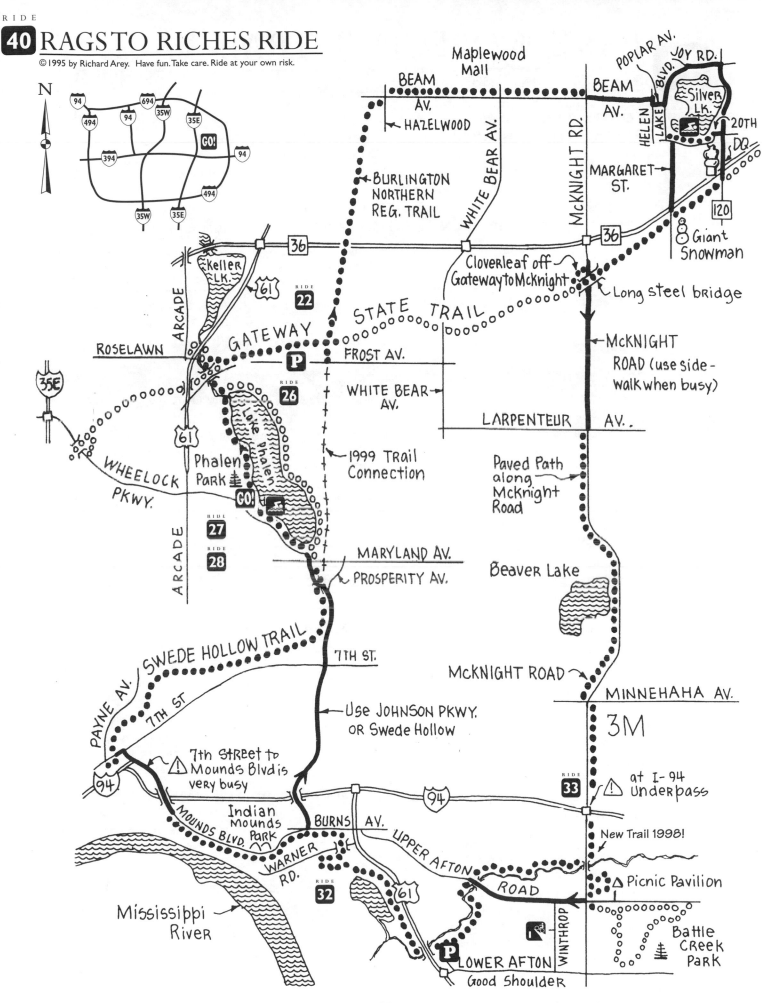

LAKE WOBEGONE TRAIL

St. Cloud

Stearns County. Phone 1-320-255-6172.

LENGTH & RATING ● 27.5 miles, 10 foot paved trail

STAY A LITTLE LONGER The Sauk Centre Chamber of Commerce (320-352-5201) can help you with area restaurants and lodging. Their web site is www. saukcentre.com. For an historic stay, and some pretty good food, check out the Palmer House Hotel on the Original Main Street in Sauk Centre. Sinclair Lewis worked here for two weeks as a night clerk in the summer of 1902.

PRAIRIE HOME COMPANION For more Lake Wobegone stories listen to MPR (91.1FM) Saturdays at 5 p.m.

FUTURE This line lies abandoned for another 70 miles up to Fergus Falls. Another rail corridor heading northeast up to Genola (and eventually Mille Lacs) is also ripe for development.

The Lake Wobegone Trail connects five small towns and two great writers. It's named for the mythical town that time forgot. In his book, Lake Wobegone Days, *Garrison Keillor locates the town via the three railway lines that form a triangle — one of which, the Great Northern, "swung west through St. Joseph, Avon, Albany and Freeport" — with each one "missing the town by miles." The trail starts in Avon and ends in Sauk Centre, about five blocks from Sinclair Lewis's boyhood home. Lewis surveyed the same small town America as Keillor with a decidedly more acidic bent that you may consider as you glide above* Main Street. *Garrison bicycled and helped dedicate the trail when it officially opened on September 30, 1998. By that Saturday afternoon he'd written, and sang on his show, a fine little tune with the refrain, "Get your bike and we'll ride, twenty miles side-by-side, down the Lake Wobegone Trail." Now it's your turn.*

GO!

Start in Avon, about 15 miles past St. Cloud on I-94. Exit on Co. Rd. 9 in Avon and go one mile north to the start of the trail.

0.0 mi Like all of these whistlestops, **AVON** is a small town with a big church (St. Benedict's Roman Catholic, 1928). It is surrounded by lakes and if you time your return just right you can enjoy the sunset over Spunk Lake before walking into the Fisher's Club for a fresh walleye dinner. Summer weekends only.

6.5 mi The first stretch of trail may be the prettiest with a nice blend of lakes, farms and woods. **ALBANY** was settled in 1863 and the big church here is a beauty – the Catholic Church of Seven Dolors (1889). Just a couple of blocks south of the trail is another architectural gem, **DAIRY QUEEN**. Try a finely constructed Banana Supreme. The next stretch of trail to Freeport closely parallels I-94. An old railroad bridge crosses over at mile 97.4.

12.4 mi In November 1969 Garrison Keillor began his stint with the fledgling Minnesota Public Radio and moved to a farm just outside of **FREEPORT**. This small burg, with its water tower, church and tiny downtown bears a striking resemblance to the cover of *Lake Wobegon Days*. It is certainly the closest model to the fabled town. And when you walk into Charlie's Cafe, with its weak coffee and thick gravy, you might even believe you're in the Chatterbox.

18.3 mi The train stops here. **MELROSE** was the railroad terminus from 1872–1878. St. Mary's Church (1898) is on the National Historic Register. Stop in at Joyce's Cafe for some homemade pie. While this stretch of trail looks to be too close to I-94, it is really quite removed and enjoyable. The Sauk River crosses the path on both sides of town.

22.0 mi **MEMORYVILLE** emerges from the mists of time and like Lake Wobegone you won't find it on any maps (until now). It's the creation of Dick Young, and his collection of historic buildings is a must stop. Young has lived a good chunk of his life along this old rail line and remembers the days when the **CIRCUS TRAINS** used to pass through. Stop and have a chat or check out his antique store to purchase your own piece of the past.

27.5 mi For now, **SAUK CENTRE** is the end of the line. The Sinclair Lewis Boyhood Home is open for tours for a small charge. There's also a town museum at the Sinclair Lewis Interpretive Center just off I-94 that's free and worth a look.

But what's most worth doing is parking your bike and taking a walk down Main Street. Before mounting up and heading back you may recall Garrison's theme song and sing, "Before insanity strikes, let's go ride our bikes, down the Lake Wobegone Trail."

Michael Doyle cruises past the 1898
St. Mary's Church in Melrose.

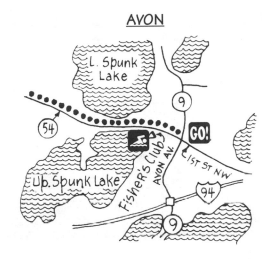

AVON

L. Spunk Lake

Up. Spunk Lake

Fisher's Club

Avon Av.

E. 1ST ST NW

54

9

GO!

94

9

SAUK CENTRE
map below

17

94

71

Sauk River

5.5 mi

MEMORYVILLE

3.7 mi

MELROSE

5.9 mi

FREEPORT

13

94

11

5.9 mi

Wood RR
Bridge

ALBANY

AVON

6.5 mi

DQ

South
3 blocks

Schwing Lake

94

Spunk Lakes

9

SAUK CENTRE

MN Home School (1911-24)
Bldgs by Clarence Johnston

HWY. 71

17

BIRCH

Sinclair
Lewis
Home

S. LEWIS AV.

Palmer House

17

MAPLE

MAIN

STREET

Sauk
River

Sinclair Lewis
Visitor Center

94

71

DQ

R I D E

41 LAKE WOBEGONE
TRAIL

N

GO! Start of ride. Parking.

────── Route – on-road

• • • • Route – off-road

© 1999 by Richard Arey. Have fun.
Take care. Ride at your own risk.

SUNRISE PRAIRIE TRAIL

Chisago and Washington Counties. Connects with RIDES 21, 24 and 43.

OWNERS Sunrise Prairie – Chisago County, phone 651-674-2345
Hardwood Creek – Washington County, phone 651-430-4300

LENGTH
- 15.0 miles **Sunrise Prairie Trail**, 10 foot wide, paved
- 9.6 miles **Hardwood Creek Trail**, rough gravel
- 35.8 miles Sunrise Prairie-Lincoln Trail Loop
- 37.6 miles Highway 61 Revisited

CAUTION The Hardwood Creek Trail is funded but awaits approval from the county rail authority that owns it. Highway 61 is quite busy but has a 10-foot-wide shoulder.

This trail follows the St. Paul and Duluth railroad. The Sunrise Prairie Trail provides daily, nonstop service from North Branch south to Forest Lake. The highway paralleling the trail almost disappears north of Wyoming. Regrettably, the Hardwood Creek Trail has been delayed and Dylan's Highway 61 is the only alternative. It's not bad, but you're sure to enjoy the rest of the on-road routes that create the loops described here.

SUNRISE PRAIRIE TRAIL AND LOOP

GO! Go north on I-35 to Forest Lake and take the first exit on Hwy. 2/Broadway Avenue, turn right (east) and go 1 mile. Trail begins on Broadway Avenue and 2nd Street.

4.5 mi It's not often that you head due north and end up in **WYOMING**. This tiny town was platted in 1869, one year after the completion of the railway. Make a mental note – **DAIRY QUEEN** here.

5.4 mi Less than a mile up from Wyoming you'll cross over the **SUNRISE RIVER**. Blink and you'll miss it.

8.8 mi **STACY** has a trailhead with parking, water, washrooms and a ballfield. It was established in 1875 and named for Dr. Stacy B. Collins, an early resident.

15.0 mi **NORTH BRANCH** is the end of the line and has a state-of-the-art trailhead – complete with a **DAIRY QUEEN**. Looks like a Tropical Blizzard on the horizon. The town was named for the north branch of the Sunrise River which crosses the active railroad tracks one-quarter mile up.

25.2 mi The on-road loop follows Lincoln and Lent Trails to the Baptist Church at the corner of County Roads 18 and 30. Traffic is light and the ride through **CARLOS AVERY WILDLIFE REFUGE** is smooth and scenic.

27.0 mi Take County Road 30 back into Stacy and Stacy Trail (County Road 19) right (west) to the trail.

35.8 mi **BACK TO** *GO!* You will hit most highlights if you start in Wyoming – a 26.8 mile loop.

HIGHWAY 61 REVISITED
If Garrison Keillor can put his blessings on the Lake Wobegone Trail then here's my nod to the state's best songwriter – Mr. Bob Dylan.

Now the rovin' gambler was very bored, tryin' to create a next world war. He found a promoter who nearly fell off the floor, saying I never engaged in this kind of thing before.

But yes I think it can be very easily done. We'll just put some bleachers out in the sun. And have it on Highway 61.

GO! Start at **LAKESIDE PARK** in Forest Lake. Same directions as for Sunrise Prairie but continue east across Highway 61 into the full-service park (washrooms, water, swimming beach). **HUGO!** makes a better starting point if you're coming from St. Paul.

10.0 mi Follow the narrow shoulder of **NORTH SHORE TRAIL** around Forest Lake and enjoy the shade.

11.5 mi A three-mile (round trip) jaunt up to the **EKO BACKEN** water slide (651-433-2422) could be just the thing on a hot summer day.

17.5 mi You'll be biking next to **BIG MARINE LAKE REGIONAL PARK**. Development is coming.

26.8 mi Follow the paved roads back to **HUGO**.

37.6 mi **BACK TO** *GO!* The Hardwood Creek Trail is probably bikable with a mountain bike but hardly worth it. It parallels the west side of Highway 61, which has a wide shoulder that is comfortable for intermediate and better cyclists.

Plus you'll want to be **BRINGING IT ALL BACK HOME** on the fabled Highway 61 Revisited. Speaking of home, I believe that's a **DAIRY QUEEN** up ahead.

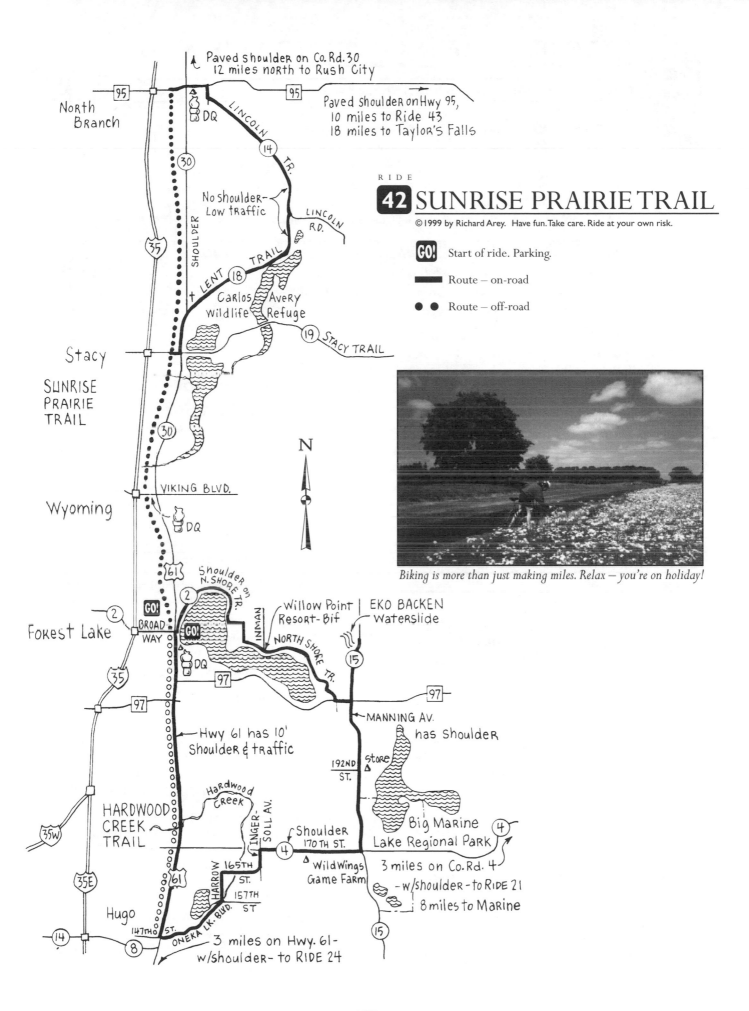

Paved shoulder on Co. Rd. 30
12 miles north to Rush City

95 North Branch 95

Paved shoulder on Hwy 95,
10 miles to Ride 43
18 miles to Taylor's Falls

30 14 LINCOLN TR.

No shoulder—
Low traffic

LINCOLN RD.

RIDE
42 SUNRISE PRAIRIE TRAIL

© 1999 by Richard Arey. Have fun. Take care. Ride at your own risk.

GO! Start of ride. Parking.

────── Route – on-road

● ● Route – off-road

35 SHOULDER LENT TRAIL 18

† Carlos Wildlife Avery Refuge

19 STACY TRAIL

Stacy

SUNRISE PRAIRIE TRAIL

30

Biking is more than just making miles. Relax — you're on holiday!

VIKING BLVD.

Wyoming DQ

61

Shoulder on N. SHORE TR.

2 Willow Point EKO BACKEN
Resort - Bif Waterslide

GO! 2

Forest Lake BROADWAY GO! DQ INMAN NORTH SHORE TR. 15

35 97 97

97

Hwy 61 has 10'
Shoulder & traffic

MANNING AV.
has shoulder

192ND ST. Store

Hardwood Creek

Big Marine
Lake Regional Park 4

HARDWOOD CREEK TRAIL

INGERSOLL AV.

Shoulder 170TH ST. 4 WildWings Game Farm 3 miles on Co. Rd. 4
- w/shoulder- to RIDE 21
8 miles to Marine

35W

35E

61 HARROW 165TH ST. 157TH ST. ONEKA LK. BLVD.

Hugo 147TH ST.

14 8 3 miles on Hwy. 61-
w/shoulder- to RIDE 24

15

- 105 -

SWEET HOME CHISAGO

Chisago County. Connects with RIDES 42, and 44.

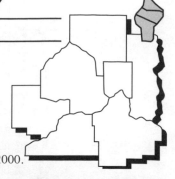

LENGTH
- 14.0 miles – Taylors Falls to Wild Mountain (and back)
- 25.1 miles – Taylors Falls Loop via Co. Rd. 20
- 32.4 miles – Taylors Falls Loop via Co. Rd. 26 and Hwy. 95
- 24.2 miles – Chisago Lakes Loop via Co. Rd. 25 (see CAUTION)
- 31.0 miles – Chisago Lakes via Hwy. 95

CAUTION Co. Rd. 3 is being rebuilt with 8 foot shoulders, construction through 2000.

The renowned Swedish author Vilhelm Moberg spent the summer of 1948 in Chisago City and explored this area by bicycle. That research helped shape his epic series of books on the great Swedish migration to America. This mostly level land of lakes is still a quiet (except for Highways 8 and 95), pretty place to explore by bike. Taylors Falls is a New England-like village nestled into the St. Croix River bluff. A stroll through the Angel Falls historic district is always a pleasure.

CHISAGO LAKES LOOPS

GO! Take I-35 north and exit at Co. Rd. 97/23. Go right (east) on 97 fourteen miles to Scandia.

SCANDIA was first settled in the winter of 1849-1850 and is the oldest Swedish settlement in Minnesota. Check to see if Co. Rd. 3 is open if you plan to return that way.

5.6 mi After curving around Bone Lake and up Lofton Avenue you'll soon see a **ROUND BARN**.

10.7 mi As you approach **CHISAGO CITY** you'll bike past the home (NE corner of Old Towne Road and Lake Avenue) where Moberg stayed in 1948. Take a short detour to the bronze sculpture of Moberg and his bike created by Ian Dudley. Chisago is contracted from the Ojibwa words **KI-CHI-SAGA** meaning "large, lovely" and referring to the nearby lake.

14.1 mi Follow Stinson Avenue and the frontage road to avoid much of treacherous Highway 8. At County Road 14 you'll need to take 8 a short ways into Lindstrom. Go for the Swedish goodies at the Lindstrom Bakery if it's open or swing up another block to **DAIRY QUEEN**. Say, "Goddag, Goddag" and order up a cone.

15.7 mi Center City can be reached via an off-road paved path. It's worth the trip just to see the **SUMMIT AVENUE HISTORIC DISTRICT**.

24.2 mi BACK TO *GO!* Olinda Trail is the easier return if County Road 3 is not under construction.

31 mi For a longer, and slightly hairier ride, take Highway 8 to **PLEASANT VALLEY ROAD** (it lives up to its name) and **BACK TO *GO*** on Highways 95 and 97.

TAYLORS FALLS LOOPS

GO! Exit I-35 at Highway 8 (just north of Forest Lake) and go 22.6 miles east into Taylors Falls.

TAYLORS FALLS is a charming town from another era. There are two terrific hikes to consider after your bike ride. You can walk up the steep, winding streets of **ANGEL HILL** to see the charming homes from the 1800s or you can step way back in time and tour the **GLACIAL GARDENS** at Interstate Park where the swirling waters of the Glacial St. Croix River scoured huge potholes – one is 60' deep! – in the rock.

7.0 mi The water slide at Wild Mountain also features swirling waters that you can ride. County Road 16 is flat and runs through thick woods – with occasional views of the river. It is a great **FALL COLORS RIDE** with almost no traffic. Families may opt to turn back here.

11.7 mi Amelund is a one-store town and Rod's Country Corner Store has **ICE CREAM CONES.**

16.3 mi Park Trail goes north into Wild River State Park or south down to Center City. For the loop, go south and left (east) on County Road 20. You will pass a couple of **ONE-ROOM SCHOOL HOUSES.**

23.9 mi Where County Road 20 intersects Mulberry Street you can go left and then right at Highway 95 to the **SCENIC OVERLOOK** and a fast ride into town or, take a right and follow County Road 20 into town.

25.1 mi BACK TO *GO* and downtown Taylors Falls.

32.4 mi Make the longer loop by continuing south on County Road 12 into Center City. Catch a breath before making your dash on Highway 8 to Pleasant Valley Road. Hwy. 95 can also get busy.

43 SWEET HOME CHISAGO

TAYLORS FALLS

95 · Mulberry · Co.Rd. 71A · Scenic Overlook of Valley · 95 · MAPLE · 16

20 · 20 · 1. 1861 Methodist Church
2. 1855 Folsom House
3. 1854 Munch House
4. 1850s Library

37 · 20 · FIRST ST. · WEST · MILITARY RD. · ST. CROIX RIVER · WILD MTN. RD. · BENCH ST. · RIVER ST. · 2ND · BASIL · GOV'T. · GOV'T. ST. · GO! · 8 · St. Croix River

ENTER →

Rod's · PARK TR. · 2 mi. · Wild River State Park

AME-LUND · 16 · REED · △Llamas

12 · Wild Mountain water slide

95

Vilhelm Moberg explored this area by bicycle in 1948 and wrote Unto a Good Land.

PARK TRAIL

No shoulder - light traffic

18 · 41 · LENT TR. · LINCOLN RD. · N. LAKES TRAIL · 20 · △1880s School · FUKUBY ROAD · 20 · 71A · TAYLORS FALLS Map above

14 · 20 · LINDSTROM · N. CTR. LAKE · 12 · One Room School · PARK TR. · 21 · 20 · 37 · GO! · 8

See Detail Map CHISAGO CITY · FRONTAGE · CENTER CITY · 37 · Summit Av. · Interstate Park · River side, 4'-6' shldr. Bluff side, 0-3' Busy! · 95 & 8

STINSON · DQ · S. CTR. LK. · LAKE 8 BLVD · L. CREEK RD. (1856!) nice alt. · Franconia Sculpture Park · 12

25 · GLADER · Chisago Lake · Karl Oskar House · 26 · PLEASANT VALLEY RD. · 21 · No shldr. · 95 · CHISAGO LAKES MAP · MAIN · LOUISE · 9 · 37

24 · 83 · CHISAGO BLVD · OLINDA TRAIL N. · △Orchard · 1882 Lutheran Church · N. Center Lake · SUMMIT AV. · Historic St. 1882-1910 · CENTER CITY

Green Lk. · 23 · △Flora Farm · 243 · ANDREW · Paved path 25 to C.C. · 8

24 · 6' Shoulder · 25 · 6' Shoulder busy! · TO OSCEOLA · LINDSTROM Bakery · 20 · DQ · HWY 8 has shldr. very busy!

2' Shoulder · △Round Barn · 238TH ST. · CHISAGO COUNTY · ST. CROIX RIVER · 14 · LINCOLN · Karl & Kris · 25 · S. Center Lake

LOFTON · MELANIE · MEADOWBRK. · WASH. CO. CONSTRUCTION 1999-2000! · ST. CROIX TR. · CHISAGO CITY · Isabel St. · LAKE BLVD. · RAIL RD. AV. · SHOQUIST · STINSON AV. · TOWNE · OLID

RIDE 42 · 1 · 3 · GO! · SCANDIA · Vil. Moberg with bike- 1996 Sculpture! · 24 · Detail maps compressed, not to scale

4.7 miles from Scandia to 41 · OAKHILL · SCANDIA TR. · ROAD · 97

97 · 7' shoulder

- 107 -

RIDE 44

ST. CROIX RIVER RAMBLES

Washington Co., Chisago Co., Wisconsin. Connects with RIDES 21, 23, 35, 43, 45 and 47.

LENGTH
RATING
- 16.5 miles – Hudson-Willow River Loop. Great quickie!
- 32.1 miles – Stillwater-Hudson Loop
- 75.1 miles – Stillwater-Taylors Falls Loop
- 101.5 miles – Stillwater-Taylors Falls-Hudson Loop

CAUTION Highway 95 has 6 foot to 7 foot wide shoulders and is busy on weekends. Wisconsin roads often have no shoulders but light traffic. Steep grades at river crossings.

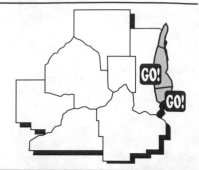

*T*he St. Croix River Valley is delightful and just far enough removed from the Twin Cities to have escaped the ills of urbanization — at least for now. Spend some time in Marine on St. Croix, Taylors Falls or Osceola and you'll be refreshed with a feeling that you've stepped away in time as well as distance. For a quick escape it's hard to beat the short Hudson-Willow River loop. Much of the route has been recently repaved and there's rustic relief around most every bend. Phone 1-800-657-6775 (Hudson) or 651-439-7700 (Stillwater) for tourist information.

HUDSON-WILLOW RIVER LOOP

GO! Take I-94 east from St. Paul 15 miles and exit on Highway 35 north as soon as you enter Wisconsin. Proceed into downtown and park. See detail map.

0.5 mi The 1855 **OCTAGON HOUSE** is open for tours and home to the local historical museum.

2.2 mi Trout Brook is a priceless **RUSTIC ROAD**.

9.1 mi River Road is almost as nice but the real treat is tiny **BURKHARDT** and the Willow River Inn.

10.0 mi **WILLOW RIVER STATE PARK** has seven miles of roads and trails but you must walk to the real highlight – the newly unveiled falls and gorge that came alive when a 70-year-old dam was removed.

16.5 mi **BACK TO GO!** You'll be back in **HUDSON** before you know it. Cruise up to Birkmose Park for a panorama and ancient **INDIAN MOUNDS**.

STILLWATER-HUDSON LOOP

GO! Take Hwy. 36 into Stillwater and turn left (north) on Greeley (two blocks past Perkins). Go 1.2 miles to Laurel and take a right (east) to **PIONEER PARK**, vantage point for one of my favorite views in the Midwest.

0.7 mi Take the down elevator on 2nd Street and Chestnut and cross the **HISTORIC LIFT BRIDGE**.

7.2 mi Angle right on County Road E going up the big hill and head east. Enjoy the new paving. A left on Valley View Road takes you up to the **BASS LAKE CHEESE FACTORY.** Mingle with the natives.

19.8 mi Follow County Roads I and A back to **HUDSON**.

24.2 mi Cross the St. Croix River and go up to **STAGE-COACH TRAIL**. You're almost …

32.1 mi **BACK TO GO!** But don't miss **NELSON'S DRIVE INN** and giant scoops of Brown's ice cream at the NE corner of Greeley and Olive Street.

STILLWATER-TAYLORS FALLS LOOP

GO! Start in Stillwater at Pioneer Park. This time head north on Owens to **STONEBRIDGE** (Highway 55).

6.3 mi Pine Point Park on the **GATEWAY TRAIL.**

11.6 mi County Road 7 is a blast and **SQUARE LAKE PARK** a real beauty.

16.5 mi **MARINE ON ST. CROIX** is always worth a stop and the **VILLAGE SCOOP** can cure what ails you.

28.3 mi **OSCEOLA ROAD** (Highway 243) is a shortcut that saves you 15.2 miles.

33.6 mi The **FRANCONIA SCULPTURE PARK** is one of the most exciting in the country. Free, open daily.

36.2 mi The descent to **TAYLORS FALLS** is a rush.

45.0 mi **OSCEOLA** has a sparkling waterfall, train rides (800-711-2591) and a **DAIRY QUEEN.**

75.1 mi **BACK TO GO!** Follow the quiet, paved roads to Valley View and go right (west). At Highway 35 it's worth going right and a bit north to take Highway 64 down across the river into **STILLWATER**.

STILLWATER-TAYLORS FALLS-HUDSON LOOP

101.5 mi This route connects all three loops.

44 ST. CROIX RIVER RAMBLES

GO! Start of ride. Parking.

━━━ Route – on-road

●● Route – off-road

○○ Off-road connector

🌲 Park. Water and toilets usually available.

© 1999 by Richard Arey. Have fun. Take care. Ride at your own risk.

N

TAYLORS FALLS

Gandy Dancer Trail

RIDE 45

Polk Co. Info. Center and Trailhead Interstate Park

Franconia Sculpture Park

RIDE 43

8

S

River Rd.

35

95

Flora Farm

Pleasant Valley

Hwy. 243

Hwy. 35

Hwy. 35 has 7' Shoulder

DQ

M

OSCEOLA

TP

OSCEOLA RIDGE ROAD

Hwy. 95 has 6' shoulder - busy!

95 St. Croix

86

River

60TH

35

CHISAGO

WASH. CO.

40TH AV.

X

280TH ST.

QUINNELL

97

Hwy 95

Wm O'Brien State Park

HUDSON

Standing Cedars Hiking

MARINE ON ST. CROIX

Launch

CO. LINE AV.

POLK ST. CROIX

35

RIDE 21

4

Square Lake Park

7

7

40TH

50TH

Tree Farm

210TH AV.

I

Phipps Arts Center on 1st

Lakeside Park

TROUT BROOK

RUSTIC ROAD

A

St. Croix St.

A

1855 Octagon House

2ND ST.

3RD ST.

VINE ST

WALNUT

55

7

59

Apple

River

35

192ND

BUCKEYE ST.

GO!

DQ

COULEE ROAD

Birkmose Park Indian Mounds, Vista!

STILLWATER

7

Pine Point Park

Gateway Trail

Norell Av.

61

RN HI BRIDGE

180TH

170TH AV

64

To MN

55

5

RIDE 23

55

5

96

95

GO!

STONEBRIDGE TRAIL

OWENS

Pioneer Park

LAUREL

CHESTNUT

2ND ST

3RD ST

64

E

35

12

Olive St.

5

Churchill

Greeley

St. Croix River

95

35TH

50TH

St. Croix River

39TH

50TH

60TH

Bass Lake Cheese Factory

140TH

Shoulder begins

Owens Laurel Orleans

Osgood Av.

47TH ST

Narrow Shoulders

E

35

V

E

I

A

St. Croix River

Crest View

River Ridge

Heggen St.

O'Keefe Rd.

HANLEY RD.

MAYER

Dog Track

F

FF

Neison's Drive-In

Orleans St.

36

VALLEY

50TH ST

47TH ST

60TH

River Road

VIEW ROAD

E

Willow River Inn

A

Willow River State Park

A has shoulders

Stagecoach Trail

22ND

River Crest Rd.

95

94

HUDSON ~ see map above

TROUT BROOK

RUSTIC ROAD

A

I

U

94

F

35

RIVER FALLS

See map

RIDE 47

Osgood Av.

Olinda St. N.

47TH

50TH ST. N.

95

RIDE 35

STAGE-COACH TRAIL

95

FF

TOWN VALLEY ROAD

GLOVER RD.

MM

APOLLO to Co. Rd. M

RIDE 45
GANDY DANCER TRAIL
Wisconsin. Phone 1-800-222-7655. Connects with RIDES 43 and 44.

NEW

LENGTH 🔵 48 miles **Gandy Dancer State Trail**, 10 foot packed limestone

RATING 〰 22 miles Lucky Loop 〰 22.5 miles Yellow River–St. Croix Run

FEE $3 daily or $10 annual trail pass required.

MOUNTAIN BIKE 〰 17.9 miles St. Croix State Forest. See map.

STAY A LITTLE LONGER Phone the Polk County Information Center (1-800-222-7655) at the Southern Trailhead or Burnett County Tourism (1-800-788-3164) for lodging, resort and restaurant listings. They'll send them out for free. I recommend splurging on an overnight stay at **Seven Pines Lodge** (715-653-2323), a secluded forest hideaway that is on the National Historic Register outside Lewis.

WEB SITES Gandy Dancer Trail (www.obnet.com/polkcounty/tourism/gandydancer.html).

FUTURE The Gandy Dancer right-of-way goes north 50 more miles to Superior, WI. It is unimproved ballast.

---

*T*his fast, gravel trail links nine little towns on the old Minneapolis, St. Paul and Sault (Soo) Ste. Marie railroad line. The "Soo Line" provides a quiet, shaded corridor without the crowds found on most rail-trails. Stop at one of the lakeside parks for a quick dip or take a detour onto a paved country road. Stick with the trail and you'll be in Luck.

In earlier times throughout the South, crews of black workers built and maintained the railroads. They used tools made by Gandy Manufacturing Company in Chicago. To help synchronize workers in the single rhythmic motion needed to lay and move track, songlike calls were created and the men sang and swayed as one.

GO! Take I-35 north and then Hwy. 8 east into Wisconsin. Turn right (south) onto Hwy. 35 and make an immediate left into the Polk County Info Center.

4.5 mi A paved path from the Info Center leads to the trail. As you approach **CENTURIA** the Ice Age Trail hops on board (and follows the Gandy up to Frederic). This 1,000 mile, path-in-progress traces Ice Age formations across Wisconsin. Centuria was founded by Cyrus Campbell at the turn of the century.

10.7 mi **MILLTOWN** is named for the sawmill that was the only structure around for several years. The stretch of trail up from Centuria is on a glacial outwash plain that has some of the best cropland in Polk County. To celebrate, Pumpkinfest takes place on Main Street the first Saturday in October.

14.4 mi You're in **LUCK**! A great little town with a beautiful lakeside park. This town began as a stopover for travelers going from Cumberland to Taylors Falls for supplies. They felt if they made it here by nightfall they'd be lucky. That's one story.

20.5 mi **FREDERIC** has restored an old train depot for use as a rest stop and small museum. There's a pleasant park on Coon Lake, a bakery and lodging. The *Frederic Lions Bike Classic Race and Tour* (phone 715-327-8750) takes place in June.

25.9 mi Just a mile off the trail from **LEWIS**, the Seven Pines Lodge is set in a grove of old-growth white pine. You can have dinner or spend the night.

27.7 mi The **WI DOT Wayside** on Elbow Lake is a good rest stop. The next five miles are quite pretty.

31.6 mi **SIREN** comes from the Swedish word for lilacs (SYREN), which surrounded the first postmaster's home and office. There is a fine swimming beach at Crooked Lake Park.

38.2 mi The North View Drive-in on Hwy. 35 and Co. Rd. FF in **WEBSTER** is a must for ice cream and burger lovers.

47.1 mi The last stretch into **DANBURY** is one of the wildest. There is a dramatic bridge crossing over the Yellow River gorge. You're in the North Woods.

47.5 mi The **ST. CROIX RIVER HIGH BRIDGE** is worth the lousy half mile of biking on loose gravel. Enjoy the pristine view. It's worth scrambling down to the river to check out this handsome bridge from below.

LUCKY LOOP Start in Luck and follow the roads south back to Centuria. You'll pass a one-room schoolhouse, some pretty lakes and a Sherman tank. Easier to follow than it looks.

YELLOW RIVER RUN Start in Webster and head west. Highlights include the historic site of Forts Folle Avoine (A rebuilt post of the Northwest Company from 1802, with interpretive facilities and a restaurant) and, for me, spotting a bobcat near dusk.

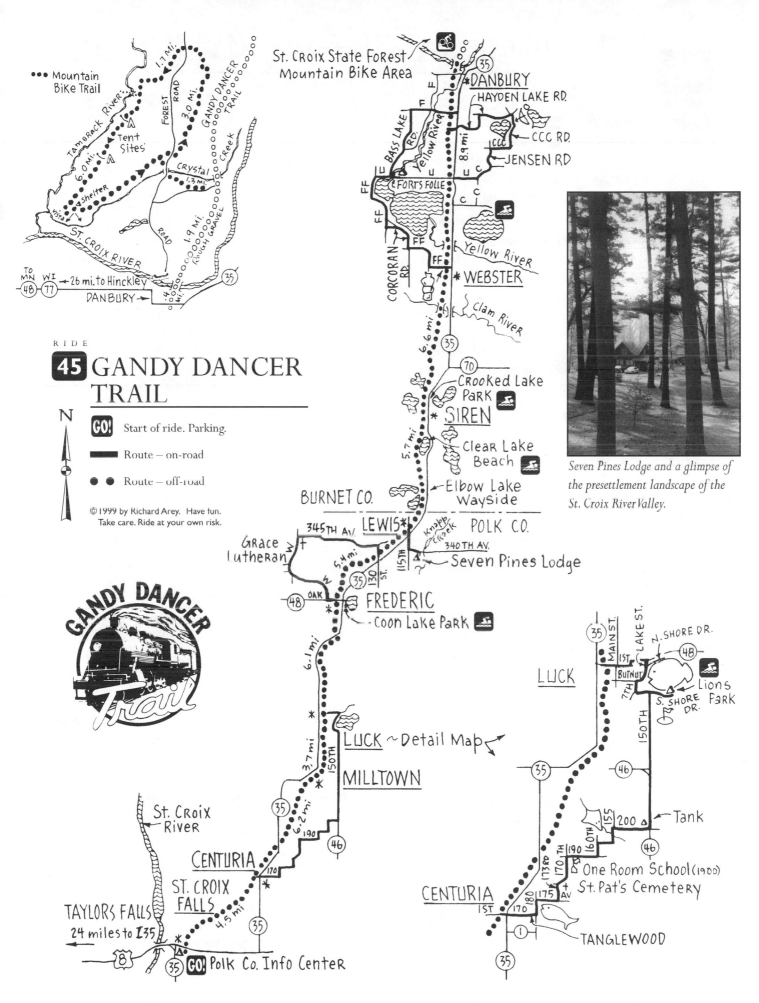

Mountain Bike Trail

St. Croix State Forest Mountain Bike Area

1.7 Mi.

FOREST ROAD

3.0 Mi.

GANDY DANCER TRAIL

Tamarack River

6.0 Mi.

Tent Sites

Crystal Creek

1.3 Mi.

Shelter

Vista

1.9 Mi. ROUGH GRAVEL

ROAD

ST. CROIX RIVER

TO MN ④⑧   WI ⑦⑦   ← 26 mi. to Hinckley

4.0 Mi.   DANBURY   ③⑤

DANBURY

HAYDEN LAKE RD.

CCC RD.

JENSEN RD

BASS LAKE RD.

Yellow River

8.9 Mi.

FORTS FOLLE

Yellow River

CORCORAN RD.

WEBSTER

Clam River

6.6 Mi.

③⑤

⑦⓪

Crooked Lake Park

SIREN

5.7 mi.

Clear Lake Beach

Elbow Lake Wayside

BURNET CO.

POLK CO.

LEWIS

345TH AV.

Grace Lutheran

5.4 mi.

Knapp Creek

340TH AV.

Seven Pines Lodge

③⑤   130 ST.   115TH

④⑧   OAK

FREDERIC

Coon Lake Park

6.1 mi.

RIDE

45 GANDY DANCER TRAIL

N

GO!   Start of ride. Parking.

────   Route — on-road

●●●   Route — off-road

© 1999 by Richard Arey.   Have fun.
Take care. Ride at your own risk.

Seven Pines Lodge and a glimpse of the presettlement landscape of the St. Croix River Valley.

GANDY DANCER Trail

St. Croix River

3.7 mi.

LUCK ~ Detail Map

MILLTOWN

③⑤   150TH

6.2 mi.

190

④⑥

CENTURIA

170

ST. CROIX FALLS

TAYLORS FALLS

24 miles to I35

⑧   ③⑤   GO! Polk Co. Info Center

4.5 mi.   ③⑤

LUCK

③⑤   MAIN ST.   1ST   LAKE ST.   N. SHORE DR.

BUTNUT   7TH   ④⑧

S. SHORE DR.   Lions Park

③⑤   ④⑥

155   200 △   ← Tank

160TH   One Room School (1900)

190   St. Pat's Cemetery

173 RD.   170 TH   340 AV.

CENTURIA   175

1ST   180   170

①   TANGLEWOOD

③⑤

-111-

RED CEDAR & CHIPPEWA RIVER TRAILS

Wisconsin. Phone Wisconsin DNR at 715-839-1602 for information.

LENGTH ◉ 15.8 miles – one way **Red Cedar State Trail** (limestone)
RATING ◉ 25.0 miles – one way **Chippewa River Trail** (asphalt-emulsion)
〰 12.8 miles – Hardscrabble Loop (on-road, see map)

RENTAL Menomonie, next to the Red Cedar Trailhead, Red Cedar Outfitters (715-235-5431); Eau Claire, Riverside (715-835-0088).

FEE A $3 daily or $10 annual trail pass is required.

STAY A LITTLE LONGER Call the Menomonie Chamber of Commerce (1-800-283-1862) or Eau Claire Tourist Bureau (1-800-344-FUNN) for lodging, food and added attractions. The **Creamery Restaurant and Inn** in Downsville (715-664-8354) is a great getaway.

The Red Cedar and Chippewa River Trails provide a car-free connection from Menomonie to Eau Claire. The trails often hug the riverbanks and a dozen historic railroad bridges cross the two rivers. This is an almost perfect blend of wildlife, scenery and history. At least that's what I was thinking on a sunsplashed evening as I stood on the 860-foot-long railroad trestle and watched an osprey diving for dinner.

RED CEDAR STATE TRAIL The trail follows the Red Cedar Junction Line built by the Milwaukee Railroad in 1888.

GO! Take I-94 60 miles east of St. Paul and exit at Hwy. 25 in Menomonie. Head south about two miles and take a left into **LAKESIDE CITY PARK.**

1.3 mi The **RED CEDAR TRAILHEAD** is in the historic railroad depot (water, washrooms, trail passes). This is a better place for families to start since you avoid crossing Hwy. 25. (Take 25 south to Hwy. 29 and 29 right to depot.)

4.0 mi The sound of the rushing river, and the rocky bluffs, make this stretch of trail a favorite. George Irvine ran a sawmill from 1854 to 1882 at the crossroads now known as **IRVINGTON**. The Chippewa Valley was the biggest source of white pine in the 1800s.

8.8 mi **DOWNSVILLE** (after Captain Downs) is a great place to stop for a bit of lunch or a short stroll. Many folks spend the night at the Creamery, and the deck overlooking the valley is pure pleasure.

11.8 mi Historic site of the Dunnville Cut Stone Quarry (trail marker is mile 10) that operated from the 1880s until the 1950s. The **MABEL TAINTER MEMORIAL THEATER** in Menomonie used Potsdam Sandstone from this quarry.

13.8 mi Overgrown stone foundations are all that remain of the former county seat of **DUNNVILLE**. Hard to imagine this was once a major steamboat landing.

15.8 mi A magnificent **860-FOOT-LONG IRON TRESTLE BRIDGE** crosses the Chippewa River and puts an exclamation mark at the end of this trail.

HARDSCRABBLE LOOP Start in Downsville or where County Road Y crosses the trail. This is a great jaunt (after the big climb) through the countryside on paved, low-traffic roads. Enjoy panoramas of the river valley and rolling countryside or stop at the **BULLFROG FISH FARM**. You may also want to go the other way up Y to make a pilgrimage to the early 1860s cottage where Caroline Woodhouse once lived. Her granddaughter, Carol Brink, memorialized her life about growing up on the wild frontier in the Newbery-award-winning book *Caddie Woodlawn*.

CHIPPEWA RIVER TRAIL This rail line was constructed in the 1870s to service the lumber industry. It was owned by the Chicago, Milwaukee, St. Paul and Pacific Railroad for most of its life.

GO! Continue east on I-94 another 23 miles past Menomonie and exit at Hwy. 85/37. Follow map.

1.5 mi The trail hugs the river as it passes through **OWEN PARK**. This stretch is quite scenic and crowded on a nice day. A second iron trestle crosses the Chippewa River at mile 1.5.

7.0 mi The **HIGHWAY 85 REST AREA** has water and washrooms about 200 yards off the trail. Look for the Silver Mine Ski Jump on the bluff across the river.

13.2 mi The village of **CARYVILLE** has some amenities.

20.0 mi **MERIDEAN** is a tiny town that marks your way.

25.0 mi The landscape gets a bit wilder as you approach the junction with the **RED CEDAR STATE TRAIL**. The towering trestle is a great place to hang out. With the lower water of midsummer the sandy beaches along the river are picnic perfect.

46 RED CEDAR & CHIPPEWA RIVER TRAILS

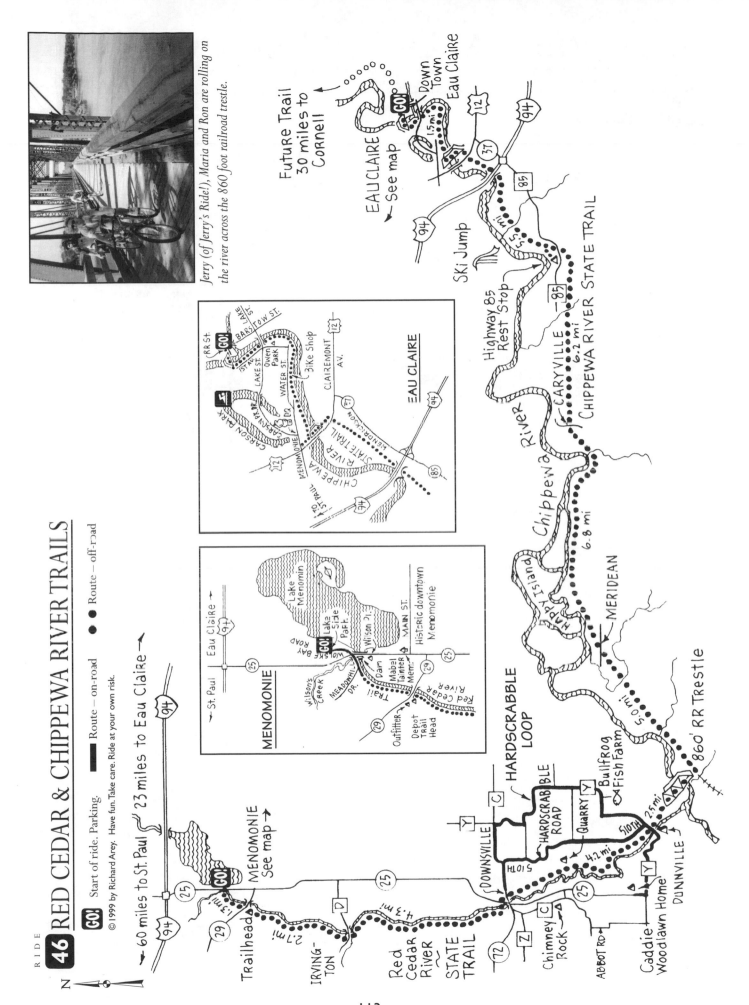

GO! Start of ride. Parking.

© 1999 by Richard Arey. Have fun. Take care. Ride at your own risk.

━━━ Route – on-road   ●●● Route – off-road

Jerry (of Jerry's Ride!), Maria and Ron are rolling on the river across the 860 foot railroad trestle.

Future Trail 30 miles to Cornell

EAU CLAIRE → See map

Down Town Eau Claire

Ski Jump

Highway 85 Rest Stop

CARYVILLE

CHIPPEWA RIVER STATE TRAIL

Chippewa River

6.2 mi

6.8 mi

5.5 mi

1.5 mi

MERIDEAN

Happy Island

5.0 mi

860' RR Trestle

EAU CLAIRE

RR St.
BARSTOW ST.
LAKE ST.
Owen Park
WATER ST.
Bike Shop
CLAIREMONT AV.
CARSON PARK
MENOMONIE
CHIPPEWA RIVER STATE TRAIL
HENDRICKSON

MENOMONIE

→ St. Paul   Eau Claire →

Lake Menomin

Lake Side Park

WOLSKE BAY ROAD

MAIN ST.

Historic downtown Menomonie

Wilson's Creek

Dam

Mabel Tainter Mem.

MEADOWHILL DR.

Trail

Red Cedar River

Outfitter

Depot Trail Head

HARDSCRABBLE LOOP

HARDSCRABBLE ROAD

QUARRY

Bullfrog Fish Farm

510TH

4.2 mi

2.5 mi

510TH

DOWNSVILLE

Caddie Woodlawn Home

DUNNVILLE

Chimney Rock

ABBOT RD.

Red Cedar River STATE TRAIL

Trailhead

IRVINGTON

MENOMONIE See map →

← 60 miles to St. Paul ⟍ 23 miles to Eau Claire →

2.7 mi

1.3 mi

4.3 mi

N

RIVER FALLS ROLLER COASTER

Wisconsin. Connects with RIDES 38, 44 and 48.

LENGTH 44.2 miles – Full loop

RATING 36.2 miles – Loop skips Hager City

CAUTION Big Hills. No shoulders on County Roads O and OO, but light traffic. Highway 35 gets busy.

CONNECTIONS From Hager City it is 12 miles to Maiden Rock (RIDE 48) and 2.5 miles to Red Wing (RIDE 38). It is 11 miles from River Falls to Hudson (RIDE 44).

> *Heartstopping hills punctuate this classic cow and coulee tour of the Wisconsin bluff country.*

GO!   Take I-94 18 miles east from St. Paul and exit on Wisconsin Hwy. 35 south. Go 8.5 miles into River Falls and through downtown. Turn right (west) on Park Street and go two blocks to **GLEN PARK**.

The little footbridge over a **SMALL GORGE** is a nice start to this ride. Hang a right at the DQ and head south. A paved path parallels Highway 35.

2.2 mi **HAPPY VALLEY ROAD** gets you going.

9.6 mi Go right on Cady Lane (950th Street) and the real fun begins. Did I mention **BIG HILLS** to Highway 10?

15.7 mi The coaster cruises up and down toward the Mississippi River. You can easily hit **40 MPH** on the final plunge to Highway 35.

21.3 mi The magnificent rock shoulders of the Mississippi River can be viewed all the way into **HAGER CITY**.

24.5 mi Cloverleaf up to VV and back to Highway 35. The scenery is gorgeous, but be careful to stay within the narrow paved shoulder on Highway 35. Go right on County O.

38.1 mi The **TRIMBELLE** (Originally two words meaning slender woman) **RIVER** dances along the gentle incline of this beautiful country road. Watch carefully for the left turn at 710 Avenue.

44.2 mi BACK TO *GO!* Did a Tropical Blizzard at **DAIRY QUEEN** ever look better?

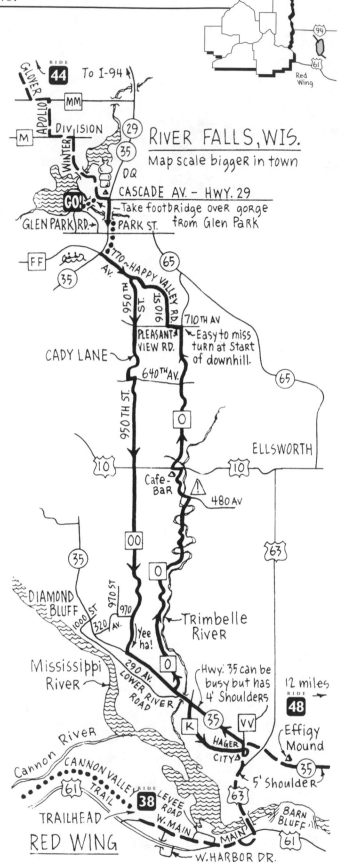

LOVELY LAKE PEPIN

Wisconsin. Connects with RIDE 47.

LENGTH ◆ 30.4 mile loop using Rustic Road
RATING ◆ 33.5 mile loop staying on paved roads
CAUTION Highway 35 gets busy but has wide (7 foot to 8 foot) shoulders. It also has some steep hills. Other roads have no shoulders and light traffic.

*T*he Great River Road between Maiden Rock and Stockholm is one of the most gorgeous in the world. Towering limestone bluffs frame the wide expanse in the Mississippi known as Lake Pepin. A perfect afternoon might begin in Maiden Rock with a leisurely ride to Stockholm for some browsing in the galleries. The glorious ride continues on to Pepin and dinner at the Harbor View Cafe. As the sun sinks into the sailboats a van would appear to whisk you back to the Harrisburg Inn — a view with a room — in Maiden Rock. You wake the next morning refreshed and ready to do the complete tour which includes the Little House in the Big Woods, the Swedish settlement of Lund and an authentic Rustic Road. Phone 715-672-5709 for a current listing of lodging and dining in Pepin County. Bon Appetit!

GO! From Red Wing cross into Wisconsin on Hwy. 63 and then go 12 miles south on Hwy. 35 to Maiden Rock.

4.5 mi The legend of **MAIDEN ROCK BLUFF** and the Indian princess Winona who leapt to her death is recounted in this beautiful wayside park.

6.4 mi Some steep climbs on the way to **STOCKHOLM** are forgotten once you enter this quaint rivertown. The Stockholm Art Fair is the third Saturday in July.

8.7 mi The historic site of **FORT ST. ANTOINE** dates to 1686 and enjoys a swell vista.

12.3 mi Turn on County Road CC for full tour.

13.2 mi The Harbor View Cafe, the Pickle Factory Bar and Grill, and the **PEPIN** Historical Museum are among the village highlights.

21.3 mi **LITTLE HOUSE WAYSIDE** re-creates the "little gray house made of logs" where Laura Ingalls Wilder was born on February 7, 1867.

23.4 mi The Sabylund Lutheran Church outside **LUND** rises above the rolling farmland.

25.1 mi If you've got a mountain bike and moxie you'll love the one-lane, gravel **RUSTIC ROAD** that winds down a coulee through a deep forest.

30.4 mi **BACK TO GO!** and perhaps a cool dip at the **BEE STOP ICE CREAM SHOP** in Maiden Rock.

33.5 mi **BACK TO GO TWO!** Take County Roads CC, H and S (for STEEP!) for a paved ride back to town.

RED LANTERN RIDE

Dakota County. Connects with RIDES 20, 29, 30, 31 and 50.

LENGTH 〰 40.0 miles – Full loop
RATING 〰 34.5 miles – Loop using Cliff Road cutoff
Road warriors apply here.

CAUTION First half of ride has no shoulders and moderate traffic. Big hills.
Good luck!

> *T*his is the training ride for L'Equipe Lanterne Rouge, which is French for "Don't try this ride if you're squeamish about hills or riding with traffic." The Red Lantern Racing Club uses this route to build strong bodies and minds. And to weed out the innocent.

GO! In St. Paul, start at the top of the **HIGH BRIDGE**. From south Minneapolis you can pick up the route by crossing the Mendota Bike Bridge and heading north on Highway 13.

0.7 mi Hop the curb and follow Cherokee Avenue along the bluff to Delaware. Head south and don't completely blow off the stop signs. The ride starts when you cross **ANNAPOLIS**.

4.6 mi Just past I-494 Delaware become **ARGENTA TRAIL**.

7.5 mi It's a bit tricky but you turn left on Jefferson Trail (Highway 149) and almost immediately left again on **RICH VALLEY BOULEVARD** (Highway 71).

8.9 mi Heads up as you take one more difficult left turn on South Robert Trail (Highway 3). This must be where Inver Grove **HEIGHTS** gets its name.

18.7 mi A long downhill and left on Rich Valley. The **CLIFF ROAD** cutoff saves about five miles. Or continue on past Koch Refinery (How long can you hold your breath?) to Highway 42. There are paved shoulders almost all the way back.

22.3 mi The Church of St. Joseph in Rosemount has a copper-clad spire with **GARGOYLE** scuppers if you can see that high.

26.8 mi **SCHULZE LAKE** in Lebanon Hills Regional Park would be a great place to cool off if you weren't in training.

35.0 mi Laugh at the slackers on the **BIG RIVERS TRAIL** as you follow North Highway 13. There are some great valley views from here when the leaves are down.

40.0 mi BACK TO **GO!** Follow Highway 13 to Smith Avenue and go left on one of my favorite downhill runs, since giving up the giant slalom.

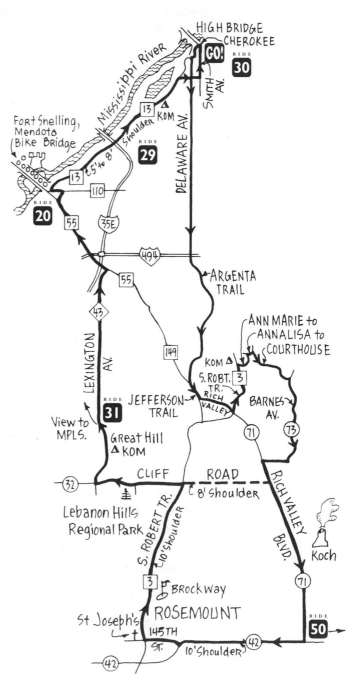

FALLS, GORGE & RIVER RIDE

Dakota County. Connects with RIDE 36, 37, 38 and 49.

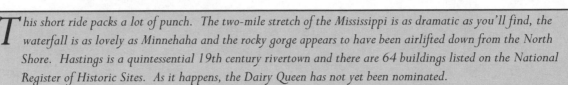

LENGTH & RATING ● 13.2 miles – quiet city streets, paths and wide shoulders

CAUTION   Be careful crossing Highway 61 at the river. An underpass will be built in 2000.

CONNECTIONS It is 4 miles to RIDE 36, 7 miles to RIDE 37, 17.1 miles to RIDE 38 and 9.5 miles to RIDE 49.

PHONE   City of Hastings 651-437-4127 or the Tourism Bureau at 651-437-6775.

This short ride packs a lot of punch. The two-mile stretch of the Mississippi is as dramatic as you'll find, the waterfall is as lovely as Minnehaha and the rocky gorge appears to have been airlifted down from the North Shore. Hastings is a quintessential 19th century rivertown and there are 64 buildings listed on the National Register of Historic Sites. As it happens, the Dairy Queen has not yet been nominated.

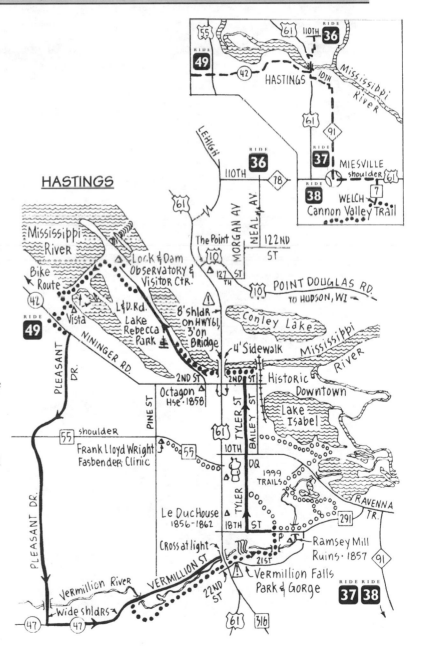

HASTINGS

GO!   Take Hwy. 61 16 miles southeast from St. Paul to Hastings. Immediately after crossing the Mississippi take a right and exit onto 2nd Street and the **HISTORIC DOWNTOWN** where you'll park.

0.3 mi   Bike east to the end of 2nd Street (just before the railroad tracks), take a left on Tyler and go **DOWN TO THE RIVER**.

2.0 mi   Bike along the Mississippi to **LOCK AND DAM NO. 2**. The observation deck, water and washrooms complement a great view of the working river. Limestone cliffs provide a dramatic backdrop.

2.9 mi   Continue along the levee and up the bluff to a **SCENIC OVERLOOK** with a picnic table.

6.6 mi   The tour continues on wide Pleasant Drive where Hasting's zoning laws have preserved some farmland. Bike the shoulder of County Road 47 and just before crossing the **VERMILLION RIVER** you have a choice. Continue on 47 and nice views of the river or go right onto the path.

7.7 mi   **VERMILLION FALLS** (a few steps from the main path) announces the start of a fascinating half mile. The **GORGE** below the falls is just out of sight until you reach the railroad trestle that leaps over it. Lock up your bike and take a stroll. Don't miss the **RAMSEY MILL RUINS** that rise like a Minnesota Stonehenge from the rapids-strewn river.

13.2 mi **BACK TO GO!** Mileage includes a short mile round-trip to the 1863 **LE DUC HOUSE** and 2.5 miles of new paved trails north of the mill. Or take the straight shot down Tyler and save three miles.

Mike Riemer – earthsports photography

Scott Hebel "catching some air" as he flies across the finish line to win the Tour de Buck at Buck Hill in 1991. Scott came in second to Greg LeMond at Chequemegon in 1990 and 1991. While mountain biking satisfies the most adventurous athletes, it also accommodates the average cyclist looking to explore new (and often quite level) territory.

MOUNTAIN BIKE RIDES AND BMX

Mountain biking is a blast. It is enjoyed by families and friends as well as more athletic types. Mountain biking can be simply a quicker way to escape into the woods on a level dirt path or it can be a vigorous workout on the steepest hills imaginable in Minnesota. While bird watchers at **Murphy–Hanrehan Regional Park** battled with mountain bikers over trail access, other bird watchers from the St. Paul Audubon Society rode their mountain bikes to observe 50 different species of birds, including a bald eagle, on the trails at **Lake Elmo Park Reserve.**

Mountain biking continues to be controversial because it is a relatively new sport and trails are already crowded. Almost every trail in this book (and thus in the metro area) is open only on an experimental basis and could be closed at any time. Always CALL FIRST to confirm that a trail is open and do your part in following the rules of the trail. Contact the **Minnesota Off Road Cyclists** at 612-895-1744 to find out about how you can help keep trails open and which rides are currently available.

See BICYCLE ORGANIZATIONS chapter for information on mountain bike and cyclocross racing clubs. There are mountain bike races year-round including bike on ice races, the 24 Hours of Afton, and the one and only Chequamegon Fat Tire Festival. See ANNUAL BIKE EVENTS chapter.

The WEB SITES listed on page 22 contain substantial information on mountain biking. A good local site is www.visi.com/~tam/mtb.html. The International Mountain Bike Association is a great advocate for sustainable mountain biking and their web site is www.imba.com.

RULES OF THE TRAIL

1. Ride on open trails only. Call first to confirm.
2. Yield to pedestrians (and horses, pets and other hikers)
3. Control your bicycle speed.
4. Leave no trace. Stay off wet trails.
5. Never spook animals.
6. Be prepared.

BASIC EQUIPMENT

I have biked the entire length of the **Minnesota Valley Trail** on an old Schwinn 10–speed with skinny tires. The easier routes listed below can be enjoyed with virtually any bike, but the day I borrowed a buddy's bike with front suspension, it became crystal clear how a really good mountain bike could turn a quiet backwoods adventure on the **Bloomington Bluff Trail** into a creek splashing, brush crashing romp. I now own such a bike.

BE PREPARED

Some of these routes will take you miles away from help, drinkable water and food. Mountain bike trails tend to be open toward fall when days are shorter and temperatures cooler. So bring:
• Helmet, water and food
• Windbreaker, gloves, hat
• Map, compass, flashlight
• Spare tube or patch kit

• Pump, tire irons, wrenches
• First aid kit, bug repellent
• Pocket knife, duct tape, cash

CHOOSING A RIDE

Call first before heading out. Most of these trails are open only for a limited season. Nothing will shut down a trail faster than riding on it when it is closed.

● Easier, Family Fun Rides
• Elm Creek Park Reserve (A)
• Louisville Swamp (G)
• Lake Elmo Park Reserve (H)
• North Hennepin Regional Trail (2)
• Biking for the Birds – dirt trail (19)

∿ More Challenging Trails
• Lake Rebecca Park (B)
• Bloomington Bluff Trail (C)
• Terrace Oaks Park (D)
• Battle Creek Regional Park (I)
• Minnesota Valley Trail (16)
• Winter trail at Baker Park (9)
• Chimney Rock Ramble (37)
• St. Croix State Forest – See Gandy Dancer Trail (45)

⧩ Most Challenging Trails
• Buck Hill (E)
• Murphy Hanrehan Park Reserve (F)
• Lebanon Hills Regional Park (J)
• Afton Alps (K)
• Red Wing Memorial Park (L)

BMX

What was big in the 1970s, disappeared by the 1980s and is coming back stronger than ever in the late 1990s. Wrong! It's BMX racing for boys and girls, moms and dads. There are now over 100,000 licensed BMX racers in the U.S. — more than mountain bike racers and road racers combined.

The sport is an adrenaline rush and a total body workout in under a minute. Kids five to 50 have taken up the sport and can be found flying through the air on high-tech bikes with tiny wheels. Tracks encourage families to spend the day together. Stop by one of the following tracks to get started or check the local **BMX web site: www.rehbeinsbmx.com.**

Buck Hill BMX Racing
Bloomington – outdoor track
Phone 612-987-4BMX Web Site: www.penncycle.com/buckhillbmx

Crow River BMX
St. Michael – outdoor track
Phone 612-497-1348

Rehbein Arena Indoor BMX
Lino Lakes – indoor/outdoor
Phone 651-784-5824

RIDE A

ELM CREEK PARK RESERVE

Hennepin County. Connects with RIDES 2 and 7.

OWNER	Hennepin Parks 612-424-5511 **FEE** $4 daily or $25 annual
OPEN	April 15 through October 31, 5 a.m. to sunset
LENGTH RATING	🌀 5 miles – turf mountain bike trail (includes 1 paved mile)
	🌀 20 miles – paved trail (10 new miles north of Elm Creek Road)
CAUTION	Trail is bumpy in spots and may be closed if trails are too wet.

Elm Creek is a good place to give mountain biking a first try. The trail is relatively short, easy and quite beautiful in places. Combine some exercise with an educational visit to Eastman Nature Center.

GO! Take I-94 north and exit at 93rd Avenue. Go right (east) about one mile to Fernbrook Lane and left (north) on Fernbrook just past Co. Rd. 81 to Territorial Road. Go right (SE) one mile to entrance.

Elm Creek is Hennepin Park's largest preserve. It contains five lakes, three streams, extensive wetlands and mature hardwood forests within the 5,400-acre site. It is easy to look across the unbuilt expanse and imagine you have stepped 200 years back in time. American Indians found good hunting grounds here and wildlife is still plentiful.

To fully enjoy this park, try some of the 20 miles of paved paths. Take a side trip up to **EASTMAN NATURE CENTER** (612-420-4300) to see the live animal exhibits. Scramble around the creative play area, take a swim or enjoy a picnic.

The mountain bike trail itself is a bit tame but allows you to visit more of the park. There are no really challenging stretches but do not get too complacent. One of the state's better woman mountain bikers took a spill and broke her collarbone in a race here.

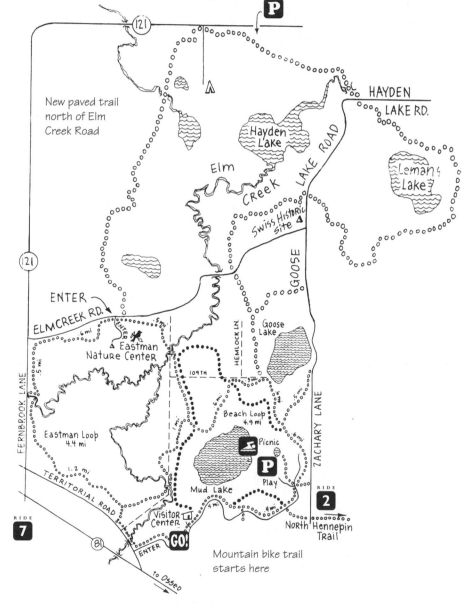

Mountain bike trail starts here

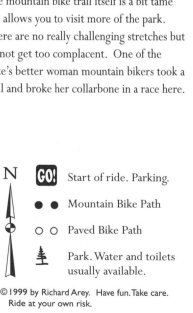

GO!	Start of ride. Parking.
●●	Mountain Bike Path
○○	Paved Bike Path
🌲	Park. Water and toilets usually available.

© 1999 by Richard Arey. Have fun. Take care. Ride at your own risk.

LAKE REBECCA PARK RESERVE

Hennepin County. Connects with RIDE 9.

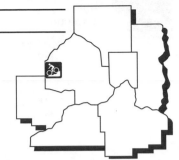

OWNER	Hennepin Parks 612-559-9000
OPEN	April 15 through October 31, 5 a.m. to sunset
LENGTH	4 mile – turf mountain bike trail
RATING	6.5 mile – paved trail
CAUTION	Trail crosses paved bike path in places.

FEE $4 daily or $25 annual

Lake Rebecca added mountain biking to its palette of summer fun on June 14, 1998. This helps offset the loss of Hyland Hills as a venue and adds an official course to the far western suburbs for the first time.

GO! Lake Rebecca is 26 miles west of Minneapolis on either Hwy. 12 or Hwy. 55. From 12 go north on Co. Rd. 139 to Co. Rd. 50 to entrance on right.

I had a lot of fun on these trails, though somebody looking for big hills or tricky single-track riding may be disappointed. The trails are mowed grass about five feet wide. There are some exciting off-camber turns and a couple of good climbs, but most beginners won't be intimidated by the course.

Fine lake views are enjoyed from the trail, and, with a bit of luck you may see a trumpeter swan. These are the world's largest waterfowl and Lake Rebecca is part of Hennepin Parks' swan restoration program.

There is plenty else to do at this sprawling 2,200 acre park. It is a little less crowded than other Hennepin parks and a great destination for a picnic with a swim after your ride. If mountain biking is not your cup of cola, try the paved hike/bike trail, the horseback trail, turf hiking trails or bring your best buddy along on the nine mile dog walking path.

N

GO! Start of ride. Parking.

● ● Mountain Bike Path

○ ○ Paved Bike Path

© 1999 by Richard Arey. Have fun. Take care. Ride at your own risk.

River

Crow

ENTER

GO!

Swan observation deck

Roy Lake

Lake Rebecca

E. LAKE REBECCA ROAD

Rattail Lake

50

55

92

TOWN LINE RD.

50

17

139

11

LOCATION MAP

ENTER

GO!

50

55

92

11

17

139

12

17 miles from 139 to I-394

RIDE BLOOMINGTON BLUFF TRAIL

Hennepin County. Connects with RIDE 11 and 19.

OWNERS   Bloomington 612-948-8877, U.S. Fish and Wildlife 612-854-5900

LENGTH & RATING 〰 10 miles one way

CAUTION   Stay on trail and out of closed areas. This is an isolated area so bring along a friend. Trail is narrow, two-way and shared with hikers. The trail may be sandy after a flood. Mosquitoes are fierce by June.

> *For my money, this is the best mountain bike trail in the Twin Cities. It has every feature desired in terms of scenery, length, technical challenges, wildlife and remoteness. There is also a rich sense of history and intimate views of the Minnesota River. Most people will cherish this ride as a great stump jumping, creek splashing romp.*

GO!   Start at the **INDIAN MOUNDS ELEMENTARY SCHOOL** located 3 blocks east of Old Shakopee Road on 98th Street and 11th Avenue South. The trail begins at the south end of 11th Avenue just before 100th Street. Follow the trail down to the bottom of the ravine and **GO RIGHT (WEST-SOUTHWEST)** at the intersecting trail near the river. Do not go left (east–northeast) into the wildlife sanctuary that is closed to bicyclists. The first stretch of trail is the most rugged.

0.4 mi   **VALLEY OVERLOOK** and small picnic area.

1.0 mi   **PARKER'S PICNIC GROUNDS** and overlook was a popular spot from the 1930s until 1965.

1.3 mi   Watch for a marked trail on the right up the bluff that takes you to the **POND – DAKOTA MISSION PARK**. The 1856 brick residence was the home of Gideon Pond. In 1842, Gideon established a mission for the local Dakota and in 1850 began publishing the *Dakota Friend*, a bilingual paper. This National Register Historic Site is open only by appointment. Phone 612-948-8878.

2.9 mi   **TRAIL ACCESS** at the end of Lyndale Avenue.

5.3 mi   A bridge now spans **NINE MILE CREEK**. The mouth of the creek is the former site of **TI TAN-KA TA-NI-NA** (habitation, large, ancient), the oldest village of the Mdewakantonwan Dakota. The French explorer Nicolas Perrot first noted this village in 1689, and parts of this trail have been trod for centuries.

7.0 mi   An old iron **SWING BRIDGE** crosses the river.

10.0 mi   County Road 18 and the end of the trail. A small **TRAILHEAD** and parking lot is located on the west side of 18. The **OLD BLOOMINGTON FERRY BRIDGE** crosses the Minnesota River and is only open to bicyclists and hikers.

¡ TRAIL IS SHARED WITH HIKERS !

RIDE
TERRACE OAKS PARK

Dakota County. Connects with RIDE 18.

OWNER City of Burnsville 612-895-4500 CALL FIRST, trail closed when wet.

LENGTH 3.4 miles

RATING 〰 Intermediate and better with some tricky single-track riding

CAUTION Stay on designated trails and be respectful of hikers. It is easy to get turned around here. Call first to confirm that trails are still open.

Terrace Oaks has a rollicking terrain of hummocks, hills and depressions thanks to the last glacier that pushed through here some 10,000 years ago. Gary Sjoquist has designed an excellent mountain bike experience with some very technical single-track riding through the oak woodlands. Riding amidst the fall colors is a real treat.

GO! From St. Paul take I-35E south 15 miles and exit on Co. Rd. 11. Go north 1.5 miles to Burnsville Parkway and right at entrance to Park Dr.

Local politics may close this beautiful mountain bike course at any time so enjoy it while you can. Mountain bike advocate Gary Sjo

quist has worked closely with the city in developing and maintaining the trails. Respectful use will help keep it open.

The narrow, twisting single-track (squirrel track?) trail segments are perhaps the most unique aspect of this park. They require some strength and superior bike handling skills. Not to mention that they are a lot of fun. Signage still needs some attention but this is a great little park that you are sure to enjoy.

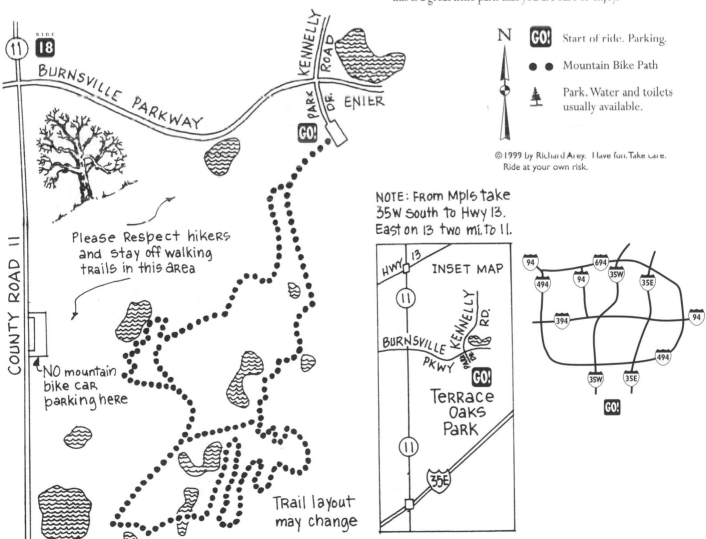

N

GO! Start of ride. Parking.

● ● Mountain Bike Path

🌲 Park. Water and toilets usually available.

Please Respect hikers and stay off walking trails in this area

NO mountain bike car parking here

NOTE: From Mpls take 35W South to Hwy 13. East on 13 two mi. to 11.

INSET MAP

Terrace Oaks Park

Trail layout may change

BUCK HILL BMX & MOUNTAIN BIKING

RIDE E

Dakota County. Connects with RIDE 18.

OWNER	Buck Hill Ski Area 612-435-7174
OPEN	May – October. Call first, may only be open weekends and for races.
LENGTH	⌁-⌁ 3 miles **RATING** Intermediate to expert
FEE	$5.00. Subject to change.
CAUTION	Casey Jones you better watch your speed.

*B*uck Hill provides a first-class mountain bike facility and great new outdoor BMX track. Experienced riders come to train or compete and Erik's Spring Cup at Buck is the annual kick-off to the mountain bike race season.

GO!   Take I-35 south and exit at Co. Rd. 46. Go right and right again on Buck Hill Road to entrance.

The 1881 *History of Dakota County* explains, "at the west end of Crystal Lake is a high hill, called by the early settlers, Buck Hill. From the top of this high eminence the Indians would watch the deer as they came to drink from the cool waters of the lake."

You will soon be ready for a cool drink because, as any suit can tell you, it takes hard work to get to the top. This is especially true at Buck Hill where you climb over 200 feet to reach the top. Your reward — burning hamstring muscles and a view of four states. Make that four lakes, and maybe one deer, if you are lucky. In any event, you are guaranteed a good workout.

The "Enchanted Forest" nicely offsets the open slopes of the main ski area. Excellent signage keeps you on track and headed in the right direction. Highlights include a beautiful little single-track trail in the woods just south of the Apex Picnic Area. And thrill seekers can really catch some air at the bottom of Don's Descent.

Sure, there is a lot of climbing here. But as a couple of kids put it, "We're here for the downhills!"

BMX

Buck Hill has embraced the youth movement and built one of the area's first BMX courses. Weekly races are held and practice sessions are available to clubs and individuals. Call 612-987-4BMX for more information or check Penn Cycle's web site at www:penncycle.com/buckhillbmx..

N

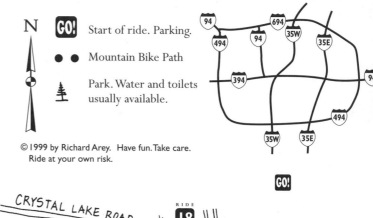

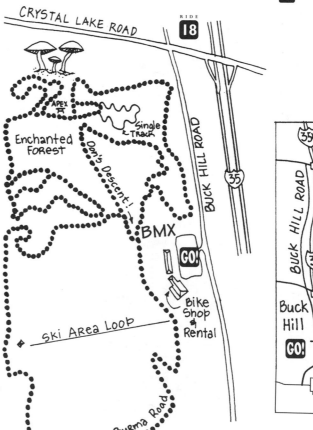

GO!	Start of ride. Parking.
● ●	Mountain Bike Path
🌲	Park. Water and toilets usually available.

© 1999 by Richard Arey. Have fun. Take care. Ride at your own risk.

- 124 -

MURPHY - HANREHAN PARK RESERVE

Scott County. Connects with RIDE 18.

OWNER	Hennepin Parks Trail Hotline 612-559-6778
OPEN	Approximately August 1 through October 31 but CALL FIRST
LENGTH	〰–〰 6 miles **RATING** Intermediate to expert
FEE	$4 daily parking or $25 annual permit
CAUTION	Bike here only when open and only on designated trails. Big hills!

A great, rugged mountain bike trail in a gorgeous setting. As suburban sprawl engulfs the surrounding landscape Murphy-Hanrehan stands out as a big (3,000 acres), beautiful oasis of woods and water. Follow all the rules and keep your fingers crossed that Hennepin Parks keeps Murphy open for mountain bikers a couple months each year.

GO! Take I-35W or I-35E south and exit on Co. Rd. 42. Turn right (west) and go about 2.5 miles to Burnsville Parkway. Take a left (you'll be on Hanrehan Lake Blvd.) and go about two miles south to Co. Rd. 75 (Murphy Lake Road). Take a left and a left again into park.

The local heavyweight champion of mountain bike courses, Murphy's been knocked down a couple of times but never out. A shortened mountain bicycling season is necessary to protect the soil and vegetation, and to prevent erosion on the trail's steep slopes. As a bird watcher, environmental advocate and mountain biker, I hope proper management and due respect by trail users will keep this trail open. It's a beauty.

Murphy-Hanrehan is a rock-and-roller-coaster-of-a-ride. Big climbs followed by plummeting drops keep you busy. This area is a favorite of racers. If the course has a drawback, it is that there is little chance to just spin and enjoy the scenery. On the plus side, if you could only choose one time to be open, then fall would be it. The oaks and maples cast a brilliant glow that is captured perfectly in the park's many ponds and lakes.

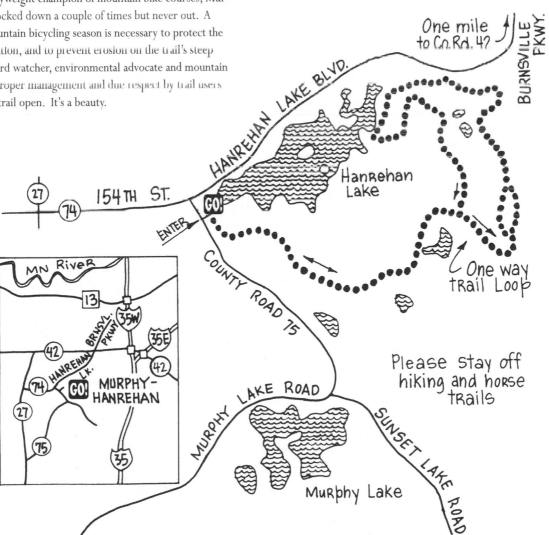

LOUISVILLE SWAMP

Scott County. Connects with RIDE 16.

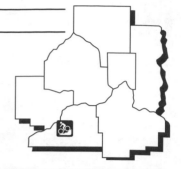

OWNER	U.S. Fish and Wildlife Service 612-854-5900
LENGTH	11.5 miles – Louisville Swamp loops
RATING	Easier, but be prepared if going a distance on the State Trail
CAUTION	Trail floods during high water in spring. Trail is shared with hikers. Mosquitoes are fierce in summer.

Louisville Swamp is one of the great unspoiled retreats in the metro area. A vast land that echoes with the ghosts of Dakota Indians, fur traders and pioneer settlers. Deer and bird life is abundant. People are not. Go now.

GO!

Take Highway 169 nine miles southwest from I-494 to Shakopee. Continue south on 169 to 145th Street (watch carefully) and turn right (west) on 145th to parking lot on left.

A wonderful place with a rich natural and cultural history that can be enjoyed by all bicyclists. The trail is mostly level as it circles the broad wetlands. Short rises take you through restored prairie and oak savanna with some surprising panoramic vistas.

The diverse habitats are home for both Northern Water Snakes (non-poisonous) and prickly pear cactus (which blooms in July). A visit with the Audubon Society yielded over 45 species of birds one morning, and wild turkeys have been introduced.

The sense of wildness belies the fact that humans have lived here for centuries. **WI-YA-KA OTI-DAN** — the "little village of Sand River" — was a thriving Dakota community when Jean Baptiste Faribault built his trading post nearby in 1802.

By the 1860s the fur trade and Indians had moved on and two pioneer families arrived. Frederick Jabs was almost as self-sufficient as the Dakota preceding him. He raised his own vegetables and hunted rabbit, otter and squirrels. The Jabs family made their own sausage using "everything but the squeal." The original stone house now serves as a trail shelter.

The trail surface is mostly packed dirt and gravel. Parts of the Little Prairie Loop are so bumpy as to be unbikeable. You may find some stretches closed or extremely muddy. Elsewhere, huge slabs of exposed granite break the trail surface and tell of this land's ancient past.

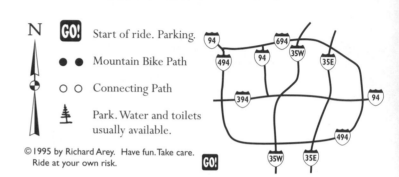

N

GO!	Start of ride. Parking.
● ●	Mountain Bike Path
○ ○	Connecting Path
🌲	Park. Water and toilets usually available.

© 1995 by Richard Arey. Have fun. Take care. Ride at your own risk.

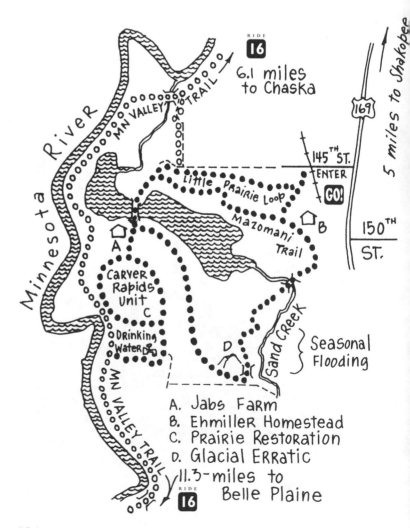

RIDE 16
6.1 miles to Chaska

145TH ST. ENTER GO!

150TH ST.

5 miles to Shakopee

Little Prairie Loop

Mazomani Trail

Minnesota River

MN VALLEY TRAIL

Carver Rapids Unit

Drinking Water

Sand Creek

Seasonal Flooding

A. Jabs Farm
B. Ehmiller Homestead
C. Prairie Restoration
D. Glacial Erratic

11.3-miles to Belle Plaine

RIDE 16

- 126 -

LAKE ELMO PARK RESERVE

Washington County. Connects with RIDE 35.

OWNER Washington County Parks 651-731-3851

OPEN Spring through fall except when very wet

LENGTH 〰 10 miles – turf mountain bike trail

RATING 6.5 miles – paved trail

CAUTION Horses and hikers share trail.

FEE $4 daily or $18 annual vehicle permit

*L*ake Elmo provides an excellent introduction to mountain biking for folks living in the east metro area. The course is long and scenic as it winds around Eagle Point Lake. The full-service park offers many other diversions — swimming, camping, picnicking, creative play areas, horseback riding, hiking and 7.5 miles of biking on paved paths.

GO! Take I-94 eight miles east from St. Paul and exit on Co. Rd. 19. Go left (north) one mile and straight into the park.

The mountain bike paths at Lake Elmo may seem relatively tame for those who have careened down the hills at Lebanon or Murphy-Hanrehan, but take note. My tour was going quite smoothly when I started descending a small hill toward a pond. Higher water had caused bikers to veer off the main path on a slight detour. I followed, and with no warning, hit a rock the size of a box hidden in some weeds. The bike stopped dead, launching me on a complete somersault over the handlebars. With Dan as my witness I landed in soft grass with nary a bruise.

Your tour is not likely to be as eventful but keep your eyes open. This is the longest mountain bike <u>loop</u> trail in the metro area. It passes through reclaimed farmland, woods and marsh. The trail is generally hard packed dirt in good condition.

Lake Elmo Park Reserve was the site for the St. Paul Audubon Society's first biking for the birds trip. On the morning of October 1, 1994, a small group spotted 50 species including six types of woodpeckers, northern harriers, a bobwhite and an immature bald eagle soaring overhead. Personally, I would recommend coming to a complete stop before getting out the binoculars.

N

GO! Start of ride. Parking.

● ● Mountain Bike Path

○ ○ Paved Bike Path

🌲 Park. Water and toilets usually available.

© 1995 by Richard Arey. Have fun. Take care. Ride at your own risk.

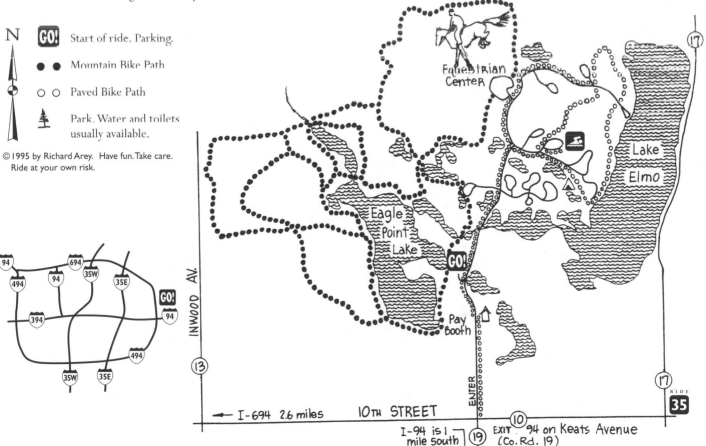

BATTLE CREEK REGIONAL PARK

Ramsey County. Connects with RIDES 30, 32, 33, 34 and 40.

OWNER Ramsey County Parks Department 651-777-1707

OPEN Daylight hours unless posted otherwise

LENGTH RATING 2.5 miles – Intermediate with some expert single-track riding.

4.5 miles – Paved paths complete in Spring of 1999 through Battle Creek Ravine to Highway 61.

CAUTION Shared trail with hikers

This is the newest experimental mountain bike trail to open in the metro area. And while it isn't exceptionally long, it is a fine addition. The 147-acre parcel commands high ground overlooking the Mississippi River and includes some nice downhill runs.

GO!

Take I-94 to the east edge of St. Paul and exit at McKnight Rd. Go south to Upper Afton Rd. and right (west) to Winthrop St. Take a left to park entrance on right.

Old timers will remember downhill skiing at this very same location. Battle Creek follows the trend of converting ski areas into mountain biking parks. The park is also blessed with an extensive oak forest on top of the bluff. By changing course you can create a variety of loops that will keep your interest for a good workout.

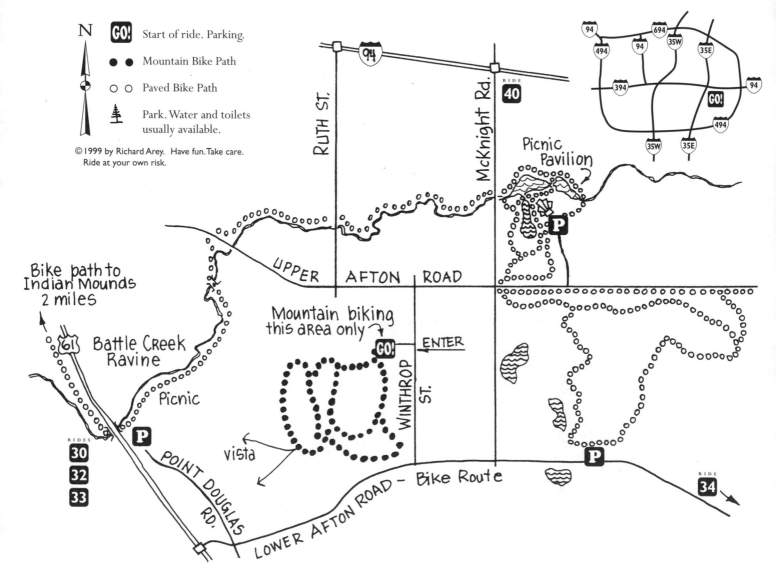

N

GO! Start of ride. Parking.

● ● Mountain Bike Path

○ ○ Paved Bike Path

🌲 Park. Water and toilets usually available.

© 1999 by Richard Arey. Have fun. Take care. Ride at your own risk.

LEBANON HILLS REGIONAL PARK

Dakota County. Connects with RIDE 31.

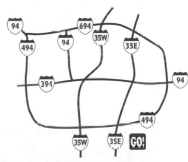

OWNER	Dakota County Parks Department 651-437-6608
OPEN	Daylight hours unless posted otherwise
LENGTH	〰 – 🔺 2.1 miles
RATING	Intermediate to expert
CAUTION	Steep hills — but that's the point.

Good things come in small packages. This is a compact course with some tough uphill grades and one memorable downhill featuring a flying banked curve. Take some time to enjoy the scenery. The course is completely wooded with a nice overlook on top where you can view the Minneapolis skyline.

GO! Take I-35E or Hwy. 77 south and exit at Cliff Road. Go east to Johnny Cake Ridge Road and then right to entrance on right.

This course is short but sweet if you have the right stuff. The fastest riders can do the outside loop in seven minutes flat. That leaves very little time to stop and smell the flowers. You will get a great workout here no matter what your times are.

Thank Dakota County for this small gem and do not be tempted to explore other parts of Lebanon Hills except on foot, skis or horseback.

N

GO! Start of ride. Parking.

● ● Mountain Bike Path

© 1999 by Richard Arey. Have fun. Take care. Ride at your own risk.

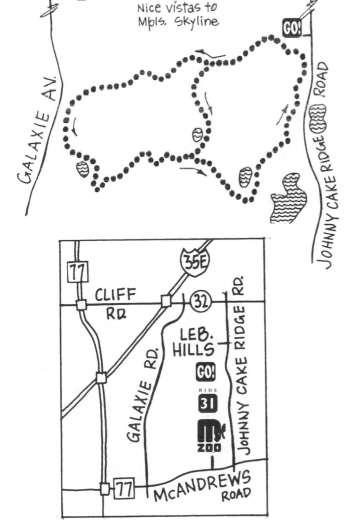

Gary Sjoquist (seen here at Red Wing Memorial Park) has been a driving force for ethical mountain bike trail development like that found at Lebanon Hills.

RIDE K — AFTON ALPS

NEW

Washington County. Connects with RIDE 36.

OWNER	Afton Alps, phone 651-436-1320
OPEN	Spring through fall, seven days a week, 7 a.m. to sunset
LENGTH	Over 7 miles of trails **RATING** Intermediate to expert
FEE	$6 daily, $85 season pass **CAUTION** Be off trails by sunset
RENTAL	Mountain bikes with or without suspension are available

When Afton Alps opened in 1995, it quickly established itself as one of the area's premier mountain bike parks. A beautiful setting, exciting single-track riding and the opportunity for a soda and burger at ride's end in the clubhouse have cemented this reputation.

GO! From St. Paul take I-94 east 7 miles to Co. Rd. 15. Exit and go south (right) 7 miles to 70th street (Co. Rd. 20). Go east (left) 3 miles to entrance.

It's not surprising that the largest downhill ski area in the Twin Cities is now one of the best mountain bike parks. Afton Alps follows Buck Hill, Hyland Hills (now closed) and Welch Village (races only) as a good place to get your kicks come winter or summer. What is a surprise is how the trails catch every grove of trees to be found. You'll think you're cruising through Afton State Park – it's right next door – instead of a ski area.

You're quickly reminded it's a ski resort with a fast descent down one of the longer runs. This is a solid intermediate and better area and you'll be glad you spent the extra bucks for front suspension on your bike. The vertical drop at Afton is 350 feet and the lifts happen to be closed all summer.

The Bridge Loop features a beautiful wooded ravine and a 30-foot-long bridge crossing. Enjoy the views from the Hideaway and the screaming downhill on Last Chance Gulch. Some of my favorite single-track trails were meticulously cut by hand into the hillsides.

They haven't posted any deer crossing signs yet but we saw ten on one visit. Afton Alps is embraced by heavily wooded bluffs, courtesy of the adjacent state park, making this a great destination for a fall ride with flying colors.

If you're still feeling strong after two or three laps you may be ready for the 24 hours of Afton race that's held here in August. Most cyclists register in teams of four, but Chad Swanson won the 1997 event with 33 laps – solo.

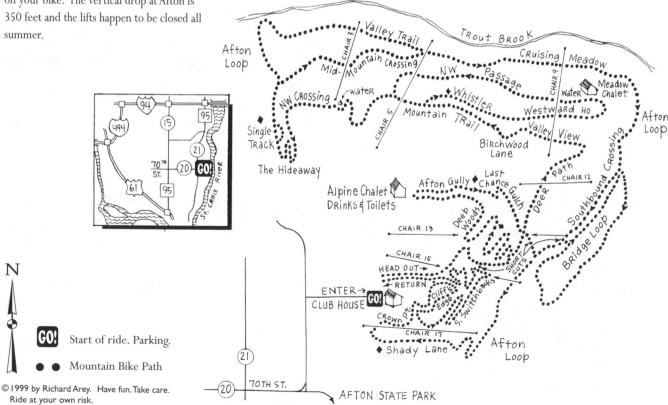

N

GO! Start of ride. Parking.

• • Mountain Bike Path

© 1999 by Richard Arey. Have fun. Take care. Ride at your own risk.

RIDE
RED WING MEMORIAL PARK

Goodhue County. Connects with RIDE 38.

OWNER   City of Red Wing, phone 651-385-3674

OPEN   Seven days a week, sunrise to sunset, from late April to ski season

LENGTH   7 miles   **RATING**   Skilled beginner to expert

CAUTION   Don't use golf course parking lot. There is bow hunting after September 15 but biking is OK from 10 a.m. to 3 p.m.

RENTAL   Quality mountain bikes (with helmets) can be rented at the Outdoor Store, 323 Main Street, in Red Wing. Phone 651-388-5358.

> *Memorial Park rivals Afton Alps as the best mountain bike course in the greater metro area. There's some terrific single-track riding, blufftop views and over 400 feet of elevation gain if you bike the trail from town.*

GO!   Take Highway 61 southeast about 50 miles to Red Wing. In downtown, take a right on Bush Street, left on 7th and right on Memorial Drive to park.

Just opened in 1997, Red Wing Memorial Park takes full advantage of its wooded blufftop setting. The park sits atop Sorin's Bluff, which was once an island in the post-glacial Mississippi River, same as nearby Barn Bluff. Trails follow the cross country ski trails that curve around the park's perimeter and plunge into the woods onto some of the most exciting single-track riding you will find in the Midwest.

You can drive to the parking lot at the top of the bluff, but if you are looking to start the day with a good burn in the quads then begin at 8th and Bluff Streets. Head up the expert single-goat-

track that climbs the bluff and think about what fun you'll have on the way back down.

An easier loop circles the prairie on top of the bluff. More challenging trails yo-yo up and down the sides of the steep slopes. A green canopy of trees obscures most views of the river but there are a couple nice bird's eye vistas. On the hairiest downhill (alright, I did walk a stretch of this), as you careen on the edge of control, you may glimpse the luxurious Mississippi National Golf Links.

The local mountain bike club, in concert with the City of Red Wing, has done an admirable job in cutting and maintaining the trails. They will be erecting signage as finances permit. As it is, Red Wing Memorial Park is a great excuse to get out of Dodge for some fine and demanding mountain biking.

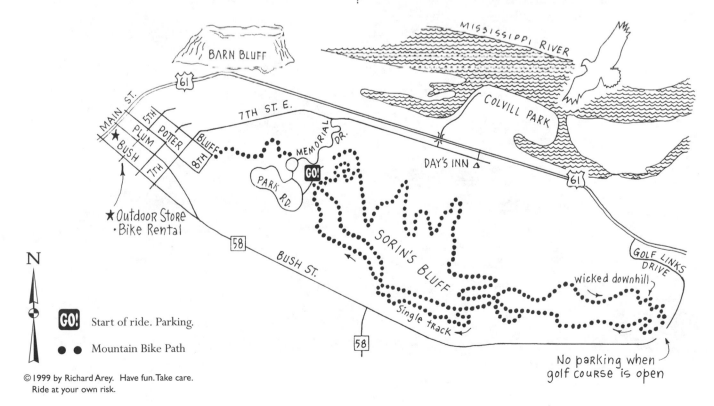

N

GO!   Start of ride. Parking.

• •   Mountain Bike Path

© 1999 by Richard Arey. Have fun. Take care.
Ride at your own risk.

Bicyclists take over Summit Avenue at the start of the 1996 Saint Paul Classic Bike Tour. Phone 612-372-3424 to find out how you can be part of the 10,000 (cyclists!) in 2000 ride when organizers plan to close the entire route to traffic. Be there!

ANNUAL BIKE EVENTS

While nobody was looking, the Twin Cities has become a place where people can — and do — ride their bikes twelve months a year. This "can bike" attitude, and the widespread use of mountain bikes, ensure that there are bicycle trips, tours and races throughout the year.

The following list highlights annual Twin Cities bicycle events. There are events for all levels of cyclists, from weekend duffers to professional racers. Contact your favorite local club (see BICYCLE ORGANIZATIONS, page 137) or sports magazine (*Cyclesport, Minnesota Sports, Twin Cities Sports*) for current listings of local events. *Silent Sports* magazine (715-258-5546) is a great place to find out about bike events throughout the Upper Midwest. The **Chequamegon Fat Tire Festival** (715-798-3811) in Hayward, Wisconsin, runs the third weekend of September. It is so popular that a lottery is now being held to determine participants.

The **Twin Cities Bicycle Club** (Hotline is 612-924-2443, web site is www.mtn.org/tcbc) schedules over 400 recreational rides throughout the year. Bicycle races are coordinated through the **Minnesota Cycling Federation** (MCF Hotline is 612-729-0702, web site is www.mcf.net).

Road and mountain biking races take place weekly, but the **Minnesota Bike Festival** may soon be the biggest annual event (see May listing). **Pro Events International** (Phone 612-378-5714) helps with some of the larger tours. Triple your pleasure by taking part in a triathlon. These events combine biking, running, swimming and, in the **Minnesota Border to Border Triathlon**, canoeing. Call Gear West at 612-473-0093 or visit their web site at www.gearwest.com. Larger tours require preregistration and helmets are almost always required.

January

POLAR BEAR RIDE
New Years Day
Start your bicycling year off right. Begun in 1983, this ride attracts 40 to 50 well-dressed cyclists for a 12-mile round trip ride down Summit Avenue in St. Paul. Starts at high noon in the SW corner of the Sears parking lot at I-94 and Marion. Phone TCBC at 612-924-2443.

BIKE ON ICE RACES
Informal races are held each winter. Check with the clubs to find out the details on this local phenomena.

HUMAN POWERED ICE RACES
Last full weekend in January
The Minnesota Human Powered Vehicle Association (612-929-2978) sponsors this annual event that began in 1992 on White Bear Lake. Contestants from throughout the Midwest use studded tires, outriggers and the wildest array of "bicycles" you are likely to see to compete in time trials, lap and drag races.

February

TCBC BIKE RIDES
Weekends and Weekdays
Check the TCBC hotline at 612-924-2443 to find out the schedule. February rides have included *Thursday Thermals* (Edina), a *Soup's on Series* (Bloomington) and a *Vibrant Valentine's Venture*. Slippery road conditions may preclude safe bicycling, but February is a great time to tune up your bike and register for the Minnesota Ironman.

March

MINNESOTA STATE BICYCLE CONFERENCE
Two days in March
Sponsored by the Minnesota Department of Transportation and the State Bicycle Advisory Board (651-296-9966), this biennial (that's every two years) conference provides an excellent opportunity to learn about the latest developments in bicycle transportation planning, trail funding, traffic calming and bike safety. On off years the Minnesota DNR (651-296-6157) will hold a trails conference that embraces all trail users.

April

EARTH DAY
April 22
On April 22, 1970, observers of the first Earth Day rode bicycles through downtown Minneapolis to protest America's addiction to the automobile. Show your gratitude to Mother Earth and leave that polluting beast in the garage for the day.

SOGN VALLEY ROAD RACE
Saturday before Ironman
This rural road race kick-starts the summer racing season. Phone the MCF Hotline at 612-729-0702.

SUMMER RACE SERIES
Weekday nights, mostly June through August
Some of the better local race series include the Black Dog Time Trials (Burnsville), the Dakota Tech Criterium (Rosemount), the Opus Criterium (Minnetonka) and the Thursday night track races at the Velodrome (Blaine). Great fun for specators and racers. Call MCF.

MINNESOTA IRONMAN
Last Sunday in April

One of Minnesota's two biggest rides is sponsored by the Minnesota Council American Youth Hostels (MN AYH), 612-924-2443. This Ironman began in 1967, years before the Hawaii triathlon that uses the same name. Minnesota's version is not a race, but a century ride with participation approaching 5,000 riders. You can bike 100 miles, 100 kilometers (62 miles) or do the 30-mile short route through scenic countryside.

May

ERIK'S SPRING CUP AT BUCK
Saturday in May

This annual mountain bike race and expo kicks off the season. Call Erik's Hotline at 612-869-BIKE or check out their web site at www.eriksbike.com.

BIKE, BUS OR CARPOOL (B-BOP!) DAY
Weekday, later in May

B-BOP Day is held each year during National Transportation Week. The idea is to leave your car at home and use an alternative — like biking — to work. Phone the B-BOP Hotline at 651-602-1602 to find out the date and how you can get your company involved. See chapter on BICYCLE COMMUTING.

MINNESOTA BIKE FESTIVAL
Mid-May, 10 days

In 1999 two national events are planned on successive weekends to celebrate bicycling and bike racing in Minnesota. Lance Armstrong's Ride to Survive will be an on-road criterium race using the State Capitol as a backdrop. This will be a great one to watch or compete in. The next weekend the Great River Criterium whistles through historic downtown Red Wing on Friday night and Welch hosts a mountain bike race with pro riders from around the country. Phone the MCF Hotline or check their web site for details.

June

MINNESOTA MS 150 BIKE TOUR
Weekend, early June

A scenic 150-mile fundraising ride from Duluth to the Twin Cities. This ride began in 1980 and its success launched fundraising bike tours around the country. The Minnesota MS 150 has raised over $6.4 million to help fight Multiple Sclerosis. Phone 651-227-8014 to register.

MOONLIGHT RIVER RAMBLE
Early June, 8 p.m. to Midnight

A benefit for the Minnesota Coalition of Bicyclists and a fine way to spend a summer's eve along the Minnesota River. Lights required. Phone 612-378-5714.

WEEKEND ON WHEELS
Mid-June

Escape to River Falls, Wisconsin with a couple of hundred TCBC (612-924-2443) enthusiasts. Rides range from 25 to 101 miles each day and the scenery can't be beat.

SUMMER SOLSTICE METRIC CENTURY
June 21 or 22

The summer solstice marks the longest day of the year, you can take off after work , bike a mere 62 miles and make it home for the evening news. TCBC.

PAUL BUNYAN DOUBLE CENTURY
Longest Saturday of the year

A one-day, 202-mile jaunt from Anoka Senior High School (4:30 a.m.!), around Lake Mille Lacs, and (ideally) back again. This ride began in 1967. Make a day of it. TCBC

A MIDSUMMER DAY'S RIDE
Sunday, late June

Tour Ramsey County's lake district and support the Northwest Youth & Family Services organization. Phone 651-486-3808.

TOUR OF SAINTS
Sunday, late June

When the Saints go biking in, they head to St. Cloud and a surprisingly handsome tour of forests and rolling hills. Phone 800-651-TOUR. Ask about their Spring Ride in late May on the new Lake Wobegone Trail.

July

WATERMELON BIKE RIDE – July 4th

Celebrate Independence Day with a relaxed 25-mile ride followed by a picnic lunch. If you get tired of spitting seeds you can do another 25-mile loop. TCBC.

THE AIDS RIDE
Six days in mid-July

The Twin Cities, Wisconsin, Chicago AIDS Ride is a major production that inspires hundreds of people to bike farther then they ever have before. Phone 612-871-0002.

MIDNIGHT-TO-DAWN METRO BIKE TOUR
Saturday night, mid-July

Now here is a Midsummer Night's Dream of a ride. Choose a 42- or 32-mile route with restaurant stops (rider's expense) and a hot breakfast while watching the sun rise over Lake Harriet (included). Phone 612-627-2463 well in advance.

MINNESOTA DOUBLE CROSS
Two days in July

Hop on your bike in Stillwater, bike across the state on Saturday and back on Sunday. That's 425 miles in two days. As Tim Nelson put it after missing a turn, "God, strike me dead." Paul Lee thought this one up. TCBC is a good contact.

HEART OF THE LAKES TRIATHLON
Mid-July

The area's largest triathlon draws 800 folks to Annandale to swim (one mile), bike (25 miles) and run (five miles). They also have a sprint category that is about half as long. Call 612-473-0093 or check their web at www.gearwest.com.

AQUATENNIAL BIKE TOUR
Later Sunday in July

This 25-mile family ride cruises along the Mississippi, through downtown Minneapolis and around the Lakes. Call 612-331-8371.

THE RIDE ACROSS MINNESOTA (TRAM)
Sunday to Friday, end of July

This is a fundraiser for Multiple Sclerosis that see 2,000 cyclists spanning the state. Small towns along the way do their best to make this a rolling parade. Call 1-800-FIGHT-MS.

August

GREAT RIVER RIDE
Three day weekend, mid-August

Here is a great trip. Start with a riverboat cruise down the Mississippi to Hastings. Then it's a leisurely 25-mile ride to Red Wing. The next two days you bike either 40 or 70 miles and wind up in Winona. Have dinner and take the Amtrak train back home. Call American Lung at 651-227-8014.

TURTLEMAN TRIATHLON
Mid-August

The Turtleman turned 15 in 1998 and happens up in Shoreview. Put that cross-training to good use. Phone 612-473-0093.

24 HOURS OF AFTON ALPS
Mid-August weekend

This epic event can be entered either as a team or as an individuals. It is a true test of wills and the sight of these riders' lights zooming through the night (night laps are just seconds off daytime numbers) is truly amazing.

September

MIDWEST TANDEM RALLY
Labor Day Weekend

Begun in 1976, the MTR draws 800 teams to this three day event. Rides range from 10 to 100 miles. Phone 612-935-9337.

DEFEAT OF JESSE JAMES DAYS
Saturday closest to September 7

On September 7, 1876, the notorious James-Younger gang rode into Northfield and started shooting. Stop on down to watch the raid be reenacted, and take your pick of scenic bike tours that range from 10 to 100 miles. Phone 507-645-5604.

SAINT PAUL CLASSIC BIKE TOUR
First Sunday after Labor Day

The Saint Paul Classic Bike Tour takes place the Sunday after Labor Day. It's a big ride and great fun with live music at the rest stops, public art and local baked goods. Two historic routes are featured — a 30-mile Grand Round and a 14-mile family ride — and both include miles of traffic-free cycling along the Mississippi River. Phone 612-372-3474.

STILLWATER BICYCLE CLASSIC
Second Sunday after Labor Day

Start in Stillwater and choose a route from 15 to 75 miles through the verdant St. Croix River Valley. Finish your ride with a beautiful view and an ice cream sundae at Pioneer Park. Phone 612-378-5714.

TOUR DE SPRAWL

An almost annual ride to look at examples of urban sprawl and some healthy alternatives. Phone 651-699-9667.

October

HALLOWEEN RIDE
Saturday closest to October 31

Boo! This is a house-to-house gobblin' (food) tour with up to 100 riders. Dress up in more eye-catching fare than your usual neon lycra. This is the last large organized bike ride of the year. Boo hoo. Pre-register with TCBC at 612-924-2443.

November and December

TCBC BIKE RIDES
Weekdays and weekends

By November and December, most folks are out hitting the ski trails or propped up in their favorite easy chair. Not that hard-charging TCBC crowd (612-924-2443). They have rides going out every week of the year. God bless 'em.

The world-class Velodrome in Blaine (785-5600) is popular with many local racing clubs and features the only wood racing track in the country. Dueling tandems are caught here at full tilt during the 1992 Olympic Trials. Left to right are Marty Northstein, Erin Hartwell, Bart Bell (right front) and Tom Brinker.

BICYCLE ORGANIZATIONS

"Never doubt that a small group of thoughtful, committed citizens can change the world — indeed, it is the only thing that ever has."
Margaret Mead

One of the great aspects of bicycling is that you can do it yourself. And you can do it right out the back door. There is no need to drive to a ski area, find a canoe partner or set up a belay. Just you, your bike and some pavement is all that's required. Heck, you could even skip the pavement.

On the other hand, there are times when it is nice to ride with a friend. If your friend can't always keep up, you can join a racing club and meet your match. There can be safety in numbers and less experienced riders will find comfort riding with a local bike riding club. Finally, making communities more bicycle-friendly requires everyone's attention. The streets and trails you ride are almost entirely owned and operated by governments. These are your officials making decisions that affect you.

GET INVOLVED! Here is a list of groups and organizations that can meet your every bicycling need. These are friendly, active folks who are helping to make a difference. Find the group (or two) you feel comfortable with. Stop by a meet-ing, call to get a sample newsletter or try out a ride with a friend. Then become a member. As the Twin City Tandems say — "you can double your bicycling pleasure."

Everyone who is interested in making their streets and cities more bicycle-friendly must take an active role. Lexington Parkway in St. Paul would have a bikeway on it today if more citizens had spoken up. Neighborhood and city council meetings are where decisions on street maintenance, trail construction, signing and striping of bicycle lanes are made. There are always people who will stand up against bicycling. You need to be there as well.

National organizations are helpful in providing ideas on how other communities solve bike issues. Federal funding through the Intermodal Surface Transportation Efficiency Act (ISTEA or "ice tea") has provided millions of dollars for bike projects throughout the Twin Cities metro area. Projects include the Stone Arch Bridge in Minneapolis, the Midtown Greenway and the Como Avenue Bikeway Project in St. Paul.

Statewide Advocacy Groups

Bicycle Industry Advocate

Gary Sjoquist, Phone: 612-941-9391 ext. 288
Quality Bicycle Products proved they were serious about promoting bike advocacy for the future of cycling by hiring one of the best. Call Gary if you are working on bike policy or facility development.

Legislative Bicycle Advocate

Representative Phyllis Kahn
Phone: 651-296-4257
The strongest advocate of bicycling at the state legislature for 20 years, Phyllis Kahn is also founder of the Hot Flashes Bicycle Club.

Minnesota Coalition of Bicyclists

Brian Rosenthal, President
P.O. Box 75452
St. Paul, MN 55175
Hotline: 651-452-9736
A statewide organization that has been working for over ten years to improve bicycling safety, education and access. Their legislative presence deserves your support. They offer a quarterly newsletter, Bicycle Minnesota.

MN Community Bicycle Safety Project

Cynthia McArthur, Bike Safety Coordinator
University of Minnesota Extension Service
340 Coffey Hall, 1420 Eckles Avenue
St. Paul, MN 55108
Phone: 612-625-9719   Fax: 612-625-1731

Cynthia is a tireless promoter of bike safety and helps communities set up bike programs for youth throughout Minnesota. Call for bike safety materials, programs or speaking engagements.

Minnesota Department of Transportation

Charles Cadenhead, State Bicycle Coordinator
395 John Ireland Boulevard, MS 315
St. Paul, MN 55155
Phone: 651-296-9966   Fax: 651-296-0590   Web Site: www.dot.state.mn.us/trim/ats/guidestar/sti/sbac.
MNDOT Bikeway Map Sales 651-296-2216
State Bicycle Program staff coordinate a bi-annual bike conference and the **State Bicycle Advisory Committee** *(651-297-1568) is helpful on technical issues. Charles has done a terrific job finding funding for a variety of bicycle projects.*

Minnesota Off Road Cyclists

Todd Powell, phone: 612-895-1744
13295 Glenhurst Avenue South
Savage, MN 55378
MORC works with local governments and land managers to gain and maintain trail access. They also work with trail users on issues of safety and trail maintenance. Members receive Knobby News.

Minnesota Rideshare

Call 651-602-1602 to get on the Chain Gang *mailing list.*
Web Site: www.metrocommuterservice.org.

Local Advocacy Groups

Hennepin County Bicycle Advisory Committee

Milt Schoen, Chair

Hennepin County Government Center, Mail Code 013

300 South 6th Street

Minneapolis, MN 55487

Phone: 612-348-3499   Fax: 612-348-3932

Current projects include implementing the Bicycle Transportation Plan and working on county highway projects like the Ford Bridge to ensure bike facilities are considered. Citizens welcome. Committee meets the second Monday of the month about 4:30 p.m.

Minneapolis Bicycle Advisory Board

Tom Becker, Chair

Room 233 City Hall

350 S. Fifth Street

Minneapolis, MN 55415-1314

Phone: 612-673-2411   Fax: 612-673-2149

The most successful bike advocacy group in the state. I came back from Europe in the fall of 1994 and found that Minneapolis was on track to become the Amsterdam of Minnesota. Citizens are welcome at meetings held the first Wednesday of each month at 10 a.m.

St. Paul Bicycle Advisory Board

Carol Andrews, Chair

Phone: Greg Reese at 651-488-6302

Advocating for better bike facilities and hosting an annual event, the Saint Paul Classic Bike Tour (first Sunday after Labor Day), are ongoing efforts. We welcome your attendance at our meetings on the first Tuesday of each month.

The Yellow Bike Coalition

Laurie Lundy, Executive Director

1101 Cedar View Drive

Minneapolis, MN 55405

Phone: 651-222-2080   Fax: 612-377-4494

Web Site: www.saintpaul.com/ybc

Their mission is connecting people and places through bikes. They take unloved bikes, paint them yellow and distribute them for public transportation.

Transit for Livable Communities

Barb Thoman, Program Staff

P.O. Box 14221, Midway Transfer Station

St. Paul, MN 55114

Phone: 651-644-6856   Fax: 612-338-1871

Citizen advocacy group promoting greater use of transit, bicycling and walking — and land use patterns that make that possible. Monthly meeting and newsletters available on request.

Sierra Club, Minnesota Chapter

Deborah Alper, Phone 651-699-9667

Web Site: www.northstar.sierraclub.org

The Sierra Club Urban Sprawl Task Force takes a holistic approach to resource preservation that includes alternative transportation.

National Advocacy Groups

Bicycle Federation of America

1506 21st Street NW, Suite 200

Washington, D.C. 20036

Phone: 202-463-6622   Web Site: www.bikefed.org

Prime movers in getting federal TEA-21 legislation moved through Congress, the Bike Federation contracts with public agencies and advocacy groups in providing training, technical assistance and program support. They have several excellent publications for sale and the Pro Bike News *is available by subscription.*

League of American Bicyclists

1612 K Street NW, Suite 401

Washington, D.C. 20006-2802

Phone: 202-822-1333   Fax: 202-822-1334

Web Site: www.bikeleague.org

Founded in 1880 as the League of American Wheelmen, the LAB is a nationwide advocacy group. Members receive the monthly magazine Bicycle USA *and the annual* Almanac. *The local representative is Lonnie Frederick, 602-839-1794.*

Rails-to-Trails Conservancy

1100 17th Street NW, 10th Floor

Washington, D.C. 20036

Phone: 202-331-9696   Fax: 202-331-9680

Web Site: www.railtrails.org

The national advocacy group for recreational off-road paths on abandoned railroad corridors. There are several of these in Minnesota. The RTC has been instrumental in saving trails across the country by purchasing corridors that would otherwise be lost.

Surface Transportation Policy Project

Check their web site at www.istea.org for daily updates on federal transportation projects and funding.

Fred cruises on a recumbent bicycle at a Minnesota Human Powered Vehicle Association meeting. Note the location of the handlebars.

Bicycle Riding Clubs

> *"I don't want to belong to any club that will accept me as a member."*
>
> Groucho Marx

Groucho's advice notwithstanding, there are plenty of good clubs to join in the Twin Cities. The **Twin Cities Bicycling Club** is the largest, with rides every week of the year. There are specialty clubs like the **Twin Cities Tandem Club** and the **Mississippi Valley Women's Cycling Association**. If you are interested in the old high-wheelers, get in touch with the **Minnesota Wheelmen**. And if you want to ride an equally eye-catching 21st century bicycle, the **Minnesota Human Powered Vehicle Association** is your club. There are bicycle clubs at several of the larger work places in town, including **3M** and **Ramsey County**. Or, you can go slumming on bike trips sponsored by the **North Star Ski Touring Club** during their off-season. Club rides are usually open to nonmembers (for a couple dollars or so) and generally require helmets.

Hennepin Parks

12615 County Road 9
Plymouth, MN 55441
Phone: 612-559-9000   Trail Hotline: 612-559-6778
Web Site: www.hennepinparks.org
Hennepin Parks leads mountain bike and trail rides summer and fall.

Mississippi Valley Women's Cycling Association

Colleen Deuberry 612-690-2116 or Sandy at 612-927-8990
This all-women's group has leisurely Wednesday night rides throughout the summer. Longer rides take place one Saturday each month. Members range from 30 to 55 years in age and receive a ride schedule and list of activities.

Minnesota Human Powered Vehicle Association

Dave Kraft, phone: 612-929-2978
4139 Brookside Avenue S.
St. Louis Park, MN 55416
Web Site: www2.bitstream.net/~mstonich
Now for something completely different — try riding a "recumbent" bicycle some time. These bikes are low slung and easy on the back as you ride low to the ground in a sitting position. The MnHPVA is home to techies, dreamers and builders. Biannual rides allow newcomers to sample these exotic, but efficient vehicles. Members receive a newsletter and meet the second Wednesday of each month.

Minnesota Wheelmen

Jon Sharratt, Captain
2322 Johnson Street N.E.
Minneapolis, MN 55418
Phone: 612-781-9954
These guys are the really big wheels of bicycling. They ride the high-wheelers and safety bikes that fueled the first bike craze in the late 1800s. Jon, on his 1885 Victor 52" highwheeler, and Melanie Steinborn, on her 1898 Hoffman Pneumatic safety bike, help kick-off the Saint Paul Classic Bike Tour each year.

North Star Ski Touring Club

P.O. Box 4275
St. Paul, MN 55104   Hotline: 612-924-9922
Web Site: www.north-star.org
Here is a big amiable group that enjoys outdoor recreation throughout the year. Rafting the Grand Canyon, trail clearing on the North Shore and, yes, bicycling in the Twin Cities. One friend who's a member confesses she has never been on a ski trip. Become a member and receive the excellent Loype *newsletter.*

Sitzmark Ski and Social Club

Nancy Wolterstorf, President
Hotline: 612-545-1151
Sitzmark has trips and parties throughout the year. With some 500 members, the emphasis is on the social life, but a little exercise never hurt anyone.

Twin Cities Bicycling Club

P.O. Box 131086
Roseville, MN 55113
Hotline: 612-924-2443   Web Site: www.mtn.org/tcbc
Formed under the auspices of Hosteling International-Minnesota AYH (612-378-3773), the TCBC is one of the premier bike riding organizations in the state, with over 1,000 members and some 700 scheduled trips in 1998. Don't worry, they don't all show up for each ride. Rides are rated for all ability levels and each has a trained leader. Members receive the Activity News *newsletter.*

Twin Cities Tandem Club

Doug and Sara Laird, phone: 612-935-9337
5445 Maple Ridge Court
Minnetonka, MN 55343-9488
Web Site: home.earthlink.net/~ewjuly/tandem/tandem.html
Double your pleasure, double your fun. This is a large active club. The Twin Cities have a unique community of tandem riders and bike builders. I love riding tandems. Nothing beats going full tilt down a big hill with your eyes closed. Tandems are more efficient and make it a lot easier to converse with your buddy. Members receive a monthly newsletter.

Twin Cities Unicycle Club

Andy Cotter, phone: 612-788-9137
1318 45th Avenue NE
Columbia Heights, MN 55421
The Twin Cities sports some of the best unicyclists on the planet. Just 18, Dana Schneider has won seven world titles and is the only rider to ever reach the sport's top level 10 ranking. I would consider myself level 10 if I could stay upright on one for more than three seconds. Here's your chance to learn from the best.

Unicycle Team of Minnesota

Tim Johnson, phone 651-633-2888
A friendly, east metro rival of the Twin Cities Unicycle Club, these folks also have weekly practices, competitions and do parades.

Bicycle Racing Clubs

> "It is a great environment here. I really believe moving here helped everything."
> Greg LeMond of Wayzata
> *after winning his third Tour de France*
>
> "Every car has a lot of speed in it. The trick is getting the speed out of it."
> A. J. Foyt, *race car driver*

There is nothing quite like the feeling of riding at high speeds in a pack of bicyclists, trading off leads and riding at a pace you could never maintain yourself. Speed, fun, and camaraderie can all be found by joining a racing club. You will also find hard work and the training necessary to compete at your highest level. The Twin Cities support a fine array of cycling clubs for those who wish to compete and for those who simply want to ride with others at a faster clip than recreational clubs can handle.

The **Minnesota Cycling Federation** (Hotline is 612-729-0702 and their web site is www.mcf.net) oversees local club and racing activities, along with the **United States Cycling Federation** (USCF, their web site is www.usacycling.org). **WISport** is an excellent source for citizens races (web site is axle.adp. wisc.edu/~alv/Wisport.html). Club sponsors and contacts change frequently so check these web sites. Competition for juniors begins at ages 10 to 12, seniors compete within the 19- to 34-year-old range and masters level begins at the ripe old age of 35.

Most clubs are open to newcomers (women and youngsters are especially encouraged to join), membership dues are reasonable and sponsoring bicycle shops offer substantial discounts on bike equipment to members. Road racing, track racing, mountain biking, cyclocross racing (you actually carry your bike for short stretches), and triathlons are now part of the mix at many clubs.

The **Youth Cycling League** (Hotline is 651-633-3416 and their web site is www.mcf.net/ycl) was begun in 1998 to help draw more kids into cycle sports. They finished their first season with 33 kids racing with three local teams and are looking to expand in the future. See page 119 for information on **BMX**.

People who have some race experience should call to ask for the location of a club's training rides. Those just starting out should call to determine if a club has beginner's rides — about half of the clubs do. The St. Paul Bicycle Racing Club started a very successful Beginner's Racing Club that is being adoped by other local clubs.

The Twin Cities have a world-class bike racing facility in the **National Sports Center Velodrome** in Blaine (612-785-5614). Located at 1700-105th Avenue NE, this all-wood racing track hosts Olympic-caliber bike races and is open to the public for club and individual use. Web site is www.nscsports.com.

Blaine Velo Club
Mark Stewart, phone: 612-783-1530
8575 Hwy. 65 NE
Blaine, MN 55434
Sponsor: Blaine Velo Sports
It should come as no surprise that one of the club's focuses is track riding. With an Olympic-caliber facility in their backyard, they have generated some of the area's better track riders. Blaine Velo was one of the first sponsors of the Youth Cycling League.

Como Wheelers
Pete Fleishhacker, phone: 651-488-9078
779 W. Wheelock Parkway
St. Paul, MN 55117
Sponsor: Como Bike Shop
Pete was a charter member of the St. Paul Bicycle Advisory Board and has been involved in local bike racing for years. The Como Wheelers hold weekly rides and the club has had a national caliber rider each of the past three years.

Erik's Bike Club
Wis Mollerud, phone: 612-869-BIKE
2020 W. 98th Street
Bloomington, MN 55431
Web Site: www.eriksbike.com
Sponsor: Erik's Bike shop
The Twin Cities' biggest bike shop sponsors a major mountain bike race series at Buck Hill, hosts bi-weekly rides at their shops throughout the Twin Cities and sponsors a "grass roots level" mountain bike team.

Flat City Cycling Club
Bruce Jenkinson, phone: 612-595-9648
Web Site: www.flatcity.org
Sponsor: Penn Cycle and Rick Lupient Saturn dealers
Races are won and lost on blown tires, so Flat City may seem an unusual moniker for a bike club, but never fear. The club has over 100 members. The focus is on racing — road, track, cyclocross and mountain biking — where club member John Sandberg won every series in 1998. They sponsor over 15 races each year.

Gopher Wheelmen Bicycle Racing Club
Scott Sandberg, phone: 612-471-8662
1380 North Arm Drive
Orono, MN 55364
Sponsor: County Cycles in Roseville
Founded in 1934, this is the oldest bicycle club in Minnesota. In fact, a founding member who participated in the old Six Day Bike Races of the 1930s — Kenny Woods — is still a member and still biking as of the publication of this book. This is a solid club for all levels of racing for men and women.

Giocatore Interno Sella
Christopher T. Smith, phone: 612-941-9391 ext. 209
4901 28th Avenue South
Minneapolis, MN 55417
Sponsor: Kenwood Cyclery
Hard to pronounce but easy to spot in their pink jerseys, Giocatore etc. loosely translates from the Italian as, "gamblers in the saddle." They ride aggressively and as a team and would rather go down in flames than wait for a race to unfold. They put on 20 races in 1998 including a series of criteriums (one in winter on frozen Bush Lake), time trials and cyclocross events.

Great River Racing

Kris Henke, phone 651-388-5358
1934 Audrey Avenue
Red Wing, MN 55066
Sponsor: The Outdoor Store, NSP, Ridell Skates
An active club for years, they officially joined the USCF in 1998. They run the gamut from young kids racing mountain bikes to older guys out for a recreational weeknight ride. They sponsor a criterium in Red Wing and the Muddy River Rock and Roll Mountain Bike Race at Memorial Park each summer.

Habanero Bicycle Club

Habanero is Latin for cowboys and these hombres have a web site at aol.com/habanero24.

Team JRA

Fred Feirn, phone: 651-787-0157
3470 Kent Street
Shoreview, MN 55126
JRA stands for the old saw "just riding around," as in, "I was just riding around and my crank fell off." That probably doesn't happen so often as this is a small but dedicated crew that races on- and off-road.

L'Etoile du Nord (Fellowship of Christian Athletes)

Dean Jarnow, phone: 612-974-0251
6729 Harlan Drive
Eden Prairie, MN 55346
As all Minnesotans know, L'Etoile du Nord is part of our state seal and translates to "Stars of the North" as one member kiddingly put it. They compete in track, cyclocross and road racing and welcome newcomers and recreational cyclists. Race promotion proceeds go to FCA camp scholarships.

L'Équipe Lanterne Rouge

Tim McNamara, phone: 651-644-5057
2137 Temple Court
St. Paul, MN 55104
Web Site: www.geocities.com/Colosseum/3232
The "red light on the end of the train" represents the last place rider in a race who is the symbol of perseverance. Much to their own surprise, Lanterne Rouge won a few races in 1998 and had their best year yet. See RIDE 49.

Long Lake Velo

Jan Guenther/Kevin O'Connor, phone: 612-473-0093
1786 W. Wayzata Boulevard
Long Lake, MN 55356
Sponsor: Gear West
Long Lake Velo's club specialty is the triathlon where long distance road biking combines with running and swimming to get you and your body totally involved. They also compete in mountain bike races.

Loon State Cycling Club

James D. Cullen, phone: 651-489-4513
1712 Lexington Avenue North
Roseville, MN 55113
Web Site: www.loonstate.org
Sponsor: Bicycle Chain
This is one of Minnesota's largest clubs with members competing at all levels and in all types of races from criteriums to road races. They have three of the ten licensed USCF coaches in the area.

Makeshift Bicycle Club

Tim Boyle, phone: 612-729-1100
4717 35th Avenue South
Minneapolis, MN 55406
Sponsor: Computer Relief
A small but up-and-coming club that has shown dramatic improvement in criterium races over the past couple of years.

Maximum Velocity

Jay Erickson, phone: 612-374-3635
2408 Hennepin Avenue S.
Minneapolis, MN 55405
Sponsor: The Alternative Bike and Board
A small, but potent off-road racing club founded by national mountain bike champion, Gene Oberpriller. They take their racing, and their fun times, seriously. Sponsored by those radical folks at Alternative Bike.

Minneapolis Bicycle Racing Cub

Scott Flanders, phone: 612-872-6994
2707 Lyndale Avenue S.
Minneapolis, MN 55408
Sponsors: Flanders Brothers Bike Shop
Scott Flanders is a perennial winner in road races and criterium races and Tim Mulrooney has been Minnesota's top rider the past two years. But most riders for the club are approaching middle age and are in it more for the rides than the races.

Minnesota Cycling Team

Kevin Lennon, phone: 612-544-3321
25 Union Terrace
Minneapolis, MN 55441
Sponsors: Tonka Cycle, Lemond and Fisher Bikes and Park Tool
The team embraces a wide range of interests — from mountain biking to road racing — and age groups. They strive for a team effort and assign experienced racers to mentor newcomers. They were one of the original sponsors of the Youth Cycling League.

St. Paul Bicycle Racing Club

Dave LaPorte, phone: 651-625-4983
3020 Simpson Street
Roseville, MN 55113
Web Site: www.spbrc.org
Sponsor: Grand Performance
Minnesota's biggest racing club was the USCF "National Club of the Year." Excellent programs in all racing modes are in place for juniors, seniors and women. The club started the Youth Cycling League and the Beginner's Racing Club that have proven very popular.

Uptown Cycling Club

Rob Lindstrom, phone: 612-824-1669
3029 Holmes Avenue, #3
Minneapolis, MN 55408
Sponsor: Boehm's Cycling and Fitness
Boehm's was named City Pages' best bike shop in 1998 and this large, active club is one of the reasons. They have over 50 members, a good mix of guys and gals, and promote cycling as a sport while competing in all types of cycling. Rob Lindstrom set a Minnesota track record at Blaine, races BMX and publishes Minnesota Cyclesport *(available at better bike shops everywhere).*

Bicycle Touring Organizations

> *"In a car you're always in a compartment, and because you're used to it, you don't realize that through the car window everything you see is just more TV.*
>
> *On a cycle the frame is gone. You're completely in contact with it all. You're in the scene, not just watching it anymore, and the sense of presence is overwhelming."*
>
> Robert M. Pirsig
> *Zen and the Art of Motorcycle Maintenance*

The following outfits offer a nice sampling of bike tours here and abroad. For the most complete listing of bike tours in the Midwest, check the back pages of *Silent Sports* magazine in the May to July issues.

Outside, Bicycling, and *Bicycle USA* (membership magazine for the League of American Bicyclists) are all good places to look for national and international bike tours. Some of the local bike clubs (listed earlier) offer special bike tours. Also check the ANNUAL BIKE EVENTS chapter and club web sites for additional tours.

American Lung Association of Hennepin County

490 Concordia Avenue, phone: 651-227-8014
St. Paul, MN 55103

Here is a way to take a bike tour, visit some wonderful places, and benefit a good cause. American Lung offers pledge (or pay) rides that include the Great River Ride from St. Paul to Winona and the Big Ride Across America.

Cycle America

P.O. Box 485
Cannon Falls, MN 55009
Phone: 800-245-3263   Fax: 507-263-0873
Web Site: www.cycleamerica.com

If you have ever wanted to ride from sea to shining sea across these United States then this is the outfit for you. Cycle America has been running since 1988. These are van supported, camping tours (motel optional) that can be done in week-long, state-wide sections. They also offer bike tours through the western national parks. Ask about their Pedal the Peaks Bicycle Challenge. Moderate in cost.

National Multiple Sclerosis Society

Minnesota Chapter
200 12th Avenue South
Minneapolis, MN 55415
Phone: 800-FIGHT MS

In 1999 the MS 150 will be celebrating its 20th anniversary. This is the pledge ride that started all the others, both locally and nationally. MS offers three great tours to help fight this chronic disease. The MS 150 goes 150 miles from Duluth to the Twin Cities each June. The MS Sixty 30 is a local ride and the MN TRAM is The Ride Across Minnesota.

Woodswomen

25 W. Diamond Lake Road
Minneapolis, MN 55419
Phone: 612-822-3809   Fax: 612-822-3814
Web Site: www.woodswomen.mn.org

Woodswomen is locally owned, with 20 years experience in leading adventure-travel trips for women throughout the world. They have Learn to Bicycle Tour trips in Wisconsin and once you get the bug you will surely want to join them in touring Tuscany, New Zealand and Ireland. I love their motto, "Adventure is the best souvenir." Moderate to expensive.

Bicycle touring is a great way to experience different lands and peoples. Everybody in the Netherlands bicycles and this couple at the Kinderdijk display the more relaxed European approach to bike attire and safety.

Fred's Photos, 1994